Restoring My Soul

The Pursuit of Spiritual Resilience

Restoring My Soul

The Pursuit of Spiritual Resilience
BILL FLATT Ed.D.

GOSPEL ADVOCATE
A TRUSTED NAME SINCE 1855

Gospel Advocate Company
P.O. Box 150
Nashville, Tennessee 37202

Other Books by Bill Flatt, Ed. D.

From Worry to Happiness

Growing Through Grief

Since You Asked

Building a Healthy Family

Personal Counseling

Counseling Homosexuals

Scriptures, unless otherwise noted, taken from the HOLY BIBLE, NEW INTERNATIONAL VERSION®. Copyright ©1973, 1978, 1984 by International Bible Society. Used by permission of Zondervan Publishing House. All rights reserved.

The "NIV" and "New International Version" trademarks are registered in the United States Patent and Trademark Office by International Bible Society. Use of either trademark requires the permission of International Bible Society.

Published by Gospel Advocate Co.
P.O. Box 150, Nashville, TN 37202
http://www.gospeladvocate.com

ISBN: 0-89225-448-3

Dedication

I dedicate this book to
our children, Steve, Tim and Danny,
and to our grandchildren,
David Madison, Kevin McFarlin, Jonathan Thomas,
Katherine Elizabeth and Benton Carl,
with our blessing and love and
with the hope that they will gain
as much spiritual resilience from their roots
as Louise and I have from ours.

Acknowledgements

No one writes a book without the help of others. That is certainly true of me.

I thank God for His providential care over the years. I thank my parents, my siblings and their spouses, and my grandparents for their spiritual resilience.

I thank my wife, Louise, for being my loving partner and encourager for more than 46 years of a great marriage. I thank her also for reading this manuscript along with my long-time friends, Jane Tomlinson, Dr. Allen Black and Dr. Don Kinder. They caught many mistakes and offered several good suggestions. I also thank Dr. Don Kinder for getting me unstuck on my computer, which I used occasionally to type this manuscript. I also thank Debbie Miller for her excellent work as typist for this book and especially for her patience in reading my writing and doing all of the changes I made throughout the process.

CONTENTS

PREFACE

This Book Is for You!

Individuals

Do you ever have struggles with guilt, worry and anxiety, excessive fears, depression, low self-esteem, anger, dysfunctional family patterns or sexual temptations? Do you grieve over significant losses in your life? Are you divorced? Have you ever thought of suicide? Would you like to grow spiritually? If you answer yes to any of these questions, this book is for you! It can help you learn to persist with discipline and faith.

Counselors

If you as a counselor ever wished you had a book to recommend to your clients, you will want to take a look at this one. In it, Dr. Bill Flatt writes about problems that his clients have talked to him about and gives helpful advice in a loving compassionate manner. Your clients will feel as though he were talking to them. His chapters on self-esteem and the Shepherd Psalm let them know that they are valuable human beings. They are made in the image of God, and they are worthwhile. His supportive messages will continue your message between counseling sessions. Take a look. You'll be glad you did!

Bible Class Teachers

Are you ready to teach a class that will capture the interest of just about everyone? Do you want to teach a class that will touch people where they, their families, and their friends live? Do you want a textbook that will give you more material than you will need to teach such a class? If you answer yes to any of these questions, this is the book for you. In it, Dr. Flatt has organized his material well. His outline of thought is easy to follow, and he gives 10 reflection questions for analy-

sis and discussion at the end of each of his 13 chapters. It's just right
for a quarter of interesting, relevant study. And remember, his writings
are always saturated with the Bible. He'll help you go into each class
well-prepared to teach, and feeling that you are giving them something
worthwhile – helping them apply God's will to their everyday struggles. They'll learn more about what discipline, persistence and faith
– spiritual resilience – really mean.

Basic Counseling Professors

Have you ever wanted a book that discusses the main problems that
people discuss with counselors, ministers and other church leaders?
Have you ever been disturbed because your textbook did not put such
discussions in a spiritual context with God, spiritual identity, spiritual resources, beliefs and values, and congruent living at the center of
the book? Were you ever disappointed that the author of your textbooks
did not seem to have the education and experience to write such books?
Did you ever want challenging reflection questions at the end of each
chapter? If your answer to any of these questions is yes, this book is
for you. Dr. Flatt is a licensed counseling psychologist, a licensed marriage and family therapist, an approved supervisor of AAMFT, and has
taught basic counseling classes at Harding University Graduate School
of Religion for more than 30 years. He knows the kind of book you
need. This book is for you and your students!

Introduction

In the Summer of 1999, I retired as Dean/CEO of Harding University Graduate School of Religion. I had served for 34 years on the faculty and administration of that good school. Since then, I have continued part-time as professor of counseling, held several weekend seminars and workshops on "Building Healthy Families" and "Growing Through Grief," and accepted several new clients in my private practice as a psychologist and marriage and family therapist. I have also rested some, traveled some, and golfed a number of times. I even bought my first computer and am trying to learn to operate it. I did my first PowerPoint presentation in my class in Basic Counseling at Harding Graduate School.

In between times, my mind keeps cranking out ideas that I would like to share with you. Because of my seminars on "Growing Through Grief" and the large number of good people I have learned from in those meetings, I thought for a while that I would write another book on working through grief. The title "Joyful Living" also appealed to me. But for several months now, I have thought of my present title for what will probably be my last book: *Restoring My Soul: The Pursuit of Spiritual Resilience!* Why this title?

Often we write about people's problems and their weaknesses, which may be helpful. We point to failures and misfortunes and the people who just don't make it in life. Yet I keep thinking about those who do make it: those who grow through difficulties; those who overcome through many trials, toils and pains; those who find strength in weakness. I think about the 85 percent of children of alcoholics who do not become alcoholics and wonder how they did that. I see people who draw spiritual strength to overcome and grow through many hardships and extra burdens and wonder how they did that.

I believe I have learned some answers and want to share them with you, although I know that some of your sorrows would be almost impossible for any of us. Read on as I lead you through many common tragedies and tell you how hundreds of good people just like you have traveled through these tough waters by spiritual resilience. They made it; you can too!

CHAPTER ONE

My Spiritual Journey

I believe that we are made in the image of God, that God breathed into man the breath of life, and man became a living soul (Genesis 1-3). I believe that the essence of a person is spirit rather than flesh although it is difficult for us to distinguish between the two.

Spirituality for me grew out of a heritage of Christian parents and grandparents, brothers and sisters, and indeed a Christian community of origin. It involved church, the Bible and a small public school that included moral teachings and some spiritual emphasis. I had many aunts and uncles who influenced my spiritual development in a positive direction.

I was born in the beautiful hills of Jackson County, Tenn., in a log house that had a dog trot down the middle and two fireplaces. My dad helped deliver me before the doctor arrived. My great-grandfather Meredith Fox had owned that place on Flynn's Creek and had died not long before I was born. I was the third of eight children born to Cleo Ann Way and Benton Madison Flatt.

Louise, my beloved wife, and I visited that place recently. Although the house is no longer there, those beautiful hills and creeks still bolster my faith. I like to go back and walk over the hills, wade the creeks, observe the birds and other wild animals – deer, squirrels, crows, hawks – look at the trees and view the beautiful stars at night. They are so bright in the country! The good people of those hills are even more encouraging to me as I search for spiritual resilience. Yet the little branch of water between the house and corncrib still reminds me of the big rock I dropped on my toe when I was 2 years old.

Spiritual life to me is a relationship between God and me. I see myself as a spiritual being accountable to God, with beliefs and values that I believe He has given us through Jesus Christ and the Bible. This abundant life in Christ makes me feel alive, and it gives meaning and purpose to my existence. It sustains me through the tough times and gives me joy even when I am unhappy. Although it is personal and less institutional than religion, it grew out of institutional religion and is nurtured by it. It is difficult for me to think of one without the other, just as it would be impossible for me to think of being patriotic without believing in the United States.

I lost my mother in 1984 and my father in 1997. In this decade, I have lost my father-in-law; my very close friend, Dr. W.B. West Jr.; and 18 uncles and aunts. Though all of this is sad, it has also been a significant spiritual experience. As I reconnected with my friends and extended family and heard numerous funeral messages, my faith, my values and my spiritual life were reinforced. Through all of this what matters is obvious – spiritual life remains. The body returns to the dust from which it came, the spirit unto God who gave it (Ecclesiastes 12:7). The real person, the spirit, continues to exist forever. This is life that is eternal in nature – abundant life in Christ (John 10). This is spiritual life for me.

I am not a spiritual giant. I have never felt that I was. Yet my spiritual life sustains me through tough times: stumped toes, meager financial circumstances, sickness and deaths.

Spiritual Giants

I have been around some people I consider spiritual giants. Dr. E.H. Ijams, a former teacher of mine, was to me a spiritual giant. He spoke in chapel at Harding Graduate School on his 87th birthday and made a great impression on us all. His topic was "Hold to God's Unchanging Hand," his favorite song, which I led that day.

Dr. Marshall Keeble, an outstanding African-American preacher, spoke in chapel several times. After one such message, I took him to lunch and interviewed him. He told me about a time when he was preaching to a white congregation in a small town in Middle Tennessee. Some of the white people in town didn't like such integration. A large man marched down the aisle while he was preaching, came up to the pulpit, and hit him in the face with brass knuckles. Several men subdued the man, called the sheriff, and took him to jail. The next morning, they called Dr. Keeble to come down to the jail and press charges, but he refused. He said, "I hold no ill-will toward that misguided man. I feel sorry for him. I'll just pray for him and leave it with Jesus." They insisted, but he refused. I really admire his love and anger management skills. I wonder how he did that. To me, he was a spiritual giant.

One time I was with Dr. West at a Christian college lectureship. The moderator of the lectureship's open forum publicly criticized Dr. West and Harding Graduate School where he served as its founding dean, even quoting comments Dr. West had written on a student's term paper – comments designed to expand the student's view of scholarship beyond authors of his own fellowship. Finally, Dr. West went to the podium and, in a very gracious voice, thanked the moderator for his interest in scholarship in religion, praised him for his love of the Bible and the church, and said that was what he and the graduate school stood for as well. I saw him unjustly criticized many times by people who knew little about what they were criticizing.

For example, in chapel one day a well-known preacher criticized all modern versions of the Bible and Harding Graduate School for using them – especially the Revised Standard and New International versions. When a graduate student asked him how he could evaluate translations since he did not know Hebrew and Greek, he replied, "That's simple. You compare them with the truth!" Dr. West remained calm as he closed out the service and thanked the preacher for all of his good work over the years. He especially appreciated one of the books he had written. I wonder how he did that. He was led by the Spirit and not by the flesh (Galatians 5:16-25).

My grandfather Hiram Way was a farmer, schoolteacher and gospel preacher. He and Ma, Ollie Fox Way, had many struggles. Although they struggled through some financially difficult times, they were able to leave each of their seven surviving children a small farm. Our family still owns what he left Mom.

On the sad side, however, they lost four of their 11 children before they were 10 years old, three to common childhood diseases and one, Jesse, to a tragic accident on their farm. Jesse, age 9, rode their mule to Flatt Hollow to give him a drink from a spring. Coming back up the steep hill, Jesse fell off the mule, caught his foot in a chain, and the mule dragged him to his death. Jesse died in Pa's arms.

How did Pa handle that? He would cry years later when he spoke of Jesse in his sermons, but he would affirm his faith that he and Ma would see Jesse again in heaven. He was a very spiritual person.

How did Ma handle it? I think it was too much for her. She seemed, as I'm sure many of us would including myself, to turn her pain and sorrow inward and became very depressed. She survived in church by prayer and Bible reading and by a network of loving family and friends.

I believe it affected my mother for life. She was older than Jesse and seemed never to shake completely the sadness. She also developed rheumatoid arthritis in her 20s soon after I was born, which bent her back considerably. She prayed through her back pain, went to church and was supported by that same network of family and friends. Her eight children were very supportive of her in her later years.

Robert Birdwell, a family friend, told me he used to drive by Pa Way's place. He would often be in the front yard under a maple tree reading his Bible. Then, Robert said, "I would drive on up the road and your mother would be sitting on the porch swing reading her Bible. That's what I remember most about them. I wonder what effect all of that had on all of you." To me they were spiritual giants although they themselves did not always feel strong. Somehow they were resilient. They lived successfully through tough circumstances.

My grandfather Flatt taught me something about thinking for myself and about understanding spirituality as an every day affair. If he saw a neighbor in need, he would help him or her. He would not wait until Sunday, give it to the church, so that the church could help him. Being a Christian was much broader than what institutions could do through their organizations. He went to church, but he was not limited to doing good by church organization. Once a neighbor's house burned. He took food and clothing to them and helped rebuild their house. Of course, all of us can see his point now.

Ma Flatt's spirituality came through to me in her relationships. I never heard her say anything bad about anyone. Once when we were talking about a distant relative who was making, drinking and selling moonshine, she said, "He has always been good to his children." Her spiritual life was obvious in a very friendly, nurturing and wholesome way.

My father-in-law, Paskell Dyer, scared me when I was young. He seemed tough and strong. He was not as restrained as my dad. Years after Louise and I married, I got to know him. He was gentle and kind. He often hugged me when I visited and sometimes cried when I left. His wife, Flora Pippin Dyer, preceded him in death by 10 years. A wonderful woman, she really took care of him. She would lay out his clothes, cook great meals, sing with him, and remind him of what he needed to do. When she died suddenly of a heart attack at age 68, we wondered how he would survive. He was lost for a while. He missed her but survived and continued to live a meaningful life. He loved to swap funny stories with me. He loved baseball and went to most Little League games in his area. He loved his children and grandchildren. He was a gentle man full of the Spirit. He lived beyond his ability by the power of his spiritual life: church, Bible, friends, children and grandchildren. It was the same combination of human toughness plus spiritual strength from God that I saw in my parents. I'm not sure I would have used the word "spiritual" to describe my dad as I was growing up. A hard worker who was disciplined and honest, a man of integrity, a man who helped his neighbors, a strong disciplinarian and a quiet man were words I would have used. These all reflect a spirituality that is deep and strong and that I saw later in his life. I asked him questions about his grandparents and what they were like. I found out that his Pa Birdwell fought in the Civil War for the North and that he was resented for this for years. I learned that Dad helped move Pa Ben Flatt's log house out of a hollow down beside the Flynn's Creek road. I learned that Pa Ben Flatt fell off a horse and died about four days later, and that Dad and his dad, Pa Henry Flatt, had just gone home right before he died. I learned that he and his brother Bill were baptized into Christ (Galatians 3:26-27) the afternoon he died, and it was in the creek within a few feet of where my brother Leamon and I were baptized years later. I learned from hearing these and other stories much more about my dad than I knew previously.

Two incidents in Dad's life inspired me more than anything else to write this book. They epitomize his discipline, determination and hard work along with his strong faith.

The first incident happened when I was 9 or 10 years old. We were gathering corn by hand one frosty morning and were complaining about being cold. Dad replied, "It's not cold. Just work a little harder boys and you'll warm up." He was tough. We didn't have gloves, which made the job colder. In his later years, he told me that his fingers were frostbitten from gathering corn with frost on the ears. Yet the principle of tough discipline he taught us still sticks with me. I have learned not to whine about so many things.

The other incident happened right before he died. He was very weak with lung cancer. He fought to live until he learned it was hopeless, and then he died in two days. Right before he died he looked up and said, "Don't worry. Everything is all right." He repeated, "Everything is all right" twice before he died.

We talked to him, told him we loved him, that he had been a good father, that we would miss him but that everything was all right. That's the way eternal life is. It goes beyond the grave. We reminded him that he and Mom taught us that. I told him that his life reminded me of what

Paul wrote in Philippians 1:21, "For me to live *is* Christ, and to die *is* gain." We quoted parts of songs he and Mom sang with us as children. Spiritual resilience. It's about discipline and toughness, faith in a God who strengthens us, and a God who cares. I saw both of these aspects of spirituality in Dad, and I think that some of it was passed on to me.

Keys to Spiritual Growth

When I wrote the above heading it seemed a bit immodest to me. It seems to imply that I am setting myself up as a spiritual model of perfection that everyone should follow. That is far from the way I feel. I see myself rather as a vulnerable human being who is strengthened by my faith in God, by church and by extended family and friends. I know that life can be hard and that it takes a certain amount of toughness and faith to have the abundant life Jesus came to give (John 10).

I know also that I need to start with me before I can encourage others. My good friend Dr. Cliff Ganus makes this point well when he quotes this poem:

God said build a better world and I said how.
The world is such a cold dark place and so
    complicated now.
And I so young and useless there is nothing I can do.
But God in his wisdom said just build a better you.

As I try to encourage you, I want to start with myself and reflect on what I believe has helped me to grow in spirit, to become more resilient than I was. This has been a painful but strengthening exercise which I encourage you to do as well. Don't just put yourself down as weak and a failure: Look at illustrations of exceptions to the "weak and failure" story. Look at how you survived. You will discover some resources and solutions you may have forgotten you have.

My goal is to become more mature emotionally and spiritually. This means to be Christlike, goal-directed, principle-oriented, inner-directed, confident of my beliefs yet not dogmatic or set in concrete to the point of being unteachable. I want to be able to listen without overreacting and communicate without antagonizing others unnecessarily. I do not want to be irresponsible. I want to be secure and yet reliant upon God and others. I want to feel okay when I am either praised or criticized. I want to respect others and assume responsibility for myself. I want to help others but not become overly responsible for them. I want to be able to reflect and think clearly, be aware of my dependence on others and free to enjoy relationships without being defensive. I want to be able to direct my passions rather than be directed by them, yet not to ignore my feelings; need others but not be needy, clingy and manipulative of them. I want to have convictions but to be kind to those who differ. I want to be an autonomous person but also able to be interdependent with others. I want to have realistic expectations. I do not want to depend upon position to feel good about who I am. I want to be able to say what needs to be said but not to be argumentative. I want to be able to tolerate discomfort that comes from life and to adapt to stress factors that I cannot change. I want to be a fully developed self, to grow, to be Christlike, to be emotionally and spiritually mature.

I have not reached this level and probably never will, but reaching for such goals motivates me. It helps me most of the time to be able to form good relationships and to develop problem-solving skills, to think rather than react, to see alternatives that are available and make choices, to leave father and mother and live a relatively autonomous life. I try to grow through difficulties (Romans 5:1-5).[1]

Let me share with you some keys to my spiritual growth.

Key 1: Learning from Others

I have learned from my study of theories of personality, which I teach at Harding University Graduate School of Religion, that we go through various stages of development. Freud gave us psychosexual stages; Erick Erickson, psychosocial stages; Jean Piaget, intellectual stages; and Lawrence Kohlberg, moral stages of development. A small child cannot reason abstractly or make moral decisions based on principles as adults do. They have not yet matured. For example, if one child accidently breaks 20 of his mother's expensive dishes and another breaks one dish on purpose, which should receive greater punishment? Most 10-year-old children will say the one that broke 20 dishes. Most adults would pick the other child because there is a moral principle involved.[2]

In the same way, we grow spiritually. We are born again of water and the Spirit (John 3:5); we become babes in Christ (Hebrews 5:13-14); our goal is to be made in the image of God's Son (Romans 8:9; 2 Corinthians 3:18), to be full-grown (Ephesians 4:13-16) and mature (Matthew 5:48; Hebrews 6:1). Jesus grew in wisdom and stature and in favor with God and man (Luke 2:52).

As I have said already, I have been greatly influenced by my good parents, grandparents, brothers and sister, aunts and uncles, my Union

Hill community of origin, and my good wife and three children. I was influenced by many good teachers including Retta Spurlock, Lola Anderson, Avo Anderson, Batsell Barrett Baxter, Joe Sanders, Jack Lewis, Don Sime, Robert Davis, Alicia Tilley and especially W.B. West Jr. There were many more too numerous to mention. I think the key to education is an attitude that my parents taught me: My teachers knew more than I did. I was there to learn. At times, when I was in a know-it-all attitude, I did not learn anything nor did I grow. My parents and teachers became much wiser as I matured.

The Bible says, "Train up a child in the way he should go: and when he is old, he will not depart from it" (Proverbs 22:6 KJV). This is a reassuring general principle to encourage teachers and parents.

Another proverb especially fits me in my journey: "As iron sharpens iron, so one man sharpens another" (Proverbs 27:17). This fits my whole life. I have been challenged, ground and sharpened by hundreds of people, but it especially fits my 36 years as a faculty member at Harding Graduate School. Faculty meetings, interactions with staff, administration, students and alumni were sometimes grinding as iron sharpened by iron, but these interactions sharpened me, challenged my weaknesses and helped me to persevere. Unjust criticisms from those outside the school circle were especially challenging to me. People often speak far beyond their knowledge. I learned, however, from Dr. West that like Nehemiah of old, I did not have time to come down and fuss continually. I had an important work to do. Not picking up on every fight is one way to be less destructive and to avoid unnecessary grinding.

Paul said, "Do not be misled. Bad company corrupts good character." To grow spiritually, I have had to choose my associations carefully, especially friends and groups that I am around the most. Even in the church, there are extremes to avoid. There are people who are super-critical, rigid and dogmatic, who are loose with the facts and who can pull you away from a spiritual life. Likewise there are extremely liberal people who continually chip away at the foundations of one's faith. These I want to keep at a healthy distance. It's not that I don't interact with them in what I hope is a loving way, I just don't stay close to them for long. They pull me away and do not nourish the abundant life I wish to live and share with those who are interested.

The Bible has given direction and substance to my spiritual life. It appeals to my reason (Isaiah 1:18) and it gives understanding (Psalm 32:8-9). Jesus answered temptation from the Devil by saying that we do not live on bread alone but by every word that comes from the mouth of God (Matthew 4:4). The Hebrew writer said that "the word of God is living and active. Sharper than any double-edged sword, it penetrates even to dividing soul and spirit, joints and marrow; it judges the thoughts and attitudes of the heart" (Hebrews 4:12). The Word provides solid spiritual food that helps me grow toward greater spiritual maturity (5:12-14). I have not, as the psalmist, meditated on it day and night; but I have had much of it in my heart for most of my life. It has often kept me, as it did the psalmist, from doing wrong things (Psalm 119:11) and has guided me toward doing constructive things. In Psalm 1, the person who meditates on the law day and night is blessed. Such a person is like a tree planted by streams of water, which yields its fruit in season, and whose leaf does not wither. Whatever he or she does shall prosper.

Key 2: A New Birth Process

If you are not religious, you may be thinking that I am tying spiritual life and resilience too much to religion. You could point out that people who are not religious see themselves as spiritual and have learned to be quite resilient. People are very resilient who never go to church. They have learned somehow to tough it out. But I have to write from my own experience.

I believe that the spirit of each person comes from God, and many forces influence that spirit. Spiritual life comes when one recognizes his Creator and lives in relationship with Him. For me as a Christian, that began when I was a young boy. I "gave myself" to God and was born of "water and the Spirit" (John 3:5). This brought me into the spiritual family of God (Galatians 3:26-29). Paul speaks of this as becoming a new creation (2 Corinthians 5:17). The fact that I did not always live up to what this called for led me farther away from God's fellowship. I then turned back to him in spiritual renewal and found peace again when I was close to 21.

All major religions that I have studied mention something like a new birth process, which brings enlightenment and fellowship with God, as they understand Him. Most atheists today speak of spiritual life. In my thinking, my spiritual life is given me by my Father in heaven. I am temporarily here in this life as Israel was in Egypt. Like Israel, Christians are redeemed from bondage by the ransom price of the blood of Jesus (Mark 10:45). He became our perfect Passover Lamb. I don't claim to understand this fully; I just accept it by faith. We are purified by our obedience to the truth by the blood of Christ through the new birth. The seed of the new birth is the Word of God (Luke 8:11), which is incorruptible, living and abiding (Mark 13:31).

When this began to take place in my life, my attitudes and activities began to change. I began to love everyone more, people of all races from all walks of life. I began to put away evil, malice, ill will toward others, hypocrisy, envy, evil speaking and slander. This has never happened completely. It happens through a lifetime of making mistakes, godly sorrow and spiritual renewal.

When this happened, I was ready for more serious study of God's Word, pure spiritual or rational milk, food for the mind and heart. A more wholesome attitude and a healthy appetite caused me to receive the Word more completely and to begin to grow toward spiritual maturity (1 Peter 2:1-3). During this new birth process, I understand that God and Jesus come and make their home with me (John 14:23), that the Spirit becomes a part of my life (Romans 8:9). I have been bought with a price and am to glorify God in my body (1 Corinthians 6:12-20).

When I was about 12 years old, I was sitting in church one Sunday morning and heard a preacher use the "n" word in referring to African-Americans. He had just been encouraging us to live by the Golden Rule, "Do unto others as you would have them do unto you." Even at that young age, I saw his blind spot. I thought to myself, "If they don't want to be called that, I won't call them that."

When I was about 19, I was stationed at Keesler Air Force Base in Biloxi, Miss. Several of us, including one African-American stopped at a drive-in restaurant to order hamburgers. They offered to serve the white airmen but not the African-American. I'm proud to say that we said "no" and drove off.

I haven't always been that true to my calling, but as I reflect on all of this, I think the spirit of Jesus had a lot to do with it. Spiritual life, discipline, faith, resilience – they started with my parents and continued as I allowed God to come into my life more fully.

Key 3: A Meaningful Church Membership

When I was a baby, my parents took me and my siblings, Rose and Leamon, in a wagon to the Antioch Church of Christ near Gainesboro, Tenn. We moved from there to the Union Hill community and the little church that met in a schoolhouse there. I was influenced a great deal by the people, the singing and the preaching. I remember that when Joe Pippin would lead a song, he would invariably lead: "Jesus paid it all. All to Him I owe. Sin had left a crimson stain. He washed it white as snow." Mr. Joe would always emphasized "He" in that song. That and other impressions remained with me and helped mold me.

Churches I have served as a minister also influenced me: Bremerhaven, Germany, where I preached my first sermon; various churches in Jackson County where I preached while in college (Union Hill, Philadelphia, Davidson's Chapel, McCoinsville, Center Grove and others). I served churches in several places as their regular pulpit minister: Spencer, Tenn.; Brownsville, Tenn.; Southeastern Church of Christ in Indianapolis, all full-time positions. While at the graduate school in Memphis, I served Marks, Miss.; McKellar Avenue in Memphis; Earle, Ark.; Como, Miss.; Macon, Tenn. Louise and I helped start the Ross Road Church of Christ in Memphis. I have also preached and conducted seminars in numerous other churches. There were painful as well as very uplifting spiritual experiences in all of these churches. I am grateful for what I learned and for the opportunity to know and serve all of these good people. They helped me continue to grow spiritually.

This is in line with what Paul said about the church in 1 Corinthians 12. It is a body with many members, and each member has a vital yet different function. As the eye can't say to the mouth, "I don't need you," neither can one member say to another, "I don't need you." I just read that Dr. Martin Luther King said that we can all work together or all foolishly perish apart. We are to bear each other's burdens and so fulfill the law of Christ (Galatians 6:2). We are to encourage one another daily so that we may not be hardened by sin's deceitfulness (Hebrews 3:13).

The church has nourished me. It is a place of fellowship, accountability, worship, study and mutual burden-bearing. I have been mistreated and disappointed in church. There were times when I felt more spiritually nourished out in the woods by myself than I did at church, but overall, church has nourished me and led me to spiritual growth and Christian service.

Key 4: Overcoming Trials

James says that overcoming trials leads to greater maturity. Jesus is a good example of this. He was tempted by the devil, made the right choices and continued to grow in favor with God and people (Luke 2:52; Matthew 4:1-11). He learned obedience by suffering and became the author of salvation to those who obey Him (Hebrews 5:8-9). James says that we are to consider it pure joy when we face trials of many kinds. How can trials be joyful? They lead to the testing of our faith and perseverance, finished work, maturity and completeness (James 1:2-4). It's as if we are not mature or complete without trials. I once read about some expensive palm trees that were transplanted from a rough, windy environment to the yard of an expensive hotel in a more perfect, calm atmosphere. Without the wind, they died.

Allen E. Bergin and P. Scott Richards wrote *A Spiritual Strategy for Counseling and Psychotherapy*, one of the best books I have read on spirituality in counseling. Here is how they say spiritual growth proceeds:

1. You see yourself as a spiritual being accountable to God who is Spirit.
2. You recognize and utilize your spiritual resources.
3. You list your beliefs and values.
4. When given choices, you live congruent with those beliefs and values.
5. Then, you grow spiritually.[3]

This is in line with what the Hebrew writer said: "But solid food is for the mature, who by constant use have trained themselves to distinguish good and evil" (Hebrews 5:14). You put what you learn into constant use, and then you grow and become more mature. That has been my experience. Many times I have been faced with serious moral decisions. Sometimes I made the wrong decision and became a little weaker spiritually; at other times, I made the right decision and became a little stronger spiritually. The next time it was a little easier to make a similar decision either way I went. A good snowball effect starts with a good spiritual decision; a bad snowball effect with a bad decision. Aim high. When you aim at nothing, you hit it every time!

When Vince, who was addicted to pornography, decided that this behavior conflicted with his spiritual identity and was inconsistent with his beliefs and values, he stopped using pornography. It was a continual struggle, yet it caused him to grow spiritually and began to loosen pornography's grip on him.

Key 5: An Active Ministry
The word ministry may scare some of you off, but stay with me. The word "minister" means servant. Ministry thus refers to service, being of service, being active in helping others. This results from spirituality, and it nourishes spirituality toward greater growth and service.

One time at the Ross Road church, I was getting somewhat discouraged. One member said to me one Sunday, "We aren't doing anything." I agreed with her that at times I was frustrated because I left so many things undone; there were so many opportunities of which I did not seem to be able to take advantage. I was a minister and an elder there and held some 12 weekend meetings and seminars in churches each year. I had a counseling practice as a psychologist and marriage and family therapist and was working full-time at the graduate school. During all of this, Louise asked me one day, "What are you trying to prove?" I started dropping some of it not long afterward. What I said to the church member was, "I wish I could do a lot more, but I feel good about what I am doing. Last week we took a refrigerator to an unemployed family that needed one. You should have seen their faces!" The point is, I think I grew some spiritually by doing that as well. Obviously, I was trying to do too much. I just needed to set priorities and not feel guilty about not doing what others expected.

This reminds me of Bill who began the Alcoholics Anonymous movement in the 1930s. He discovered accidentally that he could stay sober better when he was helping his friend stay sober. We are blessed when we minister to others.

Over the years, I have done most of my counseling at night and on Saturdays. Invariably, I would be tired when I went to a session. Yet I often felt refreshed and invigorated after such sessions. I think I was blessed by trying to help others. I forgot about my tiredness when I focused on my clients.

It is hard to imagine a spiritually mature person who only thinks, never does. Such a person will shrivel rather than grow. We had a brilliant student one time who would stay in his room and study Greek rather than go to church. He made good grades but never did well in ministry. Jesus said this is like building your house on the sand. When the rain comes, the streams rise, the wind blows, and the house will fall. It's a foolish building plan. The wise person builds his house upon a rock, a solid foundation, and when the storm comes, it does not fall. This person is the one who "hears these words of mine and puts them into practice" (Matthew 7:24-27).

Try to help others. Get involved! It's not only the right thing to do, but it will help you grow spiritually as well.

Key 6: Seeing God's Glory in Creation
Previously, I mentioned that I sometimes felt more spiritual out in the woods alone than at church. It's really not an either/or choice; both have helped me. After my Dad died, I kept my share of the old home

place, my brother Leamon kept a section, and our son Steve bought the rest including the house where we had lived when I was 4 years old. He and his wife, Linda, have restored it nicely, and we really enjoy staying there several times a year. I enjoy walking the hills, which are incidentally steeper now than they used to be, wading the creeks, and looking at the trees, wild flowers and animals. The sky looks brilliant both during the day and at night from down in Flatt Hollow. The springs we drank from as children are still flowing. The sky and the waterfalls are still there after so much water has "gone under the bridge." The spring Mom drank from when she was a child and where Jesse watered the mule that dragged him to his death is still flowing. Somehow it all reminds me of what David wrote some 3,000 years ago,

> The heavens declare the glory of God; the skies proclaim the work of his hands. Day after day they pour forth speech; night after night they display knowledge. There is no speech or language where their voice is not heard. Their voice goes out into all the earth, their words to the ends of the world (Psalm 19:1-4).

I once read that during early church history the Roman government thought that if they destroyed all of the church buildings, crosses and Bibles, they would destroy the Christian faith. They continued their destruction of these and then proudly said to a church leader, "We have destroyed all of the symbols of your faith – your church buildings, crosses and Bibles – so your faith is gone. Christianity has been destroyed." The church leader replied, "What are you going to do with the sun, the moon and the stars?"

You may not have a Flatt Hollow to visit very often, but you can look at the sky. You can notice the trees and flowers as you take a walk in your neighborhood. You can see God in a child's eyes, in the loving attitude of some of your associates. These can remind you of God and help you to grow spiritually.

Key 7: Choosing Appropriate Goals

Freud said that we are motivated by our instincts and drives. He emphasized our biological drives and concentrated upon sex, sensuality. He also thought that we have a death (destructive) instinct; yet he emphasized our biological drives. Our need for food, water, air and sex are our main motivators.[4]

Alfred Adler, a contemporary of Freud, did not repudiate these ideas, yet he said they were not our primary motivators: Overcoming our inferiority complexes and being influenced by our goals (fictional finalism) are our main motivators. He especially emphasized goals, that we are not so much driven by our drives as by our goals.[5]

I would not deny the power of my biological drives; yet I believe I am influenced a great deal by my desire to overcome and achieve my goals. I remember one Sunday afternoon when Leamon, Rose, Don and I were playing along with several friends in the front yard. The adults, as usual, were sitting on the front porch talking. Our neighbor was offering his wisdom on what each of us would accomplish in life: Rose would get married, Leamon would do okay, Don would teach school because he was so smart, and "Billy wouldn't ever amount to anything." That statement hurt me at the time, and I realize that it could have destroyed me if I had let it do so. My self-esteem was not too high anyway. Yet I think it motivated me to try harder, perhaps to prove that he was wrong about me.

When Dad was dying, I realized how much my goals motivate me. To be Christlike, to be a wholesome person, a loving husband, a supportive father and grandfather, to be useful in ministry, to help people who are struggling, to be a good teacher, to go home to be with the Lord when I die – all of these goals pull me and motivate me to grow spiritually and to do well. I want to seek those things above (Colossians 3), to put God's will first in my life (Matthew 6:33), to grow spiritually (Hebrews 6:1), to produce the fruit of the Spirit – love, joy, peace, patience, kindness, goodness, faithfulness, gentleness and self-control – to be like Christ (1 John 3:2).

I realize I am not all that I want to be. Yet these goals help me to be better, to make a difference for good, to live an abundant life of discipline, persistence and faith. This is spiritual resilience.

Reflections

1. What is your story?
2. Do you see yourself as a spiritual being accountable to God?
3. What are your spiritual resources? How are you utilizing them?
4. What are your beliefs and values?
5. Are you living by them? Which ones? Which ones have you ignored or broken? What do you need to do to get back on a spiritual track?

6. Are you growing spiritually?

7. Is spiritual resilience more human effort or divine grace and strength? Can either be left out?

8. Are you willing to learn from others?

9. Are you involved in ministry? How? How could this be more meaningful to you?

10. What are your goals? What motivates you?

CHAPTER TWO

Redemptive Guilt

I was at a national convention listening to a well-known therapist as he explained one theory of marriage and family therapy. "Above all else," he said, "the therapist must remain neutral no matter what the client has done. After all, one idea is just as right as another, and we are not to impose our values on our clients. We don't want to lay guilt on them."

I am getting a bit more bold and talkative in such situations as I get older. I thought, "That just doesn't make sense. We don't want to force our ideas on others, but we do want to influence others or we would not counsel with them." So I asked a few questions.

"How would this neutrality principle apply if you are counseling a pedophile, a child abuser or a wife beater?" "Well," he said very nervously, "I would want them to act responsibly, but I would not try to make them feel guilty." I asked what was so bad if they felt guilty. In fact, I have never counseled with a pedophile, a child abuser or a man who beat his wife who changed if he did not first feel guilty. The speaker continued by pointing to family systems and said that their family system was different, not wrong, but different – natural for them. So we should not impose our family system on them. Who are we to judge?

I asked if all family systems are equally healthy, why counsel? In such a case, there is no reason to intervene. All therapists intervene, give homework and directives.

I'm not sure I influenced the speaker, but several therapists in the audience agreed with me. I left glad that I had expressed myself.

What is guilt? What is so bad about guilt? What does it do? Can it be constructive? If so, how?

What Is Guilt?

In the objective sense, guilt is wrongdoing. When we break a law, either theological or legal, we are guilty whether we feel guilty or not. When we violate a moral principle, we are guilty whether we feel guilty or not. When someone abuses a child, he or she is guilty. When a man beats his wife, he is guilty. When we run a red light, we are guilty. When a policeman stops us, it does no good to tell him that we don't feel guilty. He would just continue to write the ticket. In fact, it does no good to argue about whether or not the red light should be there. The fact is that it is there and we ran it, so we are guilty. It does no good to say that we lost sleep the night before and were not focused on our driving. We ran the light and are still guilty. That is the objective meaning of the word guilt.

Guilt has its subjective meaning as well. It involves moral self-scrutiny. It's how we feel. We violate our personal standards and feel guilty. Sometimes we are guilty but don't feel guilty. Jan was like that. She had an affair with her boss, a very gentle, kind man who enjoyed talking with her. They grew close and became confidants. Sex just sort of grew out of the situation. She said she knew it was wrong, but she did not feel guilty. It's hard to figure, isn't it? If it's wrong, why wouldn't you feel guilty?

Sometimes people are not guilty but feel guilty anyway. I've met many people in counseling like that. "I just don't believe God could ever forgive me," Tom, a minister friend told me. "I've had my chance, and I goofed." Tom knew better than this, but he did not put his redemptive theology into practice.

Sometimes people are guilty, and they also feel guilty. They are very sorry for their mistakes. They make no excuses and don't excessively blame others. They take responsibility for what they have done and they change. Tom knew that godly sorrow leads to repentance and leaves no regret (2 Corinthians 7:10). Something constructive should result from guilt. If it doesn't, guilt is being handled inappropriately.

Causes of Guilt

What causes guilt? Sin – wrongdoing – causes guilt. This is just common sense. I have often done wrong in my life and guilt followed. I felt guilty because I was guilty.

Rachel felt guilty because she had an affair. Part of the time she thought of this affair as a beautiful experience – something she had al-

ways dreamed of. She was in love and felt guilty when she had sex –
just going through the motions – with her husband. When I asked her
if there were some other way she could look at the affair other than seeing it as something beautiful and loving, she said yes, that it was ugly,
sinful, wrong, shameful and guilt-producing. She said her guilt was her
strongest motivation for cutting off her relationship with the other man
and rebuilding her marriage. Both couples are going to counseling and
are in the process of restoring their marital bonds.

Joe was into pornography. He felt inadequate as a man when he constantly compared himself to the perfect-image Hollywood hero. He
was too short, too unattractive and too quiet to measure up. This low
self-esteem led him into pornography, lust and guilt. It was a vicious
cycle. He described himself as a slave to sex and especially impersonal,
pornographic sex. He knew this whole industry used people and was a
shallow, ugly, sleazy business. Yet he seemed to be driven and controlled, which makes me think of what Jesus said as he replied to the
Jews on one occasion in John 8:34-36: "I tell you the truth, everyone
who sins is a slave to sin."

James the brother of Jesus wrote that we are not tempted of God because he tempts no one. Instead we are tempted when we are drawn
away by our own lusts and enticed: when the lust conceives we sin, and
sin full-grown brings death (James 1:13-15). As long as we live, we
will be tempted. We sin. We let it continue until it is full-grown, and
we are enslaved, addicted. It then controls us; we do not control it: sex,
drugs and pleasure out-of-control are examples. In such cases, we hope
we can still feel guilty. We can see the discrepancy between who we
are and who we ought to be. If so, we have a chance to experience godly sorrow, repentance, new life and a clear conscience. Redemptive
guilt has done its job of making us better.

Another cause of guilt is that we have been conditioned to feel guilty.
Appropriately or inappropriately, we learned to feel guilty. Our parents
might have overdone the discipline and shame, so we feel overly guilty
about everything. They seldom forgave us, so we don't forgive ourselves. If our parents were guilt-ridden, we probably are also. We just
picked it up from them. Charlie told me that he was afraid not to continually feel guilty because if he didn't he might sin. Such neurotic,
out-of-proportion guilt does not prevent sin. It weakens our spiritual
strength and makes it more likely that we will continue to sin. This
false guilt leads to self-punishment, self-rejection, isolation, shame and

feelings of inferiority. We feel cut off from God and others as well – unworthy, hypocritical. On the other hand, many of us were conditioned to feel appropriate guilt, which is a blessing.

Men fear punishment and experience guilt as self-punishment. Women are often conditioned to feel guilty about many things, responsible for most problems. When first graders are asked why they made a poor grade, girls are likely to say it was their fault, they did not study enough. Boys say that their teacher does not like them.

Shame is the feeling of being exposed and examined by another person who is critical. We are being judged. We then experience anxiety and a fear of abandonment and isolation and want to hide. We feel unlovable and not only believe that we made mistakes but that we are a mistake, which makes us prone to depression and other mental illnesses.

In summary, guilt is caused by sin and by conditioning. Either has consequences that need to be addressed.

Consequences of Guilt

All guilt is not bad. Redemptive guilt is like a fire alarm that signals when something is wrong. The wise person is alerted to the alarm and tries to take care of the problem. Neurotic guilt would turn off the alarm or run away.

Neurotic Guilt

Susan felt guilty because she did not measure up to her mother who holds a doctorate and taught in a university. She was "only a housewife," and this just would not do. Her mother had achieved so much and she "so little." She "ought" to be like her mother. She wasn't, so she felt guilty. She was a "nobody."

Logan cheated on exams while he was in college. He had become the owner of a large grocery store, a church leader and a successful father and husband. He was well thought of in his community. He had long since repented of his cheating and had become an honest man. "Everybody cuts corners at times I guess," he said, "but I have learned from my mistakes." Yet he continually badgered himself for his "flaw in character" that led him to cheat on college exams over 20 years ago. A decent person just would not do that. How could he ever face anyone?

Debilitating guilt is shame, anger, anxiety and guilt in a never-ending vicious cycle. You feel angry, then guilty for being angry, then turn anger inward, which leads to depression.[1] Logan had done this and was suffering from major depression. He kept going back to his sin of cheating, which proved to him that he was a phony. Shame from guilt left him "helpless, powerless, worthless and lonely." The sinful act bothers his conscience, which hurts his ego, similar to Freud's id, superego and ego.[2] Fear and guilt caused Logan not to talk about and resolve these issues. This guilt is not constructive, not redemptive. All Logan and Susan did with their guilt for some 20 years was to punish themselves with it. This is not what guilt is intended to do. It should lead us to forgiveness and peace and make us better people. A growing person accepts imperfections, admits sins and learns from mistakes. That's what redemption is all about.

A biblical character named Esau knew that he had made a mistake when he sold his birthright as Isaac's first-born son to his younger twin brother Jacob for a "mess of pottage," a bowl of stew. Bitterness resulted. Yet he did not find it in his heart to truly repent (Genesis 25; Hebrews 12:14-17). He did reconcile with his brother, but it happened 20 years later. King Saul brought much glory to Israel, yet he became jealous of young, handsome, successful David who killed his ten thousands while Saul only killed his thousands (1 Samuel 17-31). This jealousy led Saul to take hundreds of soldiers to battle in order to hunt David and kill him, although David was fighting battles for King Saul and Israel. When he would try and fail in his efforts to kill David, he would feel guilty for what he had done, would cease his aggression for a while, and then start out again to kill David. His guilt brought shame, fear and sorrow. It led to misery and death. In the end, Saul fell on his own sword to avoid being killed by the Philistines. He faced his guilt like a man; he blamed somebody else. The Bible says that God rejected Saul and gave the kingdom of Israel to David (1 Samuel 17-31).

Looking back over my life, I can see myself in some of these circumstances. Guilt has not always been constructive in my own life. I have not only acknowledged my mistakes, but at times I have dwelt on them far too long. But I have learned what redemptive guilt is and accept it as my constructive model.

Redemptive Guilt

Esau and Saul were actually guilty. Judas, who betrayed Jesus and then hanged himself, could be added to the list. They just did not handle guilt constructively. They experienced the punitive but not the redemptive force of guilt (Matthew 26-27).

On the other hand, others handled guilt differently. Clayton stole some money from his company. He felt guilt for months with symptoms of depression and sleeplessness. He too felt flawed in character, worthless, ashamed and at times helpless and hopeless. Yet he did not stop there. He sought professional help, processed his sin and pain and made amends. He confessed his theft to his company, returned the money, confessed his sin at church, asked God and everyone who was involved to forgive him and found forgiveness and peace. He did lose his job, but he was not bitter. He found another job, worked extra hard and contributed some money to his old company to set out some flowers and trees. He was not the same man. His guilt had been redemptive.

King David was like that. He saw a beautiful woman named Bathsheba bathing on her roof. He sent for her and committed adultery with her. As a result, she became pregnant. He complicated his guilt by putting her husband Uriah on the front lines of battle where he was killed. David then brought Bathsheba to his house as his wife. He no doubt thought he had covered his sins adequately, but then Nathan, the prophet of God, told him a story about a rich man and a traveler. A hungry traveler came to the rich man for food. The rich man refrained from taking his own sheep or cattle to feed the traveler. Instead, he took the ewe lamb that belonged to a poor man and prepared it for the traveler to eat. David burned with anger against the rich man and said that the rich man deserved to die, that he must pay four times over because he did such a thing and had no pity. Nathan said, "You are the man" (2 Samuel 12). David then acknowledged that he had sinned against the Lord.

There were consequences to this sin both bad and good. Uriah was killed, the baby born to David and Bathsheba died and David felt miserable. In Psalm 32, he writes of these consequences: He kept silent, his bones wasted away through his groaning all day long. God's hand was continually heavy upon him, his strength was sapped. In Psalm 51, he describes the consequences in this way: he had sinned – transgressed against God. He had done evil. God was justified in judging him. He had been a sinner continually. He felt like a castaway from God's presence, a man without joy.

He acknowledged his sin and did not cover up his iniquity, and God forgave him. He was confident that God could be found in prayer, that He was his hiding place, would protect him from trouble, and surround him with songs of deliverance. He learned that the Lord's unfailing love surrounds the person who trusts in Him (Psalm 32).

In Psalm 51, David seeks cleansing, a pure heart and a steadfast spirit. He wants God to restore to him the joy of his salvation and a willing spirit to sustain him. After that happened, he will teach transgressors God's ways, and sinners would turn back to Him. He would declare God's praise. His spirit was broken and contrite, but God would not despise such a person. He would forgive and accept David's worship and service. David would become a man after God's own heart. He learned to do "everything God wanted him to do" (Acts 13:22).

Peter's story is similar. He said he would never deny Jesus. Others might, but he never would. Then, he denied Jesus three times. Yet when the rooster crowed, as Jesus had predicted, Peter, realizing his sin, went out and wept bitterly (Matthew 26). After Jesus' resurrection, the Lord questioned Peter asking him if he loved him. In fact, he asked the question three times, using a play on different Greek words for love, to see if Peter had really learned from his sin. Peter was emphatic: "You know I love you, Lord!" Then, Jesus said, "Feed my sheep" (John 21). Peter experienced godly sorrow, not just sorrow that he got caught, but sorrow that brought him to repentance, forgiveness and peace. He went out and served Jesus well. He didn't hide forever because of his sin. His was redemptive guilt. God redeemed him from his sins and for service. He saved him from spiritual death and for a useful life. That is the purpose of redemptive guilt. It involves discipline, persistence and faith.

I have learned something from David and Peter. I have learned not just to concentrate on the sins of my past but to deal with them spiritually and to learn from them. I accept God's forgiveness and the peace that Jesus gives (John 14:27). I am thankful that God has enabled me to minister to others as well. This validates the attitude of love that I have in my heart. This is redemptive guilt. It leads to godly sorrow, repentance, forgiveness, peace and service.

In summary, there can be negative or positive consequences of guilt. Consequences are negative, whether guilt is imagined, exaggerated, appropriate, ignored or used just to punish ourselves. It is positive when it is processed appropriately and leads to redemption, peace, growth and usefulness. It depends on how guilt is handled.

How People Handle Guilt

In my personal life and in my counseling experience, I have found that there are many ways people handle guilt. We will be discussing seven of those ways.

Some Ignore It

To ignore guilt seems to be a part of our national civic religion. We want people to be responsible but not to feel guilty. We don't want to lay guilt on anybody. We think some action is wrong, but we don't feel guilty about it. I've already mentioned examples of such: "I'll just ignore it, and maybe it will go away. Time will heal."

It is possible to blow our guilt out of proportion, yet time in itself does not heal real guilt that needs to be processed properly. Notice this proverb: "He who conceals his sins does not prosper, but whoever confesses and renounces them finds mercy" (Proverbs 28:13).

Jan who had "a beautiful affair" but did not at first feel guilty, found relief only when she was honest with herself, admitted wrongdoing, confessed to her husband and to God and went for marital therapy. She then began to deal with the ugly facts of having sex for 20 months with a married man. She experienced godly sorrow, repentance, redemption, forgiveness and reconciliation. She said "I know I am doing what is right, and I feel better. I can learn to love my husband again, and he's making it easy by being nice to me." That would not have happened had she continued to ignore her conscience, which told her correctly that what she was doing was wrong.

Some Minimize and Rationalize It

Clinebell says that guilt is the significant element in problems when people come for counseling. He mentions six significant types of conscience problems: appropriate guilt; neurotic guilt; self-righteous conscience; underdeveloped conscience, which lacks appropriate guilt; emptiness; and underdeveloped conscience, which lacks social responsibility.[3] Those who minimize and rationalize guilt do not have appropriate guilt but rather an underdeveloped conscience. They have been under-conditioned.

Jerry was like that. He had continually taken advantage of his parents: borrowed money from them that he never repaid, abused them verbally and did things "just to spite them." He first said that he had done nothing wrong; then, that it was no big deal; then, that they deserved what he dished out. But he changed his mind when his mom was on her deathbed. He came to feel very sorry for his actions, repented and apologized for the pain he had inflicted over the years. They also apologized to him for some of their reactions. They hugged and cried and forgave each other. His mother looked up from her bed and said, "Jerry, I love you. That's the best present you could have given me. I've longed many years for this day." Jerry quit playing the games of minimization and rationalization. He admitted his guilt, confessed and made it right. Forgiveness brought peace and reconciliation to everyone. His mother died that next week.

Rachel, whom we met earlier, fits this category as well. She minimized, rationalized her affair and lowered her standards. It was a beautiful experience, no big deal; until she really began to see all aspects of the experience. Then she saw it as ugly, sinful and guilt-producing. That's when she began to deal with it constructively.

Neil was meeting with a co-worker at work to talk, hug and kiss during breaks. Although both were married, he saw nothing wrong with their behavior. After all, they had not gone all the way and "everyone is doing it." When he processed all of this, he admitted that his behavior was inappropriate sexual activity and that he would be furious if his wife engaged in similar activity. He broke it off and began working to repair his marriage.

I hesitate to mention anything political, but I can't ignore what has happened in our highest governmental office the last few years. We saw the minimization, rationalization and lowering of standards to play down the seriousness of our president's sexually inappropriate activities. It was a right-wing conspiracy; it was because they were from Arkansas; it was not really sex; she was having sex but he wasn't; and they did not go all the way. They even tried to insinuate Kenneth Starr was a liar or some kind of oddball because he said he had never committed adultery. Minimization and rationalization did not work. Yet when our president admitted his mistake and said he was sorry, many in the nation forgave him and wished him well. Although his sexual activities seemed to be habitual and perhaps addictive, I thought I saw some pain and real remorse in his face when he faced the nation with all of this.

This scenario is similar to that of the Nixon years. At least during the early days of Watergate, those close to the president along with Nixon himself denied that he did anything wrong, then they said that he had no knowledge of what happened; then that what he did was minimal, then that everyone else had done it also, and then he resigned "for the good of the nation." Zealous Nixon supporters still say that what he did was minimal and that others did the same thing for years as though that made it right.

Pete Rose, who has more hits in baseball than anyone else, was selected as one of the greatest baseball players ever, in spite of his gambling activities, which led to his being banned from baseball for life. I was glad they let him appear at Yankee Stadium to receive his honor, but I was puzzled by the reaction of fans. They gave him the longest standing ovation of anyone who had received the award including Hank Aaron, Babe Ruth, Ted Williams, Joe DiMaggio or Mickey Mantle. I wondered what was going on. Did they not want to lay guilt on him? Did they minimize and rationalize it away? Or did they just want to forgive and reinstate him? I don't know, but I do know that many do not like anyone to "lay guilt" on others or punish them for wrongdoing.

I was on a criminal court jury in 1999. We had a case in which the accused was charged with vehicular homicide. Three children had been killed while he was driving drunk. While waiting with our jury pool, I heard one prospective juror say, "If they ask me, I'll say not guilty. I've been there myself." We have all sinned, and maybe that causes us to want forgiveness and acceptance so much that we have lost our moral courage to uphold important values and beliefs. Yet we know deep down that these values are vital to us individually and to our society as well. Neither lowering our standards nor being perfectionistic is the answer. Realistic standards with discipline, persistence and faith will help us live productive lives.

Some Exaggerate It

In cognitive therapy, thinking distortions are examined and challenged. The rationale for such therapy is that thinking affects feelings and actions. Change the thinking and feelings and actions will change as well. Exaggeration is an example of distorted thinking.

Susan, whom I introduced previously, represents a kind of exaggerated guilt, a manufactured guilt produced from internalized inappropriate standards. She thought that she must hold a doctorate because her mother had a doctorate. When she processed this, she concluded that she was doing exactly what she wanted to do; she loved being a full-time homemaker. She had always wanted to do that. She realized that she had been conditioned by modern American society to believe that full-time homemaking was not a great achievement, not a challenge. She had bought into all of that because she admired her mother so much, but she came to see that she would honor her mother most by being what she was cut out to be. She began to feel good about her role and herself, fulfilled!

Logan had done wrong by cheating on tests in college, but he exaggerated his guilt. It was as if he was the worst person in the world. He could never be forgiven, never do anything worthwhile, never hold his head up again and never be redeemed. He exaggerated his guilt and continued to punish himself. However, he learned to persist by faith, to process his guilt and to turn godly sorrow into something constructive. That's what salvation and redemption are all about!

Oscar was in a mental hospital. He had been there for years and had been treated by several competent professionals, but he was not improving. He was stuck on his guilt and specifically what he had done when he was 8 years old. He had caught a baby bird and squeezed it to death in his hand. Yes, this was terrible! Yes, it deserved considerable processing and attention by parents and perhaps by counselors. But he never dealt with it at that time. He kept it to himself and felt guilty into middle adulthood, feeling worse and worse, more and more guilty all of the time. He continually said to himself, "I'm no good. No decent person would squeeze a baby bird to death. I'm a monster. I don't deserve to live."

One day his chaplain gave him a simple, unusual bit of homework. Get some bread and feed the birds out in the mental hospital yard. He did and began to feel better. When asked why he felt better, he told the chaplain that when he was feeding the birds he suddenly realized that he was not the same person that had killed the bird when he was 8 years old. The person alive now was not one who destroyed birds but one who instead fed them. He had exaggerated his guilt but had been redeemed. He had grown through his guilt.

Some Punish Themselves

We try to deal with our guilt in many ways. Some project it onto others and become victims. They repress it into the subconscious; emotions become deadened or uncontrollable. They then react to insignificant circumstances, become rigid, legalistic and works oriented (Matthew 23). Others become obsessive and are unable to feel forgiven. Others try to redeem themselves by doing something socially acceptable.[4] Our heart is deceitful, and we can't think clearly (Jeremiah 17:9). We may handle guilt inappropriately and punish ourselves either physically or more often emotionally.

Susan who had cheated on her husband could not allow herself to be forgiven. He was willing, but she could not turn loose of the guilt of her sin for several years. She eventually did forgive herself but not until she was seriously depressed and was treated extensively in a hospital and in outpatient care with counseling and continued medication.

Logan beat himself up emotionally for some 20 years for cheating on exams in college. In his mind, his character was hopelessly flawed, and he did not deserve to be forgiven and to be at peace.

In ancient cultures, guilty people actually beat themselves physically. They often did extensive damage to their bodies with this process. We don't do this usually, but we beat ourselves emotionally and will not let something constructive happen.

Florence, a 40-year-old mother, was very suicidal. She had a list of 10 things she needed to do before she killed herself. She had done nine of them. Her background involved an abusive father who punished her as a child by whipping her with the plug end of an electric cord, often to the point of blood on her back where the plug hit her. He also punished her by burning her arms with cigarettes. She had burn marks all over both arms. At age 40, she burned herself with cigarette butts when she "was a bad girl." I'll tell you later what we did to help Florence.

Self-punishment goes far beyond appropriate godly sorrow that works repentance and leaves no regrets (2 Corinthians 7:10).

Some Do Good Works

Sam was like that. He had been in a constant argument with his neighbor for years about a property line. They fussed and yelled but never resolved anything. Finally, Sam was so angry that he hid behind a tree and shot "just to scare" his neighbor and killed him instead. No one knew who did it.

Sam tossed and turned for years trying to sleep but slept only with difficulty. He did all kinds of good works for his neighbor's wife and for others in the community. He gave more than he could afford to charity but still was not at peace with himself and with God. Good works alone did not make it right.

Some Repent, Confess and Accept Forgiveness

As we have seen, causes of guilt vary. What to do about it also varies.[5]

Charlie, who had been over-conditioned to feel guilty, learned not to feel guilty about everything. He learned to feel as though he was a worthwhile person. He challenged his negative thinking and was able to turn it around and say: "By God's grace, I'm okay."

Joe learned that he was responsible for his pornography addiction, and learned to behave differently. He learned to relate to women and view them as more than sex objects and to "stay close to God and friends to hold me accountable." He said: "I repented of my sins and accepted God's forgiveness for the way I had exploited women."

Susan adjusted her expectations of herself. She no longer had to hold a doctorate as her mother had. Her new goal was to be "what I was meant to be," which she concluded was to be a good person, wife and mother. She said she no longer felt guilty for not measuring up to her mother.

Logan still felt badly about his dishonesty in the past, but he "took it to God, confessed and prayed for forgiveness and for the courage to learn from his mistakes." He found peace and a place of useful service in "making up for cutting corners before." He read extra books, wrote useful articles and worked hard to do constructive activities that would "prove to myself that I am not the same dishonest person that I was before. What I am now is the important test," he concluded. He learned from his sins and found forgiveness and meaning in what he was doing to overcome his dishonest tendencies.

Sam, who was dying of cancer, went to a minister and lawyer for advice. The minister listened and helped him realize that God still loved him and helped him form a plan. The lawyer advised him to tell the sheriff what had happened. He also confessed to the widow of the man whom he had accidentally killed. She forgave him, and he left $10,000 in his will to her daughter for a college education. He had been a Christian before; so he and the minister prayed together for forgiveness and redemption. He died five days later.

What helped Florence? She began counseling with a Christian counselor and Bible study with a minister. The counselor, who was under my supervision, tried to gain extra time before she killed herself. The 10th item on her to-do list before she killed herself was to see her youngest daughter begin school. The counselor commended her for wanting to be a good mother and then asked her how she thought her daughter would feel when she marched across the stage and got her high school diploma with no one there to see her graduate. She adjusted her timetable for suicide until then.

Meanwhile the minister made a significant point. It was in Isaiah 53, a messianic prophecy of a savior to come:

He was despised and rejected by men, a man of sorrows,
and familiar with suffering.
Like one from whom men hide their faces he was
despised, and we esteemed him not.
Surely he took up our infirmities and carried our sorrows,
yet we considered him stricken by God, smitten by him
and afflicted.

But he was pierced for our transgressions, he was crushed
for our iniquities;
The punishment that brought us peace was upon him,
And by his wounds we are healed.

We all, like sheep, have gone astray, each of us has turned
to his own way;
And the Lord has laid on him the iniquity of us all.
(Isaiah 53:3-6).

The line that caught Florence's attention was the one that said, "by his wounds we are healed." She no longer had to wound herself; she said, "His stripes healed me." She accepted this deep theological thought at face value and gave her guilt to Jesus.

The preacher pointed her to two other passages, Acts 8 and 1 Peter 1. The Ethiopian mentioned in Acts 8 was reading from Isaiah 53 when the evangelist Philip joined him in the chariot. The Ethiopian wondered to whom Isaiah 53 referred, himself or someone else. Then Philip began with that very passage and told him the good news about Jesus, which led to his faith and baptism. They both went down into the water and Philip baptized him. The Ethiopian then went on his way rejoicing.

First Peter 1 helped explain this to Florence. The preacher pointed out that we are redeemed by the "precious blood of Christ, a lamb without blemish or defect. Through Him we believe in God so that our faith and hope is in God." He also pointed out that we are purified by obeying the truth so that we have sincere love for others, that we have thus been born again by imperishable seed through the living and enduring Word of God. Then, we put away all malice, deceit, hypocrisy, envy and slander of every kind and crave spiritual milk as newborn babes so that we may grow up in our salvation. Forgiveness, peace, renewal and constructive living follow (1 Peter 1:18-2:3). This is what Florence accepted, and she is still alive and living a good life. She watched with motherly pride as her youngest daughter graduated from high school. She still has scars from childhood abuse, but she is facing these challenges one day at a time.

Martin kept telling himself that he was no good. He learned to write on a piece of paper his negative self talk and then talk back to himself:

NEGATIVE SELF-TALK	TALK BACK
"I'm no good."	"Not so. I stole some money years ago, but that does not mean I'm no good. I gave the money back, and have sought forgiveness."
"I'll never get over this."	"Not true. I'm making progress. God still loves me."
"Everything I've ever done will be held against me on the judgment day."	"Not true. My sins have been covered by the blood of the lamb. I'll accept forgiveness, hold my head up and go on. It's what I do from now on that's important."

When Martin argued with himself in this way, he began to change his thinking, which began to change his feelings. He began to see that he was a worthwhile person who needed to live his life fully and enjoy being alive. He began to call it the "abundant life in Christ" (John 10:10).

Stella had an abortion at the age of 15. Ten years later she was still having nightmares about "the baby that never was." The night before her due date, she had her first nightmare. The baby was lying on a grocery shelf where she was shopping, crying, "Mama, why did you kill me?" She had been in therapy for six months but the nightmares continued. She learned to relax and visualize God, her Father, running with open arms to welcome her home. She learned to "hear Him saying to me that I had sinned but that He still loved me and had forgiven me. I even visualized His arms around me reassuring me that I am forgiven, that I am still His child." The nightmares stopped after three weeks of counseling which included these visualization exercises.

Some Make Restitution and Do Redemptive Things

I have mentioned these illustrations previously: Clayton paid back money he had stolen and set out a garden for his company. Logan did extra study and writing to make up for his cheating. Sam established a $10,000 college scholarship for the daughter of the man he had accidentally killed. Oscar learned to feed the birds. Stella concentrated on being a good mother to her other children instead of just thinking about the baby she had aborted. Here is one other example. J.T. raped his younger sister when she was 10 and he was 17. After he was caught and continually confronted in therapy, he experienced godly sorrow, got down on his knees before his sister and their parents, expressed his sorrow and begged her for forgiveness. After the sister was convinced that he was sincere, the counselor suggested that he needed to do something to prove his sincerity. They decided he was to begin paying into a college scholarship for his sister. He felt better, she felt better, and something redemptive came out of the ugly experience.

Restitution is an old word that can have new meaning in dealing with redemptive guilt. Zacchaeus recognized this principle some 2,000 years ago. He had gained his wealth probably by collecting more taxes than people owed, but when he met Jesus, he said, "and now I give half of my possessions to the poor, and if I have cheated anybody out of anything, I will pay back four times the amount" (Luke 19:8).

Restitution is not always possible. Redemptive service can prove to you that you have changed, that you are different. Instead of continually persecuting yourself over sins of the past that have already been processed and forgiven, ask yourself what you have learned from such sins. If you stole, do you steal now? If you cheated, do you cheat now? If you used others sexually, do you still do so now? If not, you have learned and growth has occurred, and with God's help, redemption has occurred.

Reflections

1. Define guilt: objective, subjective aspects of guilt.
2. Define neurotic guilt and redemptive guilt.
3. How can conditioning as a cause of guilt be appropriate?
4. What is over-conditioning as it relates to guilt?
5. How do we punish ourselves inappropriately for our guilt?
6. Is restitution always possible?
7. How can we tell when we have learned from our mistakes?
8. What is your understanding of the new birth process?
9. How can cognitive restructuring be helpful with guilt?
10. What do discipline, persistence and faith have to do with redemptive guilt?

CHAPTER THREE

Turning Worry and Anxiety Around

I have been around people all of my life who admitted that they worried excessively. They worried when there seemed to be no need to worry. They were often very anxious as well. Most of my clients list worry and anxiety as one of their problems. In fact, regardless of what your problem is, you may worry and experience anxiety somewhat along with that problem. Discipline, persistence and faith help overcome worry and relieve anxiety.

What is the difference between worry and anxiety? Worry is more specific and perhaps less severe. You know what you are worried about, and it may not cause any real dysfunction in your life. Anxiety is often more generalized and may cause extensive personal, social and occupational impairment. It is usually difficult if not impossible for you to say exactly why you are anxious. You just feel very apprehensive, vulnerable and threatened. You dread the future.

I have heard several amusing stories about worry. An alumna of Harding University told me about a sermon regarding worry that Jimmy Allen once preached in chapel. That night, she and her friend confronted her suitemate about her tendency to worry excessively. "You worry too much," they told her, "and God is very displeased with you."

"I know, I know," her friend replied. "I worry about that all of the time!"

My favorite story about worry is about a farmer who worried continually. When his wife saw that worried look on his face one day, she asked, "What are you worried about now?"

"I'm worried about my old mule dying," he replied.

"But you don't have an old mule," she said.

"Yes, I know," he countered, "but I was just thinking about how bad it would be if I did have an old mule, and he died."

Everybody has something to worry about. One man was living in a certain house when it began to leak. When he complained, someone replied, "You don't have anything to worry about it."

"Yes, I do," he replied. "I found this old abandoned house 9 years ago and moved in. If someone doesn't fix the roof, I'm going to move."

Jesus cautions against worry and anxiety in Matthew 6:25-34. Just notice the list of things he says people worry about: food, drink, clothing and tomorrow. Much could be listed under each of these categories.

People have their list of worries at each stage of life. Our 4-year-old grandson, Jonathan, took a deep breath recently and told his baby sitter, "I'm overwhelmed." When asked what that meant, he replied, "I just can't take it any more." He evidently had had a rough day.

Children worry about catching buses, homework and acceptance by peers. Teens worry about acceptance, dates, changes in their bodies, and measuring up to expectations. College students worry about grades, marriage and career. The list for young adults includes jobs, career, marriage, children, house payments and medical bills. After retirement, health, medical bills, taxes, income, extended family and eternity become more prominent.

Finding meaning from one's life is important. I'm at that point now and am able to see my life as very meaningful. What seems important now is spirituality, family, work, reflection on previous ministry activities, and extended family and friends.

Everybody has worries. We just need to find a way to work through them and turn them around into something that, with God's help, we can handle.

Symptoms of Anxiety

We can tell when we worry extensively. In fact, we can give a list of what we are worried about. It is more difficult, however, to diagnose anxiety. There are so many kinds of anxiety: panic disorder, agoraphobia, phobias, obsessive-compulsive disorder, post-traumatic stress disorder, anxiety disorder due to a medical condition, substance-abuse anxiety disorder and others as well. We need to see a psychologist, psychiatrist or other qualified mental health specialist to be sure of an accurate diagnosis and effective treatment.

You may recognize the following symptoms of anxiety, and that will help you to know you need help from a mental health professional. If you are having a panic attack, you will have one or all of these symptoms:

1. intense fear or discomfort, palpitations, pounding heart, an accelerated heart rate;
2. sweating, trembling or shaking, sensations of shortness of breath or smothering, feeling of choking, chest pain or discomfort, nausea or abdominal distress;
3. feeling dizzy, unsteady, lightheaded or faint;
4. feelings of unreality or detachment, fear of losing control or going crazy, fear of dying, numbness or tingling sensations and chills or hot flashes.[1]

I have seen more people with mild depression or with generalized anxiety disorder than with any other diagnosis during my practice as a psychologist and marriage and family therapist. SWICKER is my memory device for this diagnosis:

S omatic symptoms, fatigue.
W orry, excessive anxiety.
I rritability, easily agitated.
C oncentration difficulties, hard to focus.
K eyed up, on edge/muscle tension.
I nsomnia, can't sleep well usually.
R estlessness, nervous, hard to sit still.

The diagnostic key I learned recently is WORRY plus three equals GAD – generalized anxiety disorder. If you see yourself here, please call some qualified mental health therapist for help. He or she can lead you to a turnaround faster. Sometimes medication is called for; at other times, psychotherapy (counseling including relaxation) will be sufficient.

Causes of Worry and Anxiety

There are numerous causes for worry and anxiety. We will be discussing four of them.

Biological

One possible cause is biology. This word includes genetics, brain chemistry and anything biological. A heart attack or disease can cause anxiety. Brain chemistry affects mood. That's why a tranquilizer can have a calming effect on a person who is anxious. There is some evidence that genes affect chronic anxiety. It may tend to run in the family even when learning possibilities are teased out as a factor: Identical twins raised separately, for example, may tend to be equally anxious. Biology affects everything; so it obviously affects worry and anxiety. Yet there are other causes as well.

Psychological

There are psychological causes as well. People are conditioned, much like Pavlov's dogs, to be anxious. For example, parents who are excessively concerned about storms have children who react in a similar way. They use the same expressions to verbalize their worries. Other children hardly notice when a big cloud is overhead. To me, rain is a pleasant experience, probably because I used to sleep so well under a tin roof when it was raining. My parents expressed no fear of storms, and I was usually allowed to rest when it was raining. We came in from the fields, especially if there was a severe storm.

Sociological

Some worry and anxiety are primarily sociological caused by the situation. A death in the family; divorce involving you, your parents or your child; or a job loss are all situational causes of worry and anxiety. In such cases, it's almost impossible not to be anxious. It may not be healthy, but it's normal.

Spiritual

There are spiritual causes of worry and anxiety as well. This has to do with how you view yourself as a spiritual being in this vast universe. Does God care for you? Do you matter to anyone? Do you live with integrity? Will your needs be met? Do you feel okay about being you? Are you able to find meaning and significance as a person? Are you at peace with God, yourself and others? The answer to all of these questions affects worry, anxiety and contentment. It's not just what happens to you; it's what you do with what happens to you. The same fire that melts the butter hardens the egg.

Your spiritual life, as I mentioned in Chapter 1, affects you and everything you do. Some problems have no other answer other than spiritual, which brings me to the main thrust of this chapter.

What to Do About Worry and Anxiety

You have perhaps now seen that worry and anxiety are dysfunctional forces in your life. They keep you from achievement and take away your peace. So what do you do about it? Here are 10 suggestions that I have found to be helpful in my own life as well as in my private practice as a psychologist:

Analysis and Planning
Learning to analyze what is bothering you and planning what to do about it is an important first step. What are you worried about? How much of a threat to your well-being is it? Do you think it is biological, psychological, sociological or spiritual? Is it some of each? What do you need to concentrate on? What do you need to do? Read a book? Talk to a friend? A spiritual guide? See a doctor or a psychologist? What plan should you follow? Formulate a tentative plan and then begin to follow it. It takes discipline, persistence and faith. Persistence is necessary (Proverbs 18:15). Without it, we are helpless (Proverbs 24:10).

Prayer, Spiritual Growth and Strength
All of the spiritually mature people I have admired were people of prayer. Jesus prayed before major decisions in his life. Paul urged his readers to pray without ceasing (1 Thessalonians 5:17).

God knows our hearts (Proverbs 21:2). We speak from the overflow of our hearts (Matthew 12:34), our wellspring of life (Proverbs 4:23). Peaceful living comes from peaceful hearts just as fresh water comes from fresh springs (James 3:11). A new birth can change the way we are and the way we feel. Christ living in us can give us peace and the abundant life he promises (Galatians 2:20; John 10:10). Prayer and spiritual growth can give us strength to overcome, power to mount up with wings as eagles (Isaiah 40:28-31) and eternal encouragement and good hope (2 Thessalonians 2:16-17).

I can remember when my prayers were most fervent: when Louise was seriously ill, when Steve was hit with a javelin in his back, when Danny had a disc removed from his back, when I was sick at different times, when my parents were sick, when Papaw (David and Kevin's other grandfather) was seriously ill with cancer, when my boys were looking for a job, when I was looking for a job, and other times as well. Sometimes God did not respond the way I wanted, but I still prayed with persistence and faith.

I won't tell you all of the specifics, but I can remember several times when I prayed and didn't get what I wanted, and it turned out better for me eventually. For instance, I once prayed for a scholarship to go to a trade school, which probably would have kept me from doing what I have done. Another time I prayed for a job that would have taken me from my work at Harding Graduate School in Memphis. Neither prayer was answered the way I wished, but I think I am better off because of it. This gives me faith to continue my prayer life with persistence, praying specifically for the concerns of my heart. I pray every day for my children, their families, for myself, my wife, the church, my work, my clients, our health and for others. This is a part of my faith, and it makes a difference in the way I handle worry and anxiety.

Action

One day I was walking to my office and felt some gravel in my shoe. I realized I had only about a quarter of a mile to go, so I continued walking only to find that the longer I tried to ignore the gravel, the more it dug into my foot. I finally stopped, pulled off my shoe, and dumped the gravel out. The problem was solved.

Some worries are like that. You know the problem, you know what to do about it, but you haven't done it yet. Just do it!

George could not sleep. His conscience bothered him. He was having an affair with a colleague at work. His conscience was alive and well, and I was glad. When told what he needed to do, he refused saying: "I just can't do it. I'm happier than I've ever been in my life, and I believe God wants me to be happy." It's hard to think straight when passion gets involved. He said he was happy; yet he could not sleep because his conscience bothered him. Like the rich, young ruler who came to Jesus, he went away sorrowful (Matthew 19). Knowing what to do is not enough to turn it around; we have to take the needed action. Just do it!

Solomon said some 3,000 years ago in the book of Proverbs that obedience and healthy living bring happiness (10:28), protection from the Lord (10:29), life and security (11:30;12:3), confidence (14:26), smiles and happiness (15:30), goodness and honor (21:21), peace and quiet (17:1), physical health (17:22), a bright future (28:10) and help from the Lord (20:22). It sounds too good; yet I know that the way I live affects my well-being, my effectiveness and the way I feel. Living with integrity is a key to feeling good.

Acceptance

Uncle Robert told me a week before he died with cancer that he wanted more than anything to be able to get up and walk away from the hospital. He then said he knew he couldn't but that he "was ready to go," that he was "at peace." He accepted what he could not change.

When I was about 30, my hair began to fall out. I tried several remedies with no success. I prayed about it; even tried to convince God that I could preach better if I had hair. Yet it continued to fall out. My solution? I learned to accept what I could not change. It seems almost trivial now as I think about it. Some worries are like my hair – not too important in a way, but we can make them important and rob ourselves of peace, self-esteem and happiness. We make ourselves unhappy.

I have a copy of the Serenity Prayer on my office wall. I'm still trying to follow it:

> Lord, give me the serenity to accept the things
>   I cannot change.
> The strength to change the things I can.
> And the wisdom to know the difference.

Service

Bill, who founded Alcoholics Anonymous, discovered accidentally that he could stay sober better when he tried to help his friend stay sober. Service to others gets our minds off ourselves and breaks the spiral of negative thinking that perpetuates anxiety.

Before her husband died, Eva enjoyed volunteer work at the local hospital. After he died, she quit all such activity. She withdrew and thought continually about how unfair it was for "God to take him from me," a very common and understandable reaction to such a significant loss. When she forced herself to go back to her hospital work, she began to grow through her grief and get back to more normal feelings. She was not the same as before, but she had adjusted. She could "at least be helpful to others," she said.

Often when we do good for others, it comes back to us. I heard a good example of this recently. One day a poor farmer in Scotland was working in the fields when he heard a cry for help coming from a nearby bog. He dropped his tools and ran to the bog. There he found a terrified boy mired to his waist in black muck, screaming and struggling to free himself. Farmer Fleming saved the boy from what could have been a slow and terrifying death.

The next day a fancy carriage pulled up to the Scotsman's house. An elegantly dressed man stepped out and introduced himself as the father of the boy Farmer Fleming had saved. He wanted to repay Mr. Fleming for saving his son's life, but the Scottish farmer said, "No. I can't accept payment for what I did."

At that moment, the farmer's son came to the door of the family hovel. The nobleman offered to take the son and give him a good education. "If the lad is anything like his father, he'll grow into a man you can be proud of," he said.

And so it happened. Farmer Fleming's son Alexander graduated from St. Mary's Hospital Medical School in London and went on to become the noted physician who discovered penicillin.

Years afterward, the nobleman's son was stricken with pneumonia and was saved by penicillin. The name of the nobleman was Lord Randolph Churchill; his son's name, Sir Winston Churchill.

The noblest motive for service is not reward but unselfish love for others. Yet when we serve others, we help ourselves. In terms of worry and anxiety, we get our minds off ourselves, which is beneficial. Serving others distracts us and breaks our cycle of negative, dreadful thoughts about ourselves, our world and others. Our good works are not in vain (1 Corinthians 15:58).

Trust

I have found that the more I can entrust my life to God, the less I worry and experience anxiety. Faith makes a difference. The more distrustful I am about everything, the more vulnerable I feel, and the more I dread tomorrow.

Jesus addresses this problem in His Sermon on the Mount (Matthew 6:25-34). Here His answer for worry and anxiety is trust in a Father who cares. He tells us not to worry about our life, our food or clothing. He gives illustrations to make His point. The birds do not sow or reap or store away in barns, yet our heavenly Father feeds them. You are more valuable than they! Worrying does not help anyhow. Who by worrying can add a single hour to his or her life?

Don't worry about clothes, He continues. God clothes the lilies of the field beautifully, and they neither labor nor spin. Even Solomon in all his splendor was not dressed like a lily. You are more important to God than they! So don't worry! When you do, you are not remembering that you have a Father in heaven who knows and provides for your needs (Matthew 6:25-32).

I remind myself of these words when financial threats come to me or to my extended family. Sometimes I don't know how God is going to work it out, but He does. Trust is an antidote to worry and anxiety. Solomon had much to say about this in Proverbs as well. "Trust in God" He said is a safe shield (1:33; 30:5), a blessing (3:5-6; 16:20; 28:25), a fortress and a living fountain (14:26-27) and life itself (3:21-25; 4:23; 8:35). We trust and do what is right, and our worries and anxieties diminish.[2]

Setting Appropriate Priorities

I have never been able to get everything done that I thought needed to be done. School work, church work, family activities, counseling work, writing, reading, exercise and leisure activities – there are always things left over at the end of the day. I keep my sanity by prioritizing – making a list of what I need to do first, second and third. Then, I check them off my list. At the end of the day, some things that did not get done are carried over to the next day or week; some get eliminated.

My family has often wondered why I look at my schedule book so often. That's the way I keep from worrying about everything that needs to be done. I have learned that everything is not of equal importance.

Jesus recognized this as well. When asked what is the greatest commandment, He said that it was love of God and neighbor. The whole law and the prophets hang on this (Matthew 22:37-40). In His Sermon on the Mount when speaking of worry, He told us to seek first God's kingdom and His righteousness and "all these things will be given to you as well" (Matthew 6:33).

Solomon in the book of Proverbs says much about keeping priorities straight. He has several passages in which he points out that one thing is better (not valuable) than another:

- "a little with the fear of the Lord than great wealth with turmoil" (15:16)
- "a meal of vegetables where there is love than a fattened calf with hatred" (15:17)
- "a little with righteousness than much gain with injustice" (16:8)
- "a dry crust with peace and quiet than a house full of feasting with strife" (17:1)
- "a good name is more desirable than great riches" (22:1)

The way priorities help me with worries and anxiety is that they give direction to my life. I will never accomplish everything, but perhaps I will accomplish some things that are really important. That helps me to relax sometimes even in the midst of turmoil. Try to line it up for yourself: God, family, work, leisure, friends. Just think about it. Being busy is not enough. Plan. Work smart. Contentment and peace will follow.

One Day at a Time

I remember a song with these lyrics: "One day at a time, sweet Jesus. That's all I'm asking from you." That's been harder for me to do than to say, but it has also been helpful to try to practice one day at a time when I have been overwhelmed. I've also learned this from others.

Louise and I visited my brother Don and his wife, Carolyn. Don has had problems with serious depression for some 40 years; Carolyn was diagnosed last year with multiple myeloma. After two bone marrow transplants, many nauseous trips to the hospital 70 miles away, many treatments that drastically weakened her body, and other significant stresses on her life, she says she is content. Her answer, "I just take it one day at a time and that really means something to me now." Her heart is heavy because of continuing conflicts at church. She takes it one day at a time. She says that God's hand and the prayers of friends are holding her up. Who can argue with that? Don has become an encouragement to Carolyn who has been his rock. He has learned to focus on today.

Jesus said for us not to worry about tomorrow because tomorrow has enough trouble of its own. I am trying to hold on to that philosophy. It is hard in tough times, but it is then that it seems to make the most sense.

Cognitive Restructuring

Since thinking (cognition) affects feelings and actions, one effective way to change feelings is to change thinking. That is what cognitive restructuring is all about.

I have found thoughts are connected to my worries and anxieties. I think about it for a while; I can see, even when I am anxious and the anxiety seems to be automatic, that thoughts are connected to my feelings. Such thoughts as these may be present:

NEGATIVE SELF-TALK
- "I'll never get another job."
- "I'll lose my house."

- "My children will go hungry."
- "People will laugh at me."
- "I can't do what they want, and that is terrible."
- "My money will run out before I die."
- "I won't be able to pay my bills."
- "I will be embarrassed and shamed."

Thoughts like these cause more anxiety and must be challenged with persistence. I have learned to argue with myself about such thoughts. I knew one woman who was shaking all over continually when I first met her. She said I helped her primarily in three ways: By urging her to take one day at a time, by helping her challenge her negative, distorted thoughts and by teaching her how to relax.

NEGATIVE SELF-TALK
- "My husband will die before I do."
- "I can't take care of myself."
- "I won't have enough money. I'll starve."
- "I will panic and go crazy."
- "I'm losing control."

The result was that she often panicked and was very dysfunctional. Once she had a panic attack while driving and almost wrecked her car.

She learned to talk back to such distorted thinking and learned to say such as the following:

TALK BACK
- "How do I know that my husband will die first?"
- "If he did, how do I know I could not take care of myself?"
- "I have taken care of myself many times when he was away on trips."
- "I could call my children or a neighbor if I needed to do so."
- "We seem to have enough money in our retirement fund to get by. I could live simply, and that would be all right."
- "Panicky feelings won't kill me. I can tough it out. I can get professional help. All I have to do is call someone."
- "People at church care for me."
- "I'm not going crazy. I'm anxious, but not crazy."
- "I have always been able to be in control enough to get by. It just feels like I'm completely out of control."
- "I can stop the car and call someone if I get panicky."

- "I'll just take one day at a time. Why borrow trouble?"
- "God has always taken care of me, and He will do so in the future."

These thoughts helped her turn her anxieties around. She learned to relax, and the trembling stopped after about a month. Both she and her husband are still alive and enjoying good health. She may always feel a bit shaky, but with courage and persistence, she will be able to handle it.

Paul told the Roman church to be transformed by the renewing of their minds (Romans 12:1-2). He urged the Philippian church to think on certain things (Philippians 4:8). Why? Thoughts lead to actions, and actions lead to feelings. In fact, change either of these, and it changes the others as well.

In the book of Proverbs, Solomon says much about the effect of good advice and wholesome thinking. Such advice and correct thinking lead to happiness and acceptance by the Lord (12:20; 15:26), healing (12:18), and cheerfulness (12:25). It sharpens us (27:17); it is more valuable than gold (25:11); it helps us overcome problems (25:15). As we think in our heart, so are we (23:7).

Learn to write what you are saying to yourself on one side of a sheet of paper and then argue back with those thoughts that are negative and distorted on the other side of the paper. Be persistent. It works!

Relaxation

The rationale for relaxation therapy is that a person can't be relaxed and tense at the same time. So by relaxing, tension and anxiety disappear.

Anxiety affects every cell in your body. Your brain waves are faster and more intense. Your heartbeat increases and your blood pressure rises. Even the electricity in your skin is affected as well as the temperature in your limbs.

I can have a tension headache from stress and relax for 30 minutes, and it goes away. The temperature in my hands will increase from 73 degrees to 93 degrees with 30 minutes of deep muscle relaxation. If you don't know how to do this, see a mental health professional or buy some relaxation tapes and listen to them every day for two weeks. You'll learn how to let yourself relax and decrease your anxiety and worry. The effects of this are so positive they almost seem magical. What you are doing is controlling your own tension level. It's good for you!

Consider these admonitions from the Bible:

Proverbs 3:5-6: "Trust in the Lord with all your heart and lean not on your own understanding; in all your ways acknowledge him, and he will make your paths straight."

Proverbs 4:23: "Above all else, guard your heart, for it is the wellspring of life."

Proverbs 12:25: "An anxious heart weighs a man down, but a kind word cheers him up."

Habakkuk 3:17-18: "Though the fig tree does not bud and there are no grapes on the vines, though the olive crop fails and the fields produce no food, though there are no sheep in the pen and no cattle in the stalls, yet I will rejoice in the Lord, I will be joyful in God my Savior." This one is the most challenging to me.

A few days before Mom went to be with the Lord, she told Carolyn that she had learned something she wanted to leave with us. What was it? "I have learned," Mom said, "not to climb mountains until I get to them." What a lesson for all of us to learn.

Reflections

1. What is the difference between worry and anxiety?
2. What are the symptoms of anxiety?
3. What did Jesus suggest in Matthew 6:25-34?
4. How do you learn to accept what you cannot change?
5. What are some ways you can serve others?
6. What are your main priorities in life? What do you need to change to get these arranged in the right order?
7. What does it mean to borrow trouble? Can you think of ways you do this sometimes?
8. Write down some of your more persistent dysfunctional thoughts and argue back.
9. Close your eyes, take a deep breath, exhale, and say "relax." Do it several times. Draw in soothing, healing oxygen and exhale all of the tension in your life. Visualize a pleasant, relaxing scene – you are on an ocean beach looking at each wave as it comes in or you are on a mountain looking down at a creek where clear water is flowing over rocks. It's relaxing.
10. What do discipline, persistence and faith have to do with turning worry and anxiety around?

CHAPTER FOUR

Overcoming Fears

Fear can be healthy. It prevents injury, keeps us from doing wrong, and motivates us to do right. I am glad our grandchildren are afraid to wander into the street or to touch a hot stove. I am glad many of my clients are afraid of AIDS and venereal diseases. I am glad my parents taught me to fear God and keep His commandments (Ecclesiastes 12:13-14). I am glad they taught me to be afraid of copperhead snakes. Their instructions have kept me out of trouble and pointed me in constructive directions.

Understanding the theology of fear is sometimes difficult for religious people. Fear is sometimes commended in the Bible:

- Moses told Israel to fear the Lord and keep all of his statutes and commandments (Deuteronomy 6:2).
- Solomon said that the fear of the Lord brings strong confidence, a place of refuge and is a fountain of life (Proverbs 14:26-27).
- Noah was motivated by fear to build an ark, which saved his family (Hebrews 11:7).
- John told us to fear God and give him glory (Revelation 14:7).

All of this leads us to value fear. It can be very functional in a healthy way. I have counseled with people in prison who seemed to be motivated only by the fear of punishment. If it cost them, then they would consider altering their behavior. Fear of getting into trouble is not the highest level of moral development, but it does motivate some when nothing else will.

The Bible also tries to calm one's fears:

- God told Abraham to fear not because He was his shield and great reward (Genesis 15:1).
- Moses wanted Israel to fear not but to look at what God can do (Exodus 14:13).
- As in the days of old, we are to be strong and courageous, to fear not nor be discouraged (1 Chronicles 22:13).
- God did not give us a spirit of fear, but of power and love and discipline (2 Timothy 1:7).

We are not to live in a state of fearfulness to the point of living scared and being hindered from confident living and peace within. We are to face our difficulties with courage and confidence that God is encouraging us toward victory. It may be a matter of the degree of fear and the object of fear. Too much fear is bad; some reverence and fear are good. Being afraid to overcome obstacles leading to a full life is bad; being reverent toward God is good. It's productive to a good life. Jesus said, "Do not be afraid of those who kill the body but cannot kill the soul. Rather, be afraid of the One who can destroy both soul and body in hell" (Matthew 10:28). We don't use that kind of language very often, but it puts things into proper perspective quite well.

Our fears are often about people laughing at us, public speaking, the future, failure, closed spaces, blood, open spaces and heights. These can be very dysfunctional.

Symptoms of Phobias

I am especially interested in helping people with phobias, which are excessive, irrational fears. A specific phobia is marked with specific fear of certain objects or situations. This fear causes avoidance or anxious anticipation, which interferes significantly with one's daily routine, occupational functioning or social life; or the person is very distressed about having the phobia. The focus of the fear may be anticipated harm that might result, such as injury from an anticipated wreck or a dog bite. One might also fear losing control, panicking and fainting when exposed to the feared object or situation. Fear in some situations makes sense; in others it is excessive and irrational.

Subtypes of specific phobias include a fear of animals; the natural environment (storms, heights or water); blood (including injections); and certain situations (public transportation, tunnels, bridges, elevators, flying, driving or enclosed places); situations that might lead to choking, vomiting or contracting an illness; being close to walls that might fall; or loud sounds; or costume characters.[1]

Symptoms of specific phobias include the following:

- Fear that is excessive and measurable in the presence of or anticipation of a specific object or situation.
- Anxiety when in the situation.
- Recognition that the fear is excessive and unreasonable.
- The phobia situation is either avoided or is endured with intense anxiety or distress.
- This interferes significantly with one's normal routine or there is marked distress about having the phobia.
- In children under age 18, the duration is at least six months.

Females are more likely to have an animal or natural environment type of phobia. The same is true of situation and blood type phobias.[2]

In my counseling practice as a psychologist, I have seen more clients who have a social phobia (social anxiety disorder) than a specific phobia. Its essential feature is marked and persistent fear of a social or performance situation in which embarrassment may occur. Often these situations are avoided and sometimes endured with dread. The phobia interferes significantly with the person's daily routine, occupational functioning or social life, or the person is markedly distressed because of the phobia.

Specific symptoms of social phobias are similar to those mentioned previously when I discussed specific phobias. The main difference is that in the case of social phobias the fear is of social or performance situations. Such persons fear scrutiny which leads to humiliation and embarrassment. They are afraid they will not measure up and that would be awful. So they either endure with great distress or avoid social situations.

Many of my clients with fear problems are not phobic yet they experience a great deal of unnecessary stress because of such fears. They are continually anxious. If you have a full-blown phobia, I suggest that you see a psychologist, a psychiatrist or some other qualified mental health professional for therapy. Sometimes medications are indicated; usually counseling (psychotherapy) helps one to work through such phobias. They usually do not just go away without help.[3]

Some Causes of Phobias

There is ample evidence that the causes I mentioned for worry and anxiety are causes of phobias as well.

Biological

Fear of blood and injury have strong familial patterns. The same is true of specific phobias – animal type and situation type. Social phobias seem to occur more frequently among close biological relatives as well.[4] As with worry and anxiety, one may be predisposed biologically to become phobic. But learning is probably more powerful as a cause of such phobias.

Psychological

Learning may be a better word to use here than psychological. It points to overgeneralization of some experience, which often leads to phobias. A small dog bit Abby when she was 2 years old. She was phobic of all dogs at age 33. J.R. was seduced and then laughed at by an adult woman when he was 15. His fear of sex with women caused him to "never do it again" but instead to have sex with men. W.G. tried to give a book report in a high school English class. His mistakes caused the class to laugh at him. At age 31, he was petrified at the idea of speaking before a small group at work. In each of these cases, an unfortunate experience got blown up, overgeneralized; it became unreasonable and hindered the person's functioning.

Sociological

Some situations are more fearful than others and may thus be scary. They may also trigger similar fearful experiences from the past. When my bank account gets low, as it has on numerous occasions, the fear of having no money, as at times in the past, is triggered. I may have some of the same emotions I had when I was on a date in high school and did not have enough money to pay for our hamburgers or for gasoline to get home. I remember one time when six of us were out in a car and ran out of gas. We took up a collection and discovered that all of us – Leamon, Layton, Litton, Harold, Ernest, and I – only had 27 cents total. They would have been two cents short had it not been for me. We pulled into a service station and got 27 cents worth of gas.

When Regina gets around men today at age 43, she feels fearful and inadequate because they are men and she is a woman, the same feel-

ings she had when she was around her father when she was a teenager. Her father, she said, always told her that women were not as smart
as men and that they were only good for sex and homemaking. She neglects her grooming and has been unemployed for 10 years.

Obviously some situations are so fearful that most anyone would react with fear: a gunner in combat, a person close to poisonous snakes
or one who has just lost his job. Most people speaking before large au-
diences would be afraid to some extent. Such fears are not phobias;
they are normal and reasonable.

Spiritual

Spiritual is a broad word that covers our essential being and how we
feel in relationship to others and to God. When we feel too fearful of
God or very inferior and inadequate in relationship to others, we are
vulnerable to phobias that are spiritually based. When we feel worthless and helpless, we will not function well but rather will feel miserable. We will withdraw and be non-productive. We are afraid to live.

I may have been over-conditioned to fear God and to feel inferior. I
remember as a child sermons on the strong possibility of falling. "Take
heed lest ye fall" was one preacher's frequent text. "Only eight were
saved from the flood," he would continue, "and I'm not sure that many
will be saved when Jesus returns." That scared me. I knew of a lot more
than eight people who were better than me. I heard many messages that
told me not to think of myself too highly. Perhaps the intent was good,
but the message I sometimes received was that I was not important at
all. I was nothing. That conditioning is hard to shake, but I was able to
keep it from making me fail to try.

Effects of Phobias

There are both positive and negative effects from fears.

Negative Effects

Some negative effects that come to mind are as follows:
- Adam and Eve hid from God (Genesis 3).
- Abraham lied about his wife's identity to protect himself
  (Genesis 12).
- At first, Israel stood still when they should have been
  marching forward to avoid Pharaoh's army (Exodus 14).
- The 10 spies of Israel persuaded Israel not to go into the
  Promised Land because of giants in the land (Numbers 13).

- Jonah hid from God (Jonah 1).
- Regina quit looking for a job. She turns herself down before she goes on the interview and then doesn't go at all.
- At first, I did not go to college because I was afraid I could not pay the bills.
- I have seen many graduate students drop classes for fear of failure.
- Bob, age 25, would not ask for a date for fear of being turned down.

Positive Effects

Some positive effects of fears that come to mind are as follows:

- Noah built an ark and saved his family (Genesis 6; Hebrews 11).
- Israel moved forward through the Red Sea. Moses told them, "Do not be afraid. Stand firm and you will see the deliverance the Lord will bring you today" (Exodus 14:13).
- Eventually, Israel went into the Promised Land because of their fear of the Lord. They chose to serve him and pushed forward (Exodus).
- My fear of God has kept me out of serious trouble and has motivated me to seek and to know Him more fully.
- Bob's fear of being unloved forever led him to overcome his fear of being rejected. He asked for and got a date, which eventually led to a great, loving relationship, marriage and three children.
- Jonah's fear of the Lord led him eventually to preach to Nineveh (Jonah 2-4).
- Regina's fear of failure eventually led her to function in a more healthy way. She has learned better grooming skills and has had some success in her own business.
- I eventually went to college and graduate schools, at least partially motivated by my fear of failure.
- I have seen many graduate students overcome their fear of failure, graduate and become effective ministers.

So what we do with fear is the crucial point. It can make or break us depending on how we handle it.

How to Overcome Fears

I have seen many people overcome fears with discipline, persistence and faith. They work through fears that have paralyzed them and go on to find peace and live productive lives. How did they do that?

Confrontation

Confrontation of fears is absolutely necessary for victory over them. All professionals agree with this principle. Some approaches begin with other techniques yet all of them require confrontation sooner or later.

Kerry was afraid of girls, and this caused him not to ask for dates. He was lonely and miserable which led him eventually to ask. He was terrified of not having anything to say or of acting inappropriately, which caused further delay. He could just think about being on a date and become terrified – fast heartbeat, sweaty hands and a light-headed feeling. He worked on this step-by-step and dated successfully. Eventually he found the right woman and a meaningful marriage. He confronted his fears and overcame them.

Dr. George S. Benson, long-term president of Harding University, became a very successful fundraiser and leader of that good school. He raised millions of dollars, and we all thought it was so easy for him. Yet he told me one day that he often was apprehensive and so fearful of failure that he would pace back and forth several times at a prospective donor's door before getting up enough courage to go in for a solicitation visit. He faced his fears and overcame them. They then diminished with each success. Having done extensive fund-raising myself, I can readily identify with Dr. Benson's experience. Sometimes I had to really psyche myself up to get going; eventually some success would follow, and I would be on my way to more success. I'm glad I made myself do what needed to be done because I believed so much in the cause of thorough ministry preparation.

Thelma was afraid of being injured in a car wreck. As a result, at age 26 she had never learned to drive. I would think we were making progress, and then she would come for a session with a newspaper article of someone killed in a car wreck. We would be set back for a while. Her fear was so intense and real to her that she quit therapy after a few sessions and still does not drive. She did not face her fear and push beyond it. Some fear of driving is reasonable but not as much as she had. It kept her from doing what she needed to do. Her mother still has to drive her wherever she needs to go.

Phobic clients of mine often cancel appointments. This is especially true if they are afraid of people or of open spaces. They are upset at the thought of venturing outside their house and feel safer just to stay at home. They cancel their appointments and avoid confronting their fears. Yet confrontation is necessary for a cure.

Snake phobias have always intrigued me. Snakes for me mean copperheads, very poisonous snakes. Fear of them makes sense. I have killed dozens of them. Two of our dogs were bitten by them while protecting us. Yet excessive fears of all snakes can become a problem for some. They can just think about the possibility of seeing a black or a green snake, non-poisonous, and become so panicky that they avoid going out into the yard or field, behavior that can be quite upsetting and dysfunctional.

Such people have been cured of such phobias by forcing themselves to hold snakes. Just by holding on until the fear is desensitized, it goes away. Nothing else is involved in some of these experiments except confrontation of fears.

Dr. Joseph Wolpe, well-known author and psychiatrist, is called the father of systematic desensitization, probably the most successful treatment approach for phobias. During a weeklong workshop in Philadelphia in the late 1970s, he told us about one of his successful cases. His patient was a man who feared going more than five miles in any direction from his house. To be sure he didn't, he had driven stakes at the five-mile marker on all major roads from his place. He had been in traditional therapy for some 10 years with little success. He still believed he would die if he went more than five miles from his house.

Wolpe spent no time in probing the origins of this phobia, although he would admit that this is sometimes helpful information. He merely got the patient in his car and started driving. As they approached the five mile marker, the patient perspired and his heart pounded, yet Wolpe kept driving until he went six miles. He then stopped and asked, "What do you think now?" The patient replied that he must have mismeasured the mileage. They went back and did it again and again until the patient could take the ride with little or no physiological reaction. Wolpe said that in facing his phobia he had been desensitized to it.

You have probably seen examples of this. You were afraid of water but got over it by forcing yourself to go swimming. You were perhaps afraid of heights until you forced yourself to climb or drive up mountains. When you did though, you overcame your fears and could live a more normal life.

There is a strategy in the strategic approach to marriage and family therapy for treating phobias. The strategic intervention, however, is just a device to force people to confront their fears. For example, an impotent husband may have a fear of sex with his wife. One strategy to changing his behavior pattern went like this: His wife usually slept on the side of the bed against the wall. The therapist gave him a directive to change sides with her. What was the point? It forced him to get into bed by having to crawl over her. That led to more contact and eventually sex again with her. He changed his behavior in relationship to his fears.

Insight

Psychoanalysis is based upon the value of insight. The rationale for this approach to psychotherapy is that insight cures.

I have found that insight does not always cure. A person may understand why he or she is a pedophile but may continue to be that way. Yet insight sometimes leads to a cure.

I read about a singer who became phobic when she was performing publicly. She would tremble; her heart would race and pound; she would perspire greatly, and have to stop singing. She finally was able to overcome her fears when she learned that she was burned severely at age 18 months. When she smelled smoke from smokers in her audience, she would panic. The smoke triggered her early horror. After she gained insight into her problem, she forced herself to perform again and overcame her problem. Confrontation and insight were answers for her and they may be for you as well.

Faith

What you believe affects your emotions. Excessive and irrational fear is an emotion. Change what you believe, and you will therefore change your fears.

It's not quite that simple, but beliefs are part of the fear problem and solution. When Peter believed he could walk on water, he did with the help of Jesus. When he took his eyes off Jesus, he began to sink. Jesus had told them: "Take courage! It is I. Don't be afraid" (Matthew 14:27). Peter thought that if Jesus told him to come to Him on the water, he could do it, and he did until he began to look at the wind. Then he became afraid and began to sink crying, "Lord, save me." Jesus then reached out to him and saved him, saying, "You of little faith, why did you doubt?" (Matthew 14:27-31). Lack of faith set up a vicious cycle for Peter: He saw the wind and lost his faith; he began to sink which caused him to fear even more, yet his fear turned him back to his faith and to salvation.

I'm sure you realize that what we believe affects what we do. I can think of many examples of this from my family. It was fourth down in a close eighth grade football game recently. They had the ball and needed a yard for a first down. I yelled to our grandson David, "It's fourth down David. Stop him!" David moved forward from his linebacker position into a gap in the line. I could feel his determination and said to myself, "He's going to get him behind the line." He did for a seven-yard loss, which stopped their last drive and insured Harding Academy the victory. David believed he could do it, and he did.

This reminds me of a high school experience of David's dad, Tim, our middle son. Tim needed 41 points his final basketball game in high school to reach his goal of averaging 22 points per game that year. His fear was that he would not get close to 41 points. I jokingly said, "All you need to do is have the center tip you the ball to begin the game, dribble in for a lay-up, keep driving in for close-up shots until you get your confidence up, then start shooting longer and longer shots and you will score 41 points." He did exactly that and scored a career high of 46 points! Belief affects everything. It certainly affects whether or not we confront our fears.

For those close to Jesus, faith is a lot more than just the power of positive thinking. Faith can move mountains (Matthew 17:20) and trees (Luke 17:6) – problems that seem insurmountable. Jesus faced His fears and overcame them (Matthew 26-27). So can we. Paul said he had learned that he could do all things through Christ who gave him strength. That included learning to be content in all circumstances – when he was in want and when he had plenty (Philippians 4:11-14). His life proves that life does not have to be easy to be meaningful. He had been falsely imprisoned, flogged severely, exposed to death again and again, beaten with lashes and rods, shipwrecked and in danger from rivers and bandits; Yet he pressed on – pushed forward to take hold of the goal to which God had called him in Christ Jesus (Philippians 3). In such situations, he must have been afraid, yet he conquered his fears. They did not conquer him.

Maybe it's hard for you to believe any more. Perhaps you have been knocked down often like Paul. He says, "Get up. You can do it!" I say, God still loves you. You are worthwhile. You have more potential than you have yet reached. Believe in God. Believe in yourself. Keep trying. You will overcome your fears.

Love
Love is included as a part of our fear solution for several reasons:
• God is love and the more we let God into our hearts, the more power we have in our lives to overcome. He promised to come and make His home with us if we do His will (John 14:23). When He is in us, the sky is the limit!
• John says that there is no fear in love, that "perfect love drives out fear, because fear has to do with punishment. The man who fears is not made perfect in love" (1 John 4:18).
• Paul says that love never fails (1 Corinthians 13:8). It is the greatest conquering force in the universe. Where love is, there is victory and freedom from fear. Love always perseveres (1 Corinthians 13:7).

Cognitive Restructuring
The rationale for cognitive restructuring is that thinking affects actions and feelings. When we let our fears conquer us, we have gotten into a negative, irrational mindset that leads to inaction and failure, which increases our fears. Fearful thoughts go like this:
• "I can't do it."
• "Everybody else can do it better than I can."
• "I'll goof up, and everyone will laugh at me."
• "I don't really belong in this group."
• "Everybody is watching me."
Such thoughts lead to failure and more fear.

Eunice (not her real name) had a great fear of the Internal Revenue Service. Up to this point, she was normal, right? Wrong! Her fear led her not to file income taxes for six years. This increased her fear of being caught, which made her afraid to open her mail for fear she would get a notice from the IRS. Her mail piled up for months, and her phobia increased. I'll tell you later what she did to overcome her fears.

Somehow, we have to learn to talk back to our negative, irrational thoughts, perhaps along these lines:
• "How do I know I can't do it? At least I'll try."
• "What evidence is there that everyone else is better than I? And, what if they are, I'll still try."

- "How do I know I'll goof up? I do a lot of things right. The worst goof up is not to try at all."
- "Who says I don't belong? I'm on the same level as everyone else – no more important, no less important."
- "Is it true that everyone else is watching me? Not really. Most people don't think about me at all. And, if some do watch me, that will give me a chance to show what I can do. I'm not afraid of making mistakes. That's the way people learn."

Such rational thinking weakens phobias and helps us behave differently. When we behave differently and confront our fears, we overcome them. We become desensitized to them; they no longer dominate us.

Again, what we believe determines what we do. I remember two other family stories that illustrate this well. When our oldest son, Steve, was in the 11th grade, he was in a track meet for the city of Memphis shot-put championship. He had put the shot all year consistently about 47 feet. That day, however, they let him toss it four times before they measured. All four puts were over 52 feet. He won the city championships and the state title the next year. When I asked him how he had put the shot five feet farther that day, he said he wondered about that himself: "They draw those chalk lines every five feet to let us know how far we throw. All year long, they have drawn the first chalk line at 45 feet. I've always thought I've got to get it over that first chalk line. Today they drew that first chalk line at 50 feet, and I didn't know it." Our beliefs may at times limit our potential. Change the beliefs, and it changes our potential.

When our youngest son, Danny, was in ninth grade, he wanted to put the shot 60 feet. He measured off 60 feet and drove down a stake. All week long he visualized hitting that stake with the shot. On his second put, he let out a big yell as he turned to release the shot and it came down right on top of the stake and broke it. He won the city championship that year and the state championship twice later during high school. Our vision guides our actions. Without lofty visions, our fears defeat us. With overcoming visions, we overcome our fears.

Relaxation

As I mentioned in Chapter 2, the rationale for relaxation therapy is that you cannot be tense and relaxed at the same time. So one way to drive away tension caused by fears is to learn to relax. I know first hand that this works. I have practiced it for years.

Late in the day after the Old Mansion burned at the Harding Graduate School of Religion, on July 29, 1993, Mike Pridmore came up to me and said that I was so calm through it all, "a real general on the battle field. You calmed us all down by the way you handled the situation." I had done some quick exercises in relaxation all day long as well as facing the terrible situation and talking to myself: "Stay calm. Take one step at a time. This will work out somehow. Lots of people are here to help." We made fast decisions, moved almost everything out of the Old Mansion into crowded quarters in our classroom building during that long day. Discipline from my past told me that getting shook would not help. Staying calm, being persistent and faithful did.

Eunice solved her problem with her IRS fears by using several of these suggestions. She learned deep muscle relaxation until she could go limp within seconds. It's just a matter of learning how and practicing over and over again for a few weeks. She also learned to talk to herself, take one step at a time and confront her fears. Her talk back sounded something like this:

- "IRS is not out to get me. They just want what I owe them. I'm willing to pay. So what is the problem?"
- "I'll learn to open my mail. I'll make eight piles of mail and force myself to open one pile each day. If they are trying to contact me, I need to know."
- "Not opening my mail will just make everything worse. Who knows what other important mail is in that stack. Not opening it just doesn't make sense."

The way relaxation helped was that Eunice would become relaxed before she confronted each pile of mail and then visualize opening her mail one letter at a time. She learned to do this with minimal tension and then was able to open the mail. She then got a certified public accountant to advise her and they filed her taxes. The IRS accepted her payment, and she felt very relieved and victorious.

An Integrated Approach

No one technique is as powerful as several, perhaps all, used together. Confrontation, insight, faith, love, cognitive restructuring and relaxation all can help. Several people that I have mentioned previously, including Eunice, used more than one technique.

Anita is another example. A mother of three, she had served for two years as a missionary overseas. While there she ate some poisoned raisins that had been sent to her by mail. She had not only become phobic of eating raisins but also of all food as well. She had returned home weighing only 70 pounds, her health very endangered.

She overcame her excessive, exaggerated fears by using all of these techniques. Her negative self-talk went something like this:

NEGATIVE SELF-TALK

- "I'm afraid to eat anything. Somebody will poison me again."
- "I'm just not hungry."
- "I don't need to eat."
- "Eating will make me sick."
- "I don't trust anyone anymore."
- "Why didn't God take care of me? I was doing His work."

Anita's persistent talk back to herself went like this:

TALK BACK

- "I can't let my fears control me. That was just one messed-up person who put poison in my raisins. Everybody is not like that."
- "I may not be hungry now, but I need to eat. Lack of hunger is a part of my serious problem."
- "I do need to eat. I have lost 40 pounds. The doctor said I would starve to death if I don't eat soon. I don't want to die. My husband needs me. My children need me."
- "Eating might make me sick at first, but I've got to take the chance. I need nutrition. Maybe it won't make me sick. I used to enjoy eating."
- "It's hard to trust anyone, but I know my husband would not betray me. I'll let him prepare some food, eat some of it himself, and if it doesn't hurt him, I'll eat some. I've got to trust someone. I can't let that one person destroy my life."

Anita ate her first raisins in my office. She knew it was coming. First she ate different foods, very unlike raisins, in her husband's presence (her desensitizing agent). Then she ate alone, preparing the food herself. Then, she ate out with her husband. Then came raisin day in my office.

She saw them when she came in, looked and then smiled a little looking at me. I didn't say anything then, but later on in the session I said, "It's raisin time." She said, "I knew this day was coming, and I can't believe I am so uptight after all this time." We did some talk-back, got her very relaxed and then I said again, "It's raisin time." She laughed and said, "You first." I ate some. We waited a while to see if I "keeled over," and then she ate some. She relaxed again; we reinforced her talk-back rational thinking, and I dismissed her. By then, she weighed 90 pounds. Today, some 20 years later, she is a successful wife, mother and minister's wife. She must be a normal female now because she weighs 120 pounds and is worried about her weight just like many other women. Discipline, persistence and faith carried her through her phobia to peace and successful living.

Dover was afraid to fly. A very successful businessman, he would panic at the thought of flying. It was a serious problem for him because he needed to fly on business trips.

He learned the same techniques Anita learned and overcame his fears. Especially relevant for him were self-talk, relaxation and confrontation. Today, some 15 years after therapy, he tells me with a triumphant smile on his face every time he has made a successful flight. He has been overseas several times with little difficulty. Once when over the Atlantic Ocean, he felt a little panicky, saw a man who looked like me (he was bald), took a deep breath and said to himself, "Be c-a-l-m. R-e-l-a-x." He said it worked.

Jamie overcame her fear of driving to Memphis from a small town using these same techniques. Relaxation, self-talk, faith and confrontation were central for her. She has now been "all over the world." Success, you see, can have a snowball effect as well as failure. Victory leads to victory. Our son, Steve, vice president of a large insurance company, sees this continually. Salespersons tend to fail big or succeed big. What we do tends to generalize and affect what we continue to do.

As I think about the positive value of fear in my life, I summarize it like this:

• Fear of God has kept me out of much trouble and motivated me to learn more about him and his attitude toward me. I have learned more about his love and grace, and I know that his grace reaches me.

• Fear of having nothing has motivated me to work extra hard to go to school and to earn money so that I can avoid some earlier experiences of being without money. I have learned that responsibility must pair up with grace for me to succeed.

• Fear of being criticized or laughed at has caused me to over-prepare every time I speak. I want to be sure I have something worthwhile to say and not to be put down.

I could continue, but you get the picture. It's a matter of discipline, persistence and faith. Spiritual resilience has helped me overcome many fears, and it can help you as well.

Reflections

1. How does fear hinder you in your life?
2. How does it help you?
3. Define a phobia. What are some common symptoms?
4. What fears are normal? How can they hinder us?
5. What are some common phobias?
6. How would the principles I have mentioned help overcome them?
7. What does spirituality have to do with overcoming phobias?
8. List some of your fear-related negative self-talk and then talk back to it.
9. Using the athletic illustrations from Steve, Tim, David or Danny, reflect on how your vision, your beliefs, might help you overcome your fears and be more productive in the future. Your plans, your visions, your ideas, your goals will surely affect your future.
10. How do discipline, persistence and faith help you overcome your fears?

CHAPTER FIVE

Victory Over Depression

I have been around depression most of my life. My maternal grand-mother was depressed for the last 20 years of her life. So was my mother. Two of my siblings have suffered a great deal because of depression, one since about 1959. After I heard of Don's illness, I went for a drive in my car out on a mountain road near Spencer, Tenn., and just broke down crying. After many dangers, toils and snares, I visited with him a couple of weeks ago, and he is doing well although he is under a great deal of stress right now.

Let me share with you what I have learned about depression from my family and some 500 clients who have persisted through depression. First, let me tell you about some myths about depression.

Myths of Depression

There is a great deal of misunderstanding about depression. Ten of the more common myths are as follows:

Myth 1: It is sinful. "If I could just be a better Christian, that would take care of everything." This is just not true. My mother and grand-mother were wonderful Christian women, yet they were depressed. My brothers who have suffered from this illness are model Christians for me. Down through history, people have been depressed in every cul-ture and in every religion known to man with very little difference in percentages regardless of cultures or religion. This points to something beyond how religious we are as a cause of depression.

Myth 2: It is a moral weakness. "If I would just try a little harder, I could overcome this on my own." This is simply not true. My brother Dowell thought like this at first and tried for three years on his own to little avail. He was eventually convinced that he had an illness, went to a competent doctor and began to make progress. He has encouraged hundreds of depressed people by sharing his experiences. We never would think we could cure heart trouble by merely trying a little harder. Depression is also an illness.

Myth 3: The Bible has all of the answers I need. "If I would just do what the Bible says, I would not be depressed. I don't need anything else. It shows that I don't believe the Bible if I go to a psychiatrist or a psychologist. I have read in a religious paper that they are all quacks anyhow." How unfortunate! Most Bible believers do not use this kind of reasoning with other medical illnesses. Why use it with depression? I had a client once who had been very suicidal until we got him on some anti-depressant medication. Some of his fellow Christian college students convinced him that he did not need the medication but that he just needed to look to the Bible for his depression needs. A couple of days later, he called me at two o'clock in the morning saying that he had a pistol to his head and was going to end it all. We got him back on his treatment plan and he began to improve. I believe God was working through his doctors and his medication. Why limit Him in this way? Yes, some doctors and counselors are quacks, but I have found that most are not. Check around and find good ones.

My brother Dowell makes a point similar to this. The belief that depression is a lack of faith is a widespread myth, he says. He is a man of strong faith and has been seriously depressed at times for some 15 years. I admire him as well as my brother Don greatly for sharing some of their successful struggles with depression. Dowell uses our mother as an example of a giant in faith, yet often depressed. He calls this myth nonsense and irrational. He writes, "Mom's faith never cured her back problems, severe heart troubles or depression. It did help her to live a productive life and prepared her to sit with the lowly stranger from Galilee at his homecoming in the sky."

Myth 4: Depression is always due to a chemical imbalance. "If I could just get some medication, I'd be okay." Sometimes depression is primarily due to a chemical imbalance but not always, and it is not usually the only factor. I'll discuss other causes and treatments later. For now, just don't think it has to be one cause. It is not that simple.

Myth 5: Depression is all genetic. "My mom was depressed, so I have to be depressed as well. It's all in the genes." Again, this is a myth. Genetics can raise your chances for depression, but there are other factors as well. Learn to concentrate on what you can do something about.

Your thinking, your situation, and your behavior are involved as well. Concentrate on these. They make a significant difference.

Myth 6: It's all just the situation. "What is he depressed about? He has a good life. He should not be depressed." I have fielded questions like these about my family many times from well-meaning, highly educated people. They think that if one's situation is okay, the person will be all right. This implies that the situation completely controls the person. It ignores biology and years of conditioning.

Myth 7: It's all in your head. "If I would just think positive thoughts, the depression would go away. I'll just work on my thinking, and I will be well. That's all I need. Depression is not a real disease. I'm just not thinking right." I believe thinking is a possible causative factor with depression, but it is not the only factor and may not be the primary factor. I know it is not all in your head. It gets into every cell of your body as well and does not go away easily. Saying that it is all in your head is a cruel way to torture depressed people. It just makes them feel guilty for not being able to think correctly, and it makes them more depressed.

Myth 8: It is shameful. "I should not be depressed. Something is wrong with me. It's my fault, and I ought to be ashamed of myself." This is another myth, and it is related to previous myths. If I feel that depression proves that I am morally weak, an inferior person, and a less-than-serious Bible student, then it follows that I feel some sense of shame for being depressed. Yet all of these are myths. Depression is an illness that affects the whole person. We should not be ashamed of an illness. This is a passion with me.

Many of my depressed clients delayed treatment because of their shame. As my brother Dowell said, "A gospel preacher and professor of Bible at one of our respected Christian colleges is not supposed to be depressed." He finally was able to get over this hurdle, received good treatment and is back on the job preaching and teaching the gospel. He has not missed a single preaching or teaching appointment since 1990 and only twice before that time. In fact, he has led numerous mission trips overseas since his worst days of depression. Thank God he moved past his shame.

My brother Don has also shared his struggles with depression with the public many times and has encouraged others to persist in their struggle. I rejoice greatly in their often-painful victories through discipline, persistence and faith.

Myth 9: It's just a lack of faith. "Getting treatment shows that I don't have enough faith in God to heal me." Although I have heard this many times, it still surprises me. We don't use this same logic with other diseases. We go to the doctor, the hospital, take medicine – whatever is recommended by professionals. Why do we think we know best when it comes to depression? We show our faith in what God has provided for our treatment when we avail ourselves of the best treatment possible.

A similar myth very important to Dowell is that depression can be cured by becoming more spiritual. The depressed are admonished that they need to pray and study their Bible more. "Most Christians who suffer from depression," Dowell writes, "have likely prayed and studied 10 times more than their well-intended critics. Though my memory is good back to the age of 4, it is impossible for it to include a time when Bible study and prayer were not dominant forces in my life." This is good and spiritually wholesome, yet not a cure for depression.

Myth 10: It's temporary. "I'll get over it, and it'll never bother me again." I am reluctant to include this one. If you are seriously depressed for the first time, it may be discouraging for you to think that it may recur after you get well, but that may very well happen. Serious depression tends to be chronic. I don't mean that it never leaves. It does. You may go several years without a major setback, but it probably does not leave completely. What is encouraging is that serious depression can be treated and managed successfully. My brothers are good examples of this. Just be encouraged and do what you need to do. Life, though tough, can still be productive and meaningful.

These 10 myths need to be dismissed from your mind before adequate progress can be made in overcoming depression.

Symptoms of Depression

How do you recognize signs of serious depression? Here are some common symptoms that are usually present:

• A depressed mood. Depression is primarily an affective disorder.

• Markedly diminished interest in pleasure including sex, eating and other activities.

• Significant weight loss or gain. I have seen much more weight loss than gain.

• Insomnia or hypersomnia nearly every day. The person often wakes up before the alarm clock goes off after a night of fitful sleep.

• Psychomotor agitation or retardation – physical movement agitated or slowed down.

• Constant fatigue – not just tired but exhausted, depleted.

• Feelings of worthlessness or inappropriate guilt.
• Diminished ability to think or concentrate or indecisiveness – negative automatic thoughts.
• Recurrent thoughts of death, recurrent suicidal ideation.
• Low self-esteem – I'm not okay, you're okay.
• Feelings of hopelessness, despair, sadness (crying), apathy and helplessness.
• Withdrawal – desire to escape.
• Feelings of dependency.
• Anger turned inward or outward.
• Experience early mornings as the worst time of day. Just can't get going in the morning.[1]

People with mild depression will experience some of these symptoms but not all, and the experience will not be as long or as severe. If you have these symptoms, I encourage you to see a psychologist or other qualified mental health professional. If your symptoms do not begin to subside within a few weeks, I urge you to see a psychiatrist for a medical evaluation which will likely result in your taking an antidepressant medication for eight months or more. The more physical your symptoms are, the more likely you have an illness that needs medical attention: sleep loss, weight loss and other physical symptoms. Please don't resist taking medication if the psychiatrist or other medical doctor recommends it. It is not addictive if you take it as prescribed.

Types of Depression

The main types of depression are as follows:

Bipolar Disorder. A roller coaster type experience. You are up for a while and down for a while. When you are up (manic) you feel great, energetic, generous, like you can conquer the world. Often little sleep is required; you talk much faster, take on extra work and then crash exhausted and get very depressed. This is a serious illness that needs medical attention: extensive counseling plus medication.

Bipolar Disorder II. Similar but not as serious as bipolar disorder. Mood variations are not as severe.

Cyclothymia. Similar to bipolar disorder but not as serious. Hard to differentiate from bipolar disorder II.

Major Depression. Deep, severe depression. Suicidal thoughts are common. Both medication and extensive counseling are recommended. Serious depression affects every cell of your body and is hard to shake. You'll come out victorious much faster with competent help.

Dysthymic Disorder. Moderate, long-term (two years or more for adults) depression. I've seen more of this than perhaps any other type of emotional illness. Common symptoms are poor appetite or overeating, insomnia or hypersomnia, low energy or fatigue, low self-esteem, poor concentration or difficulty making decisions and feelings of hopelessness. People like this often do not think they are depressed. Life is just like this to them.[2]

Adjustment Disorder with Depressed Mood or Mixed Emotional Feature. This depression results from a reaction to some unpleasant event such as divorce, death of a loved one or loss of a job. Prognosis for recovery is usually good.

Causes of Depression

The main weakness of many counselors is that they are inadequately educated in assessment skills. Yet proper treatment is contingent upon competent assessment skills. What causes depression?

As I mentioned in my discussion of worry and anxiety, there are at least four possible causes of depression. They interact.

Biological

Although I have already said that genetics and chemistry are not the only causes of depression, I must point out that they are usually causative factors in depression. Genes and chemistry and other biological factors must not be ignored. For serious depression, you are about six times more likely to be depressed if one of your parents was depressed. Bipolar disorder and major depression tend to run in families, even in studies that allow for environmental influences – identical twins that are adopted by different families at birth.

Biological factors are much broader than genetics and body chemistry. They include one's general health. When Mom's circulation was poor, she became depressed. After my friend had a heart attack, he became depressed. College students' moods are affected by their diet, sleep and exercise habits. All of this affects how we feel and points toward lifestyle and medical interventions.

Psychological

The way we have been conditioned has an effect on our mood. Thinking affects feelings and depression is a feeling. Biology affects thinking and thinking affects biology. An interaction between these two plays out continually.

What I have seen is that a certain kind of conditioning by life experiences sets one up for depression. Biology makes it more likely and conditioning makes it even more likely. One's total experiences may lead to negative, irrational thinking which is depressing. The more typical thoughts of such people that I have seen are these:

- "I am no good, worthless."
- "Nobody likes me."
- "I can't do anything right."
- "Life ought to be easy. My life is hard. I can't stand it, I can't change it, and I can't get out."

Such thoughts set one up for depression and also help maintain it. Such people tend to overgeneralize, do all-or-nothing thinking, mentally filter out the positives, jump to conclusions, magnify faults and minimize positives. They are driven by emotions, are too perfectionistic, label themselves with negative labels such as loser and blame themselves or others inappropriately.[3] They are sad and unhappy. They see their future as hopeless. They think they are a failure and are dissatisfied. They feel inappropriate guilt and think they are being punished. They get easily irritated and have little or no interest in other people. They often feel ugly, are worried and tired.

What happens is that their environment has led them to believe down deep that they are worthless, helpless and incompetent. They are reminded in numerous ways not to get their hopes up and not to think well of themselves. "Don't think you will ever get off the farm. Remember the man who tried to go to California. His wagon broke down and he ended up in a California hollow. Remember Doc Williams, the poor farm boy who always said he was going to be a doctor? Well, he made a living selling junk. Another example of a poor boy that tried to get above his raising was farmer Jones. He was going to be a lawyer and wear a suit to work. Look where he is now – just a poor dirt farmer." These and other messages are communicated to children which conditions them not to think well of themselves. It may be something as innocent looking as being smaller and weaker than an older brother or cousin or having older siblings who are much smarter than you are. Parents may reinforce the effects by labeling each child as "smart," "good-looking" or "weak." One of my clients sees herself as dumb. Why? She finished college and continually does good problem solving, but her brother was "the smartest one in the family" – labeling and all-or-nothing thinking.

Such conditioning affects thinking and often leads to depression. Some overcome it; some don't.

Sociological

Our social situation affects our mood. When everything is going wrong, most people become depressed to some extent. The death of a loved one, divorce, loss of a job, sickness, a difficult marriage and problems with children are all hard to endure. In my marriage counseling, one or both spouses usually are experiencing depression.

Of course, biology and conditioning affect how we handle such tough situations. There is an inverse relationship between stress tolerance and emotional health. The greater degree of emotional maturity (mental health) the more stress we can tolerate before we show signs of emotional (mental) illness. As emotional health increases, the less likely stress will get under our skins. When we are emotionally healthy, fewer things bother us. The environment, however, affects all of us. We all have a breaking point somewhere. If enough stress factors are present, we tend to show depression and/or anxiety symptoms.

Spiritual

Some psychiatrists call this the existential factor. It is depressing not to find meaning in life. I call it spiritual. Your spiritual life may leave you feeling lonely, isolated, and disconnected from God and people. Living hypocritically and out of focus (disassociated) is depressing. It's a matter of how you see yourself in relationship to God, others and the world.

Spirituality helps us accept, come to grips with, and find meaning in what we cannot change. The death of a loved one, divorce, a spouse's affair are all hard to accept – devastating for anyone. Yet some come to grips with such difficulties and still find meaning in life. How, I don't always know, but I think it has something to do with spirituality.

There may be other causative factors for depression, but these are the major ones. With serious depression, the cause is probably a combination of some or all of these factors and perhaps others as well.

Outcomes of Depression

There can be both positive and negative outcomes of depression:

Positive Outcomes

A list of some positive consequences of depression includes:

• My brothers acknowledged their depression, went for treatment (and continue to go when they need to), gained a greater degree of mental and emotional health and are living productive lives as professors, preachers, husbands, fathers and grandfathers.

• Carol attempted suicide, then called for help and is now back at home functioning well in her life and in her job.

• Elijah became depressed and began to listen more closely to the small voice and returned to do great things. He learned not to focus on the threat to his life from Jezebel, King Ahab's wife, but upon God's concern for him, others who had not bowed the knee to Baal and the tasks that lay before him. He realized that he had important work still to be done. He got up, he ate, he drank, he anointed Hazael king over Aram, Jehu as king over Israel and Elisha to succeed him as prophet. They would expand his work (1 Kings 19).

• Jill went for counseling, learned to forgive her penitent husband who had had several affairs and found meaning again in their life together. She learned that forgiveness does not mean endorsement of her husband's behavior; it just meant that she was being Christlike in giving him what he needed to redeem his life and their marriage. Very thankful for his second chance, he became a thoughtful, faithful husband and a spiritual leader for their children.

• Jim, a college student, learned to think differently and to live a healthier lifestyle. He learned to balance his graduate studies with physical exercise, a more healthy diet and regular appropriate sleep. He also learned to challenge his negative, irrational thinking that had continually pulled him down.

Negative Outcomes

The negative consequences I have seen are twofold: The symptoms of depression are devastating, and what people did with them was not productive. Depression pulled them under, took away their happiness and caused them to be dysfunctional.

• When Judas realized what he had done in selling Jesus for 30 pieces of silver, he went out and hanged himself (Matthew 27).

• When King Saul saw the odds against him in battle, he fell on his own sword and killed himself (1 Samuel 31).

• Gene would not go for treatment and lived a sad, lonely, unproductive life. He lived a long time but, by his own description, was miserable. He continually wished he had never been born.

• Jody went for medical treatment, received medication from a succession of doctors who knew nothing of her medication history, became addicted to prescription drugs and became worse off than she was before. She graduated to illegal drugs, had an auto accident and killed herself.

• Abby "never could" forgive her husband for his affairs. She kept telling herself that if she forgave him it would go against everything she had been taught about the sacredness of marriage. After three years, she divorced him but did not get over it. She kept telling herself these things and rehearsing what he had done for the rest of her life.

What I have seen is that people can have the same depression symptoms and the ultimate consequences can be drastically different. It depends upon what they do with their depression.

How to Turn It Around

How you begin to overcome depression depends upon the causes of depression.

Biological

If the main cause of your depression is genetic, nothing obviously can be done about that. Yet depression is not totally genetic. In fact, genetics is often only a small part of the problem. In such cases, look at other possibilities.

If it is biochemical, see a psychiatrist or another medical doctor. Medication is probably indicated if your depression is serious. Antidepressant medication affects chemicals in the brain, which affect mood. Be sure to follow instructions precisely and give the doctor feedback on what the medication is doing to your system, including side effects. Most of the newer antidepressants have fewer side effects than do older medications. If one medication does not work, don't give up. Perhaps another will.

Electroconvulsive therapy (ECT) is also sometimes effective, and it's not painful now as it once was. I have had clients who did not respond to any other treatment but who did respond well to ECT. I still look at it as the last treatment to try rather than the first, yet I would not rule it out if other treatments are ineffective and medical experts recommend it.

If there are biological problems, they can be treated medically as well. Everything from poor circulation to malnutrition can be treated and will affect one's mood. Treatment for heart trouble or cancer may elevate one's mood.

Counseling can also help since it can affect body chemistry. The way we think affects chemical flow in the brain, which affects mood. Just because something is medical does not mean that psychotherapy is not indicated. Thinking and behavior affect mood. If they can be changed in counseling, then mood can be changed as well. This is even more obvious when the cause of depression is psychological.

Psychological
   There are at least three ways mood is affected: by medication, by changes in thinking and by changes in behavior. Medication is given by a medical doctor; thinking and behavioral changes are brought about in counseling. Directives are given to change behavior. Cognitive restructuring can change thinking. The person learns to talk back to negative, irrational thoughts that are depressing. Jill, whom we met before, did homework along these lines:

NEGATIVE SELF-TALK

"My husband broke his covenant with me, and I can never forgive him."

"If I forgive him, that means I am saying what he did was all right ... just glossing it over."

"He is getting off too easy. He has not suffered enough yet."

TALK BACK

"What he did was awful, forgiveness will be very difficult, but it is not impossible."

"Not true. When God forgives us, that does not mean He is endorsing what we did."

"How much do I have to punish him before I can forgive him? What if I do it for a lifetime? Will that solve anything?"

   Jill finally decided to reconcile with her husband. Her hardest assignment was to have sex with him again. She kept thinking of the other women, but she decided not to let her feelings dominate her. She wanted to rebuild her marriage, so she learned to act better than she felt. After the first time, she said it got easier. He helped too by saying and doing the right things. His love and appreciation grew, and she felt validated by him as never before. She began to come out of her depression and did not have to feel continually hurt after that. I admired her discipline, persistence and faith.
   Often a person's automatic self-talk has been negative and irrational since childhood. In such cases, cognitive restructuring can proceed along these lines:

NEGATIVE SELF-TALK

"I'm no good."

TALK BACK

"Not true. God says that I am valuable and I am."

"I'm ugly."   "People don't seem to be turned
                                off by the way I look. Other things
                                are more important anyhow. I'll
                                just try to look the best I can."

"I never do anything right."   "Not true. I do many things right.
                                I can try harder."

"God will never forgive me."   "Where did I learn that? No
                                religion in the world teaches that.
                                God is gracious. He wants me to
                                be sorry and to learn from my
                                mistakes."

This kind of cognitive challenging has to be done continually over a
long period of time to turn it around. Don't give up. Be persistent. I know
from experience that it works. You'll feel better when you think better.

Let me share with you now a summary of cognitive therapy techniques designed to change cognitions, the eye of the storm of depression, and to change behavior and feelings as well.

- Fill out a schedule listing activities designed to help you
  be more effective.
- Do graded task assignments designed to give you suc-
  cesses and help you view yourself as a winner rather than
  a loser. Do projects that become progressively more challenging. This assignment can build your confidence.
- Keep a record of things you do well and things you
  enjoy.
- Challenge your faulty thinking patterns. Identify thinking
  distortions; then talk back to them. Identify underlying assumptions and premises.
- Look at alternative ways of dealing with problems.
- Imagine steps you will take with specific activities. Look
  at obstacles and conflicts and ways to overcome them.
- Act on rational, reasonable thoughts.[4]

Cognitive therapy for depression grew out of the work of Albert Ellis
and his A-B-C Approach. In this approach, the A is the activating event
or experience. The B is the belief about the experience; the C, the con-
sequence. We usually think that A causes C, but Ellis says that it does-
n't; instead, B causes C.[5] It is not what happens to us so much as what

we believe about what happens to us. This approach gives us a chance to examine our thoughts and change our feelings.

Megan was devastated when Melanie did not speak to her at school. She concluded that nobody likes her and that she is a nobody. Is there another way of looking at this situation? Perhaps Melanie was preoccupied. Perhaps she doesn't like Megan and was deliberately rude to her. What then? Do we have to conclude that Megan is a nobody and that she has to feel terrible? No, that doesn't follow at all.

Most of us have a few people who don't like us, but that does not make us nobodies. It just means that people have different tastes, different personalities, different sore spots. Too bad; just don't let it make you unhappy for life. Maybe we should try a little harder to communicate and to get along, but our happiness should not depend upon how others treat us. Cognitive restructuring can affect how we see A, can change B and thus change C. It's worth a try. I know it works. I use it personally as well as with my clients. It saves me a lot of heartache although I have not perfected it yet.

My brother Dowell in a letter to me wrote that when he was at his lowest point of depression in 1986 he often thought that we are not in the Garden of Eden or Heaven. "This was a great comfort to me," he said. He also reminded me that when we were boys and it got dry on the farm and the corn was already wilting from lack of rain, Mom would often say, "We have not starved yet." "That," Dowell said, "was a source of strength. God will take care of us in tough situations. It's faith! It's a healthy perspective."

The psalmists of the Bible often proceed from negative to positive thoughts. In Psalm 77, the writer asks if the Lord will cast him off forever and never be favorable to him again. Will His promise always fail? Has He forgotten to be gracious? Has He in anger shut off His tender mercies? The psalmist is pessimistic, doubtful and despairing.

He then remembers the wonderful things God has done for him and his people. He remembers the works of the Almighty, His wonders worked in the past. He meditates on God's gracious work and tells of His doings (Psalm 77:7-12). He then continues with a hymn of praise to God who is great and does wonders (Psalm 77:13-20). He has talked his way out of despair and is able to express thanksgiving and praise to God.

Psalm 18 is a psalm David sang when the Lord had delivered him from the hand of his enemies.

I love you, O Lord, my strength.
The Lord is my rock, my fortress and my deliverer;
My God is my rock, in whom I take refuge.
He is my shield and the horn of my salvation, my
    stronghold.

Therefore I will praise you among the nations, O Lord;
I will sing praises to your name (Psalm 18:1-2, 49).

Other examples of praise and thanksgiving by the psalmists may
be seen in Psalms 21, 30, 43, 107 and 116. Psalms 96, 104 and 113 are
good examples of praise.

It isn't that happy people never feel sad or have negative thoughts.
Rather, they look at those thoughts, process them, argue back, change
them (beliefs) and feel better (have a different C).

Perhaps that's enough about cognitions for now. What about the situation, the activating event?

Sociological

Sometimes activating events seem to have a life of their own. We
can't do anything about them. Things happen that hurt. That's when
we think it through and see if we can look at the events differently.
Perhaps someone did not minister to us, but the meaning of that may
vary. What we do with it makes a big difference in how we feel.
Somebody didn't speak to me: it would be nice if they did, but not necessary. My life can go on in spite of this event.

Sometimes, however, stress factors can be changed. Follow me
through these examples:

• Roy improved his communication with his wife and improved his
marriage. His situation was not depressive any more. It was easier
for him to be happy.

• I have simplified my schedule and my life has become less hec-
tic. I teach, I preach, I counsel, I write, I golf, but I don't have to get
it all done at once. I have not given myself an absolute deadline on fin-
ishing this book or set a number on the weekend seminars I have to
hold. I take new clients when I have enough time to effectively counsel them and refer them to other professionals when I don't. I've worked
on keeping my schedule reasonable most of my life, often without much
success. I have finally learned that I am responsible for at least some
of my stress factors.

Ask yourself what you need to change to make your life less depressing and more enjoyable. Are these changes possible? Would they bring on additional problems worse than the ones you have now? For example, I worked more than is desirable most of my life, but I thought I needed to pay the bills, help send our boys through college and give my family more than I had. It was a trade-off that I was willing to make.

Just ask yourself about your situation. What could you change to get you out of despair? What could you change to make you happy? Weigh all of the consequences carefully, then decide. Your situation influences your feelings as well as biology, psychology and spirituality.

Spiritual

If your depression is related to spirituality, you can take a different approach that addresses spirituality, the core of your being. Depression is related to how you see yourself in relationship to God, people and the world. It is related to the quality of your life. I often remember that Jesus came to give us abundant life. I wonder what the full meaning of that statement is. I know that abundant life is life lived "to the full" (John 10:10). It is life full of vigor, optimism, integrity and meaning. Such a life would surely be an antidote to depression. The good people I mentioned before who were depressed were not depressed because of their badness, yet they realized that they were not living life, while depressed, fully.

Since spirituality affects our whole life, it is a logical focal point for changes that need to be made. Good people can be too perfectionistic, too sensitive, too self-blaming, which can cause a downward pull toward depression. They seldom are satisfied with themselves, and this is unsettling.

I have developed a worksheet on spirituality and problem solving that might prove to be helpful to you. It was influenced by a good book I read by Richards and Bergin.[6] They follow a similar theme throughout their book. My line of questions is as follows:

- Do you see yourself as a spiritual being accountable to God? What is your spiritual identity? Does your problem relate to this identity?
- What spiritual resources do you have? The church? The Bible? Other good books? Spiritual friends? Other? Have you been utilizing them?
- What are your spiritual values and beliefs? Please write a list. Is your problem related to these? How?

- Do you live congruently, in accord with, these values and beliefs? How does this relate to your problem and spiritual well-being?
- Are you alive spiritually? Are you growing spiritually? What do you need to do differently to grow spiritually? Are you willing to do this? When?

The key here is your spiritual identity and your integrity. When I try to focus on who I am as a child of God, it helps me to be genuine and to grow spiritually. I'm still trying to reach that goal of congruent living, but just trying helps me to do better and to feel better. Just make an honest effort, make adjustments when needed, and go on. Don't continually look back and second-guess yourself.

My clients and I have selected several scriptures that help them when they are depressed. Our Top 10 list is as follows:

Psalm 23:1: The Lord is my Shepherd, I shall not want.

Psalm 46:1-3: God is our refuge and strength, an ever-present help in trouble. Therefore we will not fear, though the earth give way and the mountains fall into the heart of the sea, though its waters roar and foam and the mountains quake with their surging.

Isaiah 40:28-30: Do you not know? Have you not heard? The Lord is the everlasting God, the Creator of the ends of the earth. He will not grow tired or weary, and his understanding no one can fathom. He gives strength to the weary and increases the power of the weak. Even youths grow tired and weary, and young men stumble and fall; but those who hope in the Lord will renew their strength. They will soar on wings like eagles; they will run and not grow weary, they will walk and not be faint.

Matthew 6:25: Therefore I tell you, do not worry about your life, what you will eat or drink; or about your body, what you will wear. Is not life more important than food, and the body more important that clothes?

Matthew 6:34: Therefore do not worry about tomorrow, for tomorrow will worry about itself. Each day has enough trouble of its own.

Philippians 4:12-13: I know what it is to be in need, and I know what it is to have plenty. I have learned the secret of being content in any and every situation, whether well fed or hungry, whether living in plenty or in want. I can do everything through him who gives me strength.

Philippians 4:19: And my God will meet all your needs according to his glorious riches in Christ Jesus.

1 Peter 5:7: Cast all your anxiety on him because he cares for you.

Psalm 121:1-3: I lift up my eyes to the hills – where does my help come from? My help comes from the Lord, the Maker of heaven and earth. He will not let your foot slip – he who watches over you will not slumber;

Revelation 21:4: He will wipe every tear from their eyes. There will be no more death or mourning or crying or pain, for the old order of things has passed away.

I hope you can find strength and encouragement in these words, as have hundreds of my clients over the years. One friend of mine told me he would cling at times, when deep in depression, to the hope and strength found in such verses of scripture. In fact, he mentioned over half of the verses I just listed.

Take another look at some psalms that deal with various emotions often experienced by depressed persons.

Despair. This feeling was expressed in Psalm 6. David asked God not to rebuke him in His anger but to be merciful. He was faint and asked for healing: His bones were in agony. He asks, "How long, O Lord, how long? ... I am worn out from groaning; all night long I flood my bed with weeping and drench my couch with tears?" (vv. 1-6).

Hopelessness. In Psalm 69, David felt as though he were coming up to his neck, that he was sinking in miry depths where there is no foothold. He had come to deep water and the floods engulfed him. Then, he called out for God to rescue him from the mire, not to let him sink, to deliver him from those who hate him, from the deep waters. "Do not," he continues, "let the floodwaters engulf me or the depths swallow me up or the pit close its mouth over me" (vv. 1-15).

Abandonment. The psalmist sometimes feels lonely and confused. He asks why the Lord stands far off, why He hides himself in times of trouble. He asks the Lord not to forget the helpless (Psalm 10:1, 12). He is honest with God in admitting such fears.

Desire to escape. David expressed a desire to escape in Psalm 55, to just fly away with the wings of a dove into the desert. There he would find rest and shelter, far from the tempest and storm.

Guilt. In Psalm 51, David wrote of his guilt which was always before him. He had sinned against God and done evil in his sight. God is thus proved right when He speaks and justified when He judges. David is probably referring here to his sin with Bathsheba and against her husband, Uriah (2 Samuel 11-12).

David knew that it is healthy to be honest and work through emotions. He did and found answers. In Psalm 30, he acknowledged that

God had lifted him out of the depths, had healed him, had brought him up from the grave and spared him from going down into the pit (Psalm 30:1-3). There was hope in despair. He waited patiently for the Lord who turned to him and heard his cry. God, he said, lifted him out of the slimy pit, out of the mud and mire; "he set my feet on a rock and gave me a firm place to stand" (Psalm 40:1-2).

Other passages point out the following:

- God, as I have mentioned, was David's refuge and strength (Psalm 46:1-4; 71:1-4; 121).
- God forgave him of his sins, redeemed his life from the pit and crowned him with love and compassion. He satisfied him with good things and renewed his life like the eagle's (Psalm 32; 103:1-5).
- God had intimate knowledge of David. He knew everything about him. David found comfort in Him (Psalm 139:1-8). He is always with us. He will never leave or forsake us (Matthew 28:18-20; Hebrews 13:5-6).
- God was his shepherd who would lead him through the valley to better times (Psalm 23).
- God listens to our cry for help. He will not despise or disdain the suffering of the afflicted one. He will not hide His face from him but will listen to his cry for help (Psalm 22). He will be there in desperate situations, when "The cords of death entangled me" (Psalm 18). He will draw me out of deep waters (Psalm 18:16).

Sometimes when you are deeply depressed, you don't believe in yourself, and it's hard to believe anything. These are times to hold on to words of hope and strength. When tempted, Jesus quoted passages of scripture (Matthew 4:1-11). It helps by giving structure, content and direction to your emotions. It restructures your thinking and changes your behavior and feelings.

We are back to spiritual resilience: discipline, persistence and faith through struggles. If you are seriously depressed, reach out for help. Read; pray; talk to trusted, healthy friends; see a psychologist, psychiatrist or some other qualified mental health expert; tie a knot in the end of your rope and hang on until others can help you climb back up.

This reminds me of a story from my childhood about a mule that fell into a well. The farmer tried every way he knew to pull him out but to no avail. Finally, he decided to just throw dirt over him and bury him. But when the dirt came down, the mule shook it off and stepped up on top of it. After a while, the mule, battered and exhausted, stepped over the wall of the well. The key to his victory: shake it off and step up!

I enjoy success stories about people who persisted when prospects of success were slim. Einstein did not learn to talk until he was 4 or read until he was 7. Beethoven's music teacher once called him hopeless. Thomas Edison's teachers said he was so stupid that he could not learn anything. F.W. Woolworth was not allowed to wait on customers because he "didn't have enough sense." Walt Disney was once fired by a newspaper editor because he did not have any good ideas. Caruso was told by one music teacher that he couldn't sing; Louisa May Alcott was informed that she was incapable of writing anything that would have popular appeal. They achieved success because they talked back to their negative critics and persisted. They refused to say, "I can't."

Thomas Edison performed 10,000 experiments before he perfected his hard rubber disc phonograph record – 1,500 experiments before he found a filament that would carry electric current. He even tried a hair out of a redheaded woman to see if it would carry electricity. Trial and error: He didn't quit. He persisted, and he succeeded.

Alfred C. Fuller lost his first three jobs. He was shy and could hardly read or write. No one would give him a fourth job, so he started making brushes and selling them door-to-door. Again, it was discipline, persistence and faith toward success.

When I watch my grandchildren, I wish I could spare them disappointment. David misses a shot in basketball; Kevin's team loses a soccer game; Jonathan and Kate fall and skin themselves. Benton is sore from his circumcision operation and cries. They are hurt and disappointed, and I can't do anything about it. Yet perhaps that is the way they learn. Without some failure, we probably would not learn much.

A little boy, for example, watching a little chicken trying to crack its egg and get out, cracked the egg for it. The chick died. His father then told him that a chick gains strength to survive from its struggle to crack its egg and get out. There may be value, you see, in our struggles. I wish there were an easier way, but in this world, there is no royal road to healthy growth and emotional maturity. Some struggle and persistence are involved. We learn simple math before we learn algebra. We gain strength through difficulty.

I'll close with my favorite illustration of success through discipline, persistence and faith.

He had a difficult childhood.

Less than one year of formal schooling.

He failed in business in 1831.
He was defeated for the legislature in 1832.
Again failed in business in 1833.
Elected to the legislature in 1834.
His fiancée died in 1835.
Defeated for Speaker in 1838.
Defeated for Elector in 1840.
He married, and his wife became a burden in 1842.
Only one of his sons lived past age 18.
He was defeated for Congress in 1843.
Elected to Congress in 1846.
Defeated for Congress in 1848.
Defeated for the Senate in 1855.
Defeated for Vice President in 1856.
Defeated for the Senate in 1858.

Yet this man, Abraham Lincoln, was not a loser. He was elected president in 1860 and is now thought of as perhaps our greatest president.

Finally, get help if you are seriously depressed. I have seen hundreds of depressed people get such help and live good lives. Most scholars today think that Abraham Lincoln was depressed. He just kept trying. You can too!

Reflections

1. What are the four possible causes of depression I mentioned?
2. What are some common myths about depression?
3. What are its symptoms?
4. What are some consequences of depression?
5. How does medication help depression?
6. What does counseling do?
7. Give some examples from your life of how thinking affects behavior and feelings.
8. What scriptures are most uplifting to you?
9. Are there changes in your life you need to make that would perhaps enable you to be happy? What?
10. Can you think of examples of friends who like Abraham Lincoln and Thomas Edison never gave up? What success did they achieve because of their discipline, persistence, and faith?

CHAPTER SIX

Building Self-Esteem

Y ou may not have symptoms of anxiety or depression, but you
may struggle because of low self-esteem. Or, you may be a parent and wish to build self-esteem in your children. How is it possible to build self-esteem in my children or in myself? It's a slow process,
but here are some ideas that work.

Building Self-Esteem in Children
Children are a heritage of the Lord and His reward (Psalm 127:3).
Parents should receive them with love and gratitude and not provoke
or discourage them (Colossians 3:21). Such an approach will help children learn to have good self-esteem.

Coopersmith found that many factors influence the development of
self-esteem in children: power, effectance, significance, acceptance,
affection, virtue, morality and ethics.[1] Competence, achievement, success, relationships, a sense of belonging, support from others and money are important as well. It has also been demonstrated that physical
appearance, intelligence, competition and the family and community
situation also influence self-esteem. Family strengths are so important
that they can sometimes overcome social rejection. For this to happen,
parents must have definite values, a clear idea of what they perceive as
appropriate behavior, and be able and willing to present and enforce
their beliefs that self-esteem is highly influenced by our beliefs about
who we are. God made us; therefore, we are worthwhile. If we are
worthwhile, then we have good reason to have good self-esteem. Our
self-esteem is not a selfish sort of thing but is rooted in faith in our
Creator. He made us worthwhile!

As a parent, you may want some specific guidelines for building self-
esteem in children. Although there are no cookbook approaches that

will always be completely adequate, here are some ideas that have
proven themselves worthwhile in child rearing:

Try to improve your own mental health. It is impossible for you to
contribute toward good self-esteem in your child if your self-esteem is
extremely low. You can try, but you will probably be unsuccessful
unless you start with yourself. In dealing with your children, you teach
more by what you are than by what you say. Ask yourself such questions as the following: Since God accepts me, why can't I accept myself? Since God loves me, why can't I love myself? Since God says I
am worthwhile, why will I not accept this evaluation? Who am I to
question God? Since I forgive others, why can't I forgive myself?
Perhaps there is something in me that is worthwhile.

If you are married, establish a healthy marriage. If your marriage is
unhealthy, you no doubt have unhealthy patterns of interaction in your
home that affect your children. The starting place for family therapy is
with the individual parents and with the patterns of interaction between
them. If you can't work it out yourself, get some help in doing so. It is
not a sign of weakness to see your own faults and to try to overcome
them. In fact, it is a sign of maturity and strength to do so. Weak people try to avoid such reality.

Provide for your family's needs: physical, emotional, psychological,
social and spiritual. When such needs as these are not met, children
will be affected. They need to be loved, fed, clothed, given shelter and
safety, given understanding, acceptance, responsibility, a sense of effectance and spiritual training. If parents are relatively healthy themselves, they can provide the kind of atmosphere children need to feel
good about themselves.

Spend time with your children. In these days of two-career families,
it is sometimes difficult for either parent to spend much quality time
with the children. Parents are often not only busy but also tired and need
rest themselves. However, children are a priority and must be given some
attention. Try to restore the family table to its rightful place. Eat as many
meals together as possible. Make such meals a time of pleasant interaction. No distractions should normally be allowed, such as watching
television while you are eating. This is a time for togetherness. It is also
good to find other times for mutual participation. I have always had a
basketball goal in our yard and have often played basketball with our
children as they grew up. I believe this time together helped us to form
some bonds that are still very strong. You may think of many other

situations in which you can find some quality time together. Use your imagination and make this a real priority in your family.

Teach them proper values. Children will pick up your values. If they see you living for money and prestige, they will value money and prestige. If they see you laying up treasures in heaven, they will usually value heaven (Matthew 6:19-21). Show them that you value them and that you value spiritual realities. God, family, individuals, church, responsibility and Christian character should have a high priority in your life!

Let your children be children. As parents, we sometimes rush our children into adulthood. We put them into competitive activities sometimes even before they start school. They pick up the spirit of competitiveness and create for themselves extreme pressure to achieve beyond what is desirable or possible. Such achievement is often not that important in the overall scheme of things. This is especially true if they get so competitive and so involved in such activities that they miss the opportunity of being children. Children need to have some time to just play around and do nothing. Let them be creative, try themselves out at different tasks. Encourage them; do not thwart initiative.

Focus upon strengths rather than weaknesses. Be realistic, yet recognize strengths. Get the child to thinking of what he or she can do rather than what can't be done. If we are unrealistic, we set our children up for defeat. Rosenberg found that high self-esteem children tend to have mothers who are satisfied with average or below average performance.[2] This goes against the grain with most of us because we do not want our children to be just average. Yet if everyone pushes his or her child to be above average, about half of them are going to be frustrated and dissatisfied with themselves.

Help them overcome setbacks and compete. We cannot completely overlook the need for our children to perform. We need to help them to learn, to keep trying when they fail, to overcome setbacks and to compete. Competition is not everything, but self-esteem is related to how well one does in relationship to others. This means doing as well as possible in school, continuing to try when mistakes are made.

Discipline your children with love. Set certain limits and enforce them. Several researchers have found that low self-esteem is highly correlated with permissive parents. Discipline pays off. Show your love by your warmth, encouragement, consistency, realistic expectation and a balance between permissiveness and being overly strict. Use reward more often than punishment. When you discipline your children, tell them why you are doing so if they are old enough to understand at all. Discipline with moderation. Discipline according to the age level of the child.

Encourage achievement in school. Motivate, help maximize potential, yet accept them for what they are and not for what you wish them to be. I know of one young man who committed suicide the day after his father forced him to change his educational and career goals. To the son, this demand meant that the father did not accept him for what he really was. God gave each of us different aptitudes and abilities; we need to maximize these to the fullest.

Try to avoid over protection and dependency. Give children appropriate responsibilities at different age levels, ask for their input, interact with them, give them responsibility and praise them for their achievements. Let them try things out. Give them wings as well as roots.

Explain changes that will occur at puberty. There are still children from good homes who do not know what is going to happen to them at pubescence. They often are embarrassed and scared. We need to teach them that these changes are a part of God's plan and interpret them in terms of becoming mature. Then they will see them as a positive rather than a negative factor.

Forgive them. Most children are corrected, but many are not forgiven. Children need to hear their parents say, "I forgive you. You did wrong, but you have done what you could to correct it. I still love you and I forgive you. We are going to go on from here."

Don't be partial to one child. Some believe that this caused Joseph problems with his brothers. Jacob had given him a special coat, indicating some preference for Joseph over his brothers This may have caused them to turn against him. It isn't fair to any of the children when we show partiality.

Learn to show affection. This is difficult for you if you were reared in a family that did not show such affection. But you can learn to make some kind of appropriate physical contact with your children and show affection. This will help them to feel accepted, valuable and secure.

Help them to belong. God helps Christians to have a feeling of belonging by saying that we are vital parts in the body of Christ (Romans 12; 1 Corinthians 12). Each part of the body has its function. Each child has a place of his or her very own in the family. Giving chores that are appropriate to the children's age level may help them have a sense of belonging. Telling them will also help.

Help them develop a strong faith in God, the source of our true value. We are worthwhile because God made us, and we are His. His grace is sufficient for us (2 Corinthians 12:9). We can therefore glory in our weaknesses because the power of Christ rests upon us.

Don't be afraid to act for fear of doing the wrong thing. You can make mistakes and still do a good job with your children. Remember that self-esteem is self-perpetuating, either high self-esteem or low self-esteem. Once we get something going in a certain direction, it seems to perpetuate itself. This can be encouraging as we, with God's help, work to develop self-esteem in our children.[3]

Building Self-Esteem in Adolescents

Adolescents often experience low self-esteem. They may develop a sense of inferiority instead of good self-esteem. They feel lonely, uncomfortable and self-conscious and tend to focus on themselves during this stage from age 13 to 19. Bodily change, menses for girls, sexual development, zit-in-the-mirror, voice changes and acceptance by peers can bring emotional upheaval. As Erickson says it, it is a time of identity vs. identity confusion.[4]

Factors in our culture that may influence self-esteem the most are good looks, intelligence, money and position and strength and athletics for boys. Even children's stories put down the ugly duckling and Dumbo the elephant. Shackelford found that teachers give higher grades to attractive children and blame unattractive ones for offenses.[5] Such children may come to believe that they are not worthy of their aims and do not have the ability to achieve them.

Adolescents may vacillate between the extremes of narcissism and being dependent before becoming a healthy personality. Who am I? What are my strengths and weaknesses? Where do I fit in? What will I do with my life? These are vital questions to be answered. We need to see adolescents not as potential rebels but as individuals with potential for growth, happiness and service.

During this stage, what can be done to build self-esteem? Please consider these suggestions.

Positive Reinforcement

There is no better way to build self-esteem in adolescents than by valuing them and finding ways to give them credit for who they are and what they do. Parents, siblings, grandparents, teachers, ministers and

others all have an impact on teens. We may get what we expect to get.
A friend of mine told me about how two of his teachers began their classes. One said, "I see all of you as 'F' students until you prove otherwise." A second teacher's view was expressed this way: "Until you prove differently, I see all of you as 'A' students." Guess which students worked the hardest and got the best grades?

If you are a teenager, you need to learn self-reinforcement principles. Give yourself credit for every small success and continue to try. What you think of you can over-ride many negative factors that pull you down.

Cognitive Restructuring

Teens often feel badly about themselves because they have internalized negative messages they have heard from significant others. They need to talk back to these messages: "I am worthwhile. I can amount to something. Everybody does not dislike me. I don't have to be the most popular person in school to be worthwhile." Talk back to that internal critic.

Carlson's Suggestions

David Carlson in his book *Counseling and Self-Esteem* lists several steps to help adolescents:

• Acknowledge the problems low self-esteem produces including guilt, over sensitivity, hypercriticalness, shyness, clowning, arrogance, blaming, feeling blamed, self-negation, insincerity, addictions and marriage and family problems.
• Believe that loving yourself is acceptable to God.
• Believe that God chooses to need you.
• Discover your place in relationship to God and His people.
• Validate yourself.
• Make realistic demands on yourself.
• Reflect on the truth about yourself.
• Live with God's love and forgiveness as a way to implement change.
• Nurture yourself.
• Serve others.
• Meditate on who you are in relationship to God.
• Be as patient with the process of learning to love yourself as God is.[6]

Scott Peck in his book *The Road Less Travelled* expressed a vital thought when he said, "Once we perceive the reality of grace, our un-

derstanding of ourselves as meaningless and insignificant is shattered."[7]
We matter. We are somebody! We belong. Self-esteem is not found
from a humanistic view of self worth; the basis of self-esteem is found
in God who made us and accepts us. It gets back to our perception:
How we see ourselves in relationship to God, people, and the world.

Neil, age 16, had done well until his teen years. He then began to
doubt himself, feel like he was a freak, and perform poorly in school.
His self-esteem was a one on a 1-10 scale. He began to turn it around
by using some of Carlson's principles. A summary of some of his homework in counseling looked like this.[8]

NEGATIVE SELF-TALK	THINKING MISTAKE	FEELING	TALK BACK
I can never measure up.	Fortune telling	Shame	Not true. Never is a long time. I some-times do well.
I am worthless. Nobody likes me.	Labeling Exaggeration Overgeneralization	Depressed Low self-esteem	Everybody is worthwhile. I am too! Jason spoke to me this morning
I am helpless.	Exaggeration Labeling	Suicidal	I feel helpless but I know I'm not. I can't do every-thing, but I can do some things. I'll do what I can.
I can't do anything right.	Overgeneralization	Depressed	Not true. I goofed on the math exam, but I did well in his-tory. I can do lots of things right.
I look awful. People think I'm a freak.	Labeling Exaggeration	Low self-esteem Depressed Suicidal	Not true, really. Some people say I look good. I just have a few zits on my face. I'm getting that treated. It's not that big a deal any-how. There is more to me than zits.

Neil continued for a year in therapy working on his perceptions and
his life. As he processed his pain, he began to see himself differently,
which changed his feelings. His self-esteem improved, as did his grades
and his social life. He has now graduated from college, is married and

has a good job. All of this happened because of his discipline, persistence and faith as he worked through the changes and struggles of his life.

Acceptance

I wish you could change our culture so that intelligence, good looks, strength, achievements, money and position were not so important, but you can't. I can't either. Other things are more important: character, love, joy, peace, effort, faithfulness, consideration, thoughtfulness and service to name a few. Self-worth that is built in is much more important than popularity based upon our culture's standards. It is hard not be affected by them, but we must constantly try. They are very real, and we can't change them overnight and perhaps never. We can, however, accept the fact that our culture's values are not what they should be and that we have values that are more elevated, nobler: Everyone has self-worth. We can determine not to let our culture dictate how we feel – push our button. We march to a different drummer. We change our perspective, which changes our feelings.

Neil learned that everyone does not have equal opportunity for attractiveness, economic status, education level, intelligence, strength and athletic ability and thus have value as the world defines value. He learned that he was valuable apart from all of this. "God," he said, "has chosen to value me. I am made in his image. What he created is good. I have been redeemed by Jesus. I am loved. I have a place." He began to not only have faith but to practice it and feel better. This is in line with the findings of Adcock and Noaker that: Those who just claim to have faith have a significantly lower self-esteem than those who practice their faith, and adolescents with positive self-esteem scored higher on a measure of religiosity than did those with low self-esteem.[9]

Communicating Effectively

Constructive communication can lead to higher self-esteem. This is true of both parent and teen communication. Teens who constantly listen to negative communication often pick up the pattern and pass it on, thus having a double negative effect on their self-esteem. They get negative input from parents, pass it on and then get negative feedback, which pulls them down.

Barber reported that the quality of marriages affects self-esteem, especially in boys.[10] Parents who perceive God as loving and accepting, integrate their faith and practice, perceive themselves as worthwhile and competent usually communicate effectively and help their children build self-esteem.

A Practical Solution

If you are a teenager, get a 4" x 6" card and write the following on it. Then, read the card several times each day.

• God loves me. He knows me personally.[11]
• Others love me.
• God created me.
• I belong to Him.
• I'll not try to grow up too fast. I need time to be an adolescent.
• I'll learn to listen and to talk.
• I'll learn how to solve problems. If I don't know, I'll ask.
• I'll pick out good role models to follow.
• I'll not hold grudges against my parents or others. They mean well. Nobody is perfect.
• I'll take responsibility. I have some control over what happens to me.
• I'll show interest in and respect for others.
• I'll try.
• By God's grace, I'm okay.

Working together with parents, teachers, church leaders and other adults, you can learn to be all that God meant for you to be. Your future can be interesting and productive.

Dobson's Suggestions for Parents

Before I close out this section about teens, I would like to encourage parents to read James Dobson's book *Hide or Seek* on building self-esteem in adolescents. He lists 10 strategies:

1. Examine the values in your home.
2. Reserve adolescence for adolescents.
3. Teach your children a no-knock policy.
4. Help them compensate.
5. Help them compete.
6. Discipline them without damaging their self-esteem.
7. Keep a close eye on the classroom.
8. Avoid over protection and dependency.
9. Prepare for what to expect in adolescence.
10. Improve your own self-esteem.[12]

This last point prepares us for our next section. What can you do to build self-esteem in yourself?

Building Self-Esteem in Yourself As an Adult

Building self-esteem in yourself is a hard and slow process. Yet it is not an impossible one. It's worth the effort because you influence so many people and because of your own happiness.

What is self-esteem? It is how you feel about being you, how you feel about being alive. It results from an evaluation of your self-image, how you feel about the way you see yourself. It is influenced by the distance of the gap between your self-image and your ideal image. You can, for example, see yourself as being of average intelligence, feel all right about it and experience high self-esteem. Or you can feel badly about it and experience low self-esteem. You can feel worthy or unworthy, competent or incompetent, significant or insignificant, valuable or worthless, hopeful or hopeless, truthful or deceptive, confident or fearful, withdrawn or sociable, preoccupied or spontaneous. You may have accurate perceptions of others or be preoccupied with self, feel loved or unloved, overly sensitive to criticism or open to a healthy interaction with others. Self-esteem has an evaluative element: How do you feel about the way you see yourself?

Self-esteem has many correlates. Low self-esteem has been correlated with psychological distress, depression, preoccupation with self, fatigue, chronic health problems, negative attitudes toward self and others, being trapped in a self-defeating cycle, a concept of being a nobody, rigidity, authoritarian families, neurosis, anxiety, defensiveness, drug abuse, alcoholism, interpersonal problems, child abuse, low academic achievement, hostility and even suicide in some cases. High self-esteem is correlated with good health, confidence, accurate perceptions of reality, flexibility, good ability to interact with others, trust, happiness, success, involvement with others, openness, competence, good home life, good decisions, academic success and self-respect. A person with good self-esteem has a sense of self worth, yet recognizes his or her limitations. Such a person is not conceited but rather is glad to be himself. Self-actualized persons tend to have accurate perceptions of reality and adapt well to it. They accept themselves and others but want to correct their own shortcomings. They are problem-centered, not self-centered: They appreciate the simple things of life, are ethical, able to discriminate between means and ends; they get along in their culture yet resist enculturation and have a genuine desire to help others – a good description of self-esteem.

Self-esteem may be classified into two divisions: basic self-esteem and functional self-esteem. Basic self-esteem is established in childhood, is hard but not impossible to change; whereas functional self-esteem is derived from daily experiences and changes more readily.

To build self-esteem, you need to know its roots. Parents probably have the greatest influence on self-esteem. A close relationship between parents and children leads to high self-esteem in children; indifferent relationships, to low self-esteem. Positive reinforcement and acceptance teach children to value themselves. They develop attitudes toward themselves similar to those expressed by significant others in their lives. Parents who love, show concern, give attention, direction and approval to their children teach them to value themselves positively. There is not, however, a direct cause-effect relationship in the building of self-esteem. Persons are involved themselves and thus help create their own environment. One who is honest and lives with integrity tends to have good self-esteem; whereas dishonest persons do not. It's how you feel about what you have thought, felt and done that determines your self-esteem.

Healthy self-esteem in men is thought to be derived to some extent from vocations, intelligence, wealth, achievements, education, positions of power and competition. Female self-esteem results more from the achievement of goals, self and body image, education, money, everyday concerns and family relationships. Both sexes are usually affected by their view of how they are evaluated by significant others in their lives.

In summary, there are probably at least 17 influences on one's self-esteem: one's self, one's sex, significant others, social role expectations, family relationships, community influence, psychosocial developmental issues, communication and coping strategies, standards, unrealistic expectations, education, wealth, intelligence, achievements, competition, theology and thinking. These should be kept in mind as you begin to build your own self-esteem.

Here are some specific suggestions for building self-esteem:

Personal Responsibility

Accept personal responsibility for your own low self-esteem (carry your own burden – Galatians 6:5). The past and the present influence you, but you are a creative factor in the formation of your own thoughts, actions and feelings. If you do not take such responsibility, you will never change. The mind does not automatically generate ideas in a direct cause-effect fashion similar to the way the heart pumps blood.

There is a volitional element involved in the mind's creation of ideas. The person himself or herself is involved. We add a creative part to the production of ideas and self-esteem. We must therefore take responsibility for what we are doing. Your locus of control must become internal rather than external (other people, circumstances). You must become less passive and more active. You must realize that it is not outside events that directly cause feelings but rather your interpretation of those events. We need to learn that we choose to think, act or feel a certain way. We can thus choose to perceive the past differently and to see ourselves differently. That I was treated badly does not mean that I am worthless any more than a dog's barking at the moon makes it disappear. I am of value even if others do not think so. And I feel good about it! These sorts of self-statements will start us on the road toward better self-esteem.

Restructure Your Thinking

Restructure your thinking (Philippians 4:8-9). Thinking affects feelings and feelings affect thinking. When you feel worthless, you think negative thoughts that reinforce and perpetuate this feeling. People who are down on themselves tend to make many thinking mistakes such as the following:

• They *overgeneralize*. From one mistake, they conclude that they can't do anything right.

• They *eternalize*. From one failure, they conclude that they will never do anything right.

• They *personalize*. They are too absorbed with themselves. They inappropriately apply comments and criticism from others to themselves: "They are all talking about me." They blame themselves too much: "Others had nothing to do with it, circumstances had nothing to do with it, I caused it all. I'm completely to blame."

• They *catastrophize*. What they do is the worst thing that has ever been done: "If you only knew what I did, you would not want me in your group."

• They *filter*. Many positive things may have happened to them, yet they do not see them. They filter them out. Their whole world is thus negative.

• They *neutralize*. If they do see positive things in their lives, they negate them: "He doesn't really like me. He just needed a date." We can make anyone look bad by filtering out his or her good points or by concentrating on bad points.

• They *absolutize*. Everything becomes a must. "People *must* like me, life *must* be easy, and I *must* be competent. If not, I am worthless and life is not worth living." Albert Ellis encourages people to make a distinction between desire and demand: "It would be *nice* if everyone liked me, but it is not necessary."[13] Persons with low self-esteem often jump to conclusions without adequate evidence.

• They *dichotomize*. Everything is either black or white; there is no gray. Such persons are often very perfectionistic.

• They *self-destruct*. They set up negative self-fulfilling prophecies: "No one likes me." So when a person does like them, they are suspicious and uncomfortable, which cause them to send out negative signals, which cause the other person to back off. When they back off, the person says to himself: "I was right. No one likes me." It seems impossible for a person with low self-esteem to feel loved.

Building self-esteem involves several steps such as the following:

• Discover thinking mistakes that contribute to your low self-esteem: by looking at your history, by writing down statements about yourself (automatic self talk) or by keeping a daily journal.

• Challenge the validity of each self-statement: dispute, challenge, contradict and reverbalize them one at a time. One idea that is often effective is to try to prove that you are worthless. If you tie feelings of worthlessness in with competency, you can learn that the sense of being worthwhile has nothing to do with competence. You only think that it makes you worthless! If you are alive, you have worth! Learn to test your judgment and validate the relationship between thoughts and feelings. Your belief system can be challenged and changed, and thus your behavior and feelings of self-esteem change also. Beliefs have consequences.

• Learn how these misconceptions originated and see that they are inaccurate, unrealistic and distorted. Learn to view yourself differently and to understand that you are not a victim of thoughts and feelings but rather a participant.

• Write the new list of correct beliefs on a card and read the list several times each day. They become your new self-talk.

• Role-play situations in which you have felt inferior in the past. Learn to perform tasks that you normally avoid.

• Practice these new behaviors during the next week; perform needed tasks you previously avoided because of feelings of inferiority; and then properly assess the outcome. Do not be prejudiced against yourself because of improper assessment of outcomes.

Set Realistic Goals

Paul pressed on toward the mark of the high calling of God (Philippians 3:13-14): That was a realistic goal for him. But it is not realistic for us to think that we can all become the richest, the most attractive, the most effective, the most powerful person in the world. If we set unrealistic goals, we set ourselves up for defeat and low self-esteem.

Be Fair to Yourself

If you would forgive others for doing what you have done, forgive yourself. Don't be prejudiced against yourself. It's not fair!

Learn Thought-Stopping

Think inappropriate negative thoughts about yourself, and yell, "stop," and slam a book down on your desk. Repeat this practice several times. Then repeat the process. Next, repeat the process and say, "stop," to yourself. This helps you to stop thinking such inappropriate thoughts.

Substitute Incompatible Thoughts

Substitute incompatible thoughts that interfere with inappropriate negative thoughts. For example, one older friend of mine learned to say, "I'll be better off in heaven," instead of "I'm afraid to die." Another, "I've been successful in many ways," rather than "I'm a failure." Such statements divert one's mind from negative, irrational thoughts.

Change Your Attitude

People with low self-esteem usually have an attitude of "poor me," "stupid you" and "poor stupid world." They seem to be stuck in their past, their unconscious memories and their present situation. Yet we are not prisoners of these circumstances and can change. If you have had a setback, get help with your burdens and restore your hope in an interesting future.

Take Small Steps Toward Success

Persons who experience success tend to manifest higher self-esteem. Persons with low self-esteem may have known little else but failure. Structure attainable goals or tasks which, when completed, will have a positive effect. Give yourself credit for making small improvements.

Institute Self-Improvements Projects.
Something as simple as losing excessive weight, an exercise program, physical work, taking a course in school or just doing some things you believe you ought to do can improve your self-esteem. If you do better, you feel better (Philippians 4:9).

Build on Strengths
Emphasize and build on strengths rather than weaknesses. One way to do this is to write down positive self-evaluations daily for several weeks. List personal, intellectual, physical and spiritual assets on cards. Then read these several times a day for a few weeks. Such exercises have been shown to help increase self-esteem. You may compensate for deficiencies by accenting strengths. Think more about what you like about being you and less about what you don't like.

Learn Coping Skills
It has been found that training in progressive relaxation, anxiety management, social skills and self-reinforcement procedures can help build self-esteem. Learn to avoid argumentative comments that will merely alienate others, to give encouragement to others, to compliment and to listen.
The attainment of other skills may also help. If you experience academic failure, learn better study habits and discipline. Learning how to communicate may help you to be less self-absorbed and more aware of others. Additional education may give greater self-confidence.

Build Relationships
People who have low self-esteem think of themselves as inferior, so they behave that way and expect others to reject them. This blocks the building of relationships. Since the roots of relationship problems are usually in childhood, they need to learn a more mature interaction pattern by making regular contact with each member of their family of origin. A study of their family tree might facilitate interactional patterns in the family and increase understanding. Remembering that we belong to one another also helps us. Fellowship in Christ and mutual edification help secure my mind and emotions (Hebrews 10:19-25;1 Peter 4:7-11).
Group counseling or group discussions at church is a good context for relationship building. Anything that encourages us in constructive

interaction may help actualize self-esteem. If we feel good about ourselves, we should feel good about interacting with others. If we do not, something is wrong. Learn to interact and to give to others. Learn to receive and to give.

Visualize

Learn to relax and to visualize yourself with high self-esteem in different situations of life, enjoying being alive and acting with good self-esteem. We tend to become what we visualize.

Reframe Experiences

Pictures often look different in different frames. So do experiences, past, present and future. There is a difference between saying, "I've hit the bottom," and saying, "There is no way for me to go but up." The latter statement leaves you with hope; the former, without hope. Get used to thinking in terms of reframing your negative experiences. It is a powerful tool.

Build Strong Spiritual Lives

Learn to build strong spiritual lives. I believe that you are of inestimable value in the sight of God. He created you in His own image (Genesis 1:26-27) and endowed you with a measure of Himself. You are not a curious accident of evolution. God loves you (John 3:16): While we were yet sinners, Jesus died for us (Romans 5:8). Christ would not die for worthless individuals. God created the world for us (Genesis 1); He listens to us when we pray (John 15:16); He provides many blessings every day. By His grace, we are significant! We have a high purpose for living. Our labor in Him is not vain (1 Corinthians 15:58). Self-worth implanted by God is the solid basis of our self-esteem.

We are not totally depraved as some interpret the Bible to say. Such a faulty theology leads to low self-esteem. We are much more than worms. God has given us value. Note the exalted view of mankind reflected in Psalm 8:3-8:

> When I consider your heavens,
>   the work of your fingers,
> the moon and the stars,
>   which you have set in place,
> what is man that you are mindful of him,
>   the son of man that you care for him?

You made him a little lower than the heavenly beings
    and crowned him with glory and honor.
You made him ruler over the works of your hands;
    you put everything under his feet;
all flocks and herds,
    and the beasts of the field,
the birds of the air,
    and the fish of the sea,
all that swim the paths of the seas.

We are to have sound judgment (Romans 12:3), to mature into the "whole measure of the fullness of Christ" (Ephesians 4:13). We need to be close to God. We find extreme closeness and spiritual life in giving up self (Matthew 10:39) to allow God to make His home with us (John 14:23). We come closer to God by modeling Jesus in our lives.

It is not wrong to love yourself (Matthew 22:37-39). Love of others and a belief that others love us necessitates such love. God accepts us, forgives us, loves us so we can accept, forgive and love ourselves.[14] We must value ourselves in order to believe that we can cope in all situations through Christ (Philippians 4:13). To say that we are no good and worthless is to make God a liar, and God cannot lie! To condemn ourselves as faithful Christians is sinful because God justifies us (Romans 8:31-39). To judge ourselves is to judge the servant of another, which is wrong since we serve God (Romans 14:4). He is our judge. Let us rejoice and be glad! He has delivered us from our sins and given us hope of everlasting life. As we accept these facts and serve others, our minds are less on self and more on other things, and our self-esteem improves. The more we believe in self worth as given by God, the more self-esteem we have. God is able to help us live productive lives.

Consider these thoughts:

• Think in terms of what God had in mind for you as a fully functioning person. Choose to become that person. Visualize yourself that way in different situations. Pray for God's help. Then, carry your vision out in action.

• Live a life of integrity so that by the grace of God you can enjoy being you, enjoy being alive.

• Model Jesus in your life. Accept personal responsibility; practice rational thinking, realistic goal setting and fairness to yourself. Learn to change your attitude, to take small steps toward success, to initiate self-improvement projects, to learn coping skills, to assert yourself, to build relationships, to visualize yourself with high self-esteem, to reframe destructive experiences and to build strong spiritual lives. You will grow through these experiences. Your discipline, persistence, and faith will see you through to better self-esteem. This will then enable you to help others, including your children, think well of themselves. It's a long struggle, but it's worth it. It helps you to go on your way rejoicing. I know this from experience.

Self-esteem is both a cause and an effect. I believe it is a causative factor underneath anxiety and depression.

So if you have low self-esteem, ask yourself these questions: What causes me not to accept myself, to be down on myself? What can I do about it? Then hit it head on, do what you need to do and you will feel better about being who you are, and you can help build self-esteem in your family. God bless.

Reflections

1. What is self-esteem?

2. Do you feel good about being you?

3. How would you describe the self-esteem of Jesus?

4. Why is it important to take responsibility for your own self-esteem?

5. How can a parent who has just gone through divorce build self-esteem in his or her children?

6. Think of some experience that has lowered your self-esteem and reframe it.

7. List some of your negative thoughts that have kept your self-esteem low and talk back to them.

8. What could you do for a child or a teenager to build his or her self-esteem?

9. List some things you could do to build your self-esteem.

10. How do discipline, persistence, and faith affect self-esteem?

CHAPTER SEVEN

Conquering Anger

C onquering anger is an ambitious title for this chapter. Anger, as you know, is hard to conquer. Yet if you don't conquer anger, it will conquer you.

I sometimes get angry, and I know I don't have it completely conquered yet. I don't strike out at people when I'm angry; my mistake is turning it inward. I'm more likely to feel hurt and get quiet than to yell or lash out at people. It doesn't help me to kick things or to hit a punching bag. I just sit silently and think it through. While I have not yet conquered anger, I have made some progress with it over the years and am still willing to learn. It's a tough emotion to control. Usually it controls us and does significant harm to us or to others.

A Description of Anger

Anger in itself is not sinful, but it usually results in sin. Almost always in the Bible it results in sin and is condemned. We are admonished to put it away (Ephesians 4; Colossians 3).

Notice how anger is described by biblical writers. Elihu became very angry with Job for justifying himself rather than God. He was also angry at Job's three friends because they had not found a way to refute Job, yet had condemned him (Job 32:2-3) – frustration, anger! The psalmist wonders why God has continually rejected him and why his anger smolders against the sheep of his pasture (Psalm 74:1). Why does God not destroy their enemies (Psalm 74:10-11)? God had acted on their behalf when the anger of their enemies flared against them; otherwise, they would have been swallowed alive; the raging waters would have swept them away. Their help was in the name of the Lord, the Maker of heaven and earth (Psalm 124). They praised God when He did what they wanted and were disappointed and angry at Him when He didn't.

Jacob became angry at Rachel when she asked him to give her children or she would die. He replied, "Am I in the place of God, who has kept you from having children?" (Genesis 30:1-2). She demanded more than he thought he could give, and he got mad. God became angry with Moses when he wanted God to send someone else to deliver His people from Egyptian bondage. His anger burned against Moses, and He suggested that Moses speak through his brother Aaron who could speak well. His anger caused him to find a way to do what needed to be done (Exodus 4:1-17). God's anger burned against the people of Israel on another occasion, and he wanted to destroy them. Moses intervened and asked God to turn from His fierce anger, relent and keep His promise to make a great nation out of Abraham's descendants. God relented and gave His people the Ten Commandments (Exodus 32:1-16). God's anger could result in dead bodies, or He could relent and bless (Isaiah 66:24). His indignation would be turned against Jerusalem, and He would punish those who were complacent, plunder their wealth and demolish their houses (Zephaniah 1:11-13). His wrath could bring destruction on His people for their sins (Ezekiel 16:35-42). Following other gods can provoke God to anger (Jeremiah 25:4-7). God's anger can lead to destruction or He can change his mind.

The fool rages and scoffs, and there is no peace. He gives full vent to his anger, but a wise man keeps himself under control (Proverbs 29:9-11). An angry man stirs up dissension, and a hot-tempered one commits many sins (Proverbs 29:22). King Nebuchadnezzar was furious with rage when he heard that Shadrach, Meshach, and Abednego refused to bow down and worship the image of gold. So what else could he do but throw them into the furnace of fire (Daniel 3)? Of course, this story has a good ending. God protected them from the fire, and they came out unharmed. Most people aren't so blessed when they are the object of someone's wrath.

Pharaoh's anger drove him to imprison some of his servants (Genesis 41:10). Bijthana and Teresh, officers of King Xerxes, became angry and tried to assassinate the king. Mordecai reported their plot to Queen Esther, and they were executed (Esther 2:19-23).

King Nebuchadnezzar once had a dream that his wise men could not interpret. This made the king so mad that he ordered their execution (Daniel 2:1-13). He couldn't make things happen the way he wanted, so he became angry. The anger conquered him, and he executed all of his wise men.

So far I've reviewed several different words for anger, and they all scare me. Anger burns and often drives people to do destructive things! It is scary and needs to be conquered. It is a subjective reaction that needs to be controlled in a healthy way. Yet to do this, we need to understand what causes it.

Causes of Anger

From what I have said so far and from additional reflections, I can think of several possible causes of anger.

Biological

We may have a biological, genetic tendency to become angry. Some people seem to be born with a short fuse. Lorenz considers anger a product of the brain's primitive structures such as the limbic system and hypothalamus. Biological theories of anger emphasize gene structure, blood chemistry or brain disease.[1]

Learned Behavior

We may be conditioned to be angry. Severe punishment seems to breed anger. Children who are beaten by parents and others usually have a lot of pent-up anger. Children may also learn violence by watching it on television or in their own family. Lopez and Thurman found in a study of anger among students that the family environments of high-trait angry students were significantly less cohesive, emotionally repressive, more conflicted and more disorganized than those having low-trait anger.[2] Hogland and Nicholas found that childhood learning, work noise and crowds were environmental contributors to anger.[3] The Bible says for us to make no friendship with an angry or furious man, lest we learn his ways (Proverbs 22:24-25).

Character Flaws

Our sinful inclinations may cause us to become angry. From a biblical perspective, this tendency may be a flaw in our character. We are thus told to put off anger, wrath, malice, blasphemy and filthy language (Colossians 3:8).

Situational

The situation we are in may cause us to become angry. We get hurt, then get mad. We get frustrated, then get mad. Life is unfair and we get mad. When I started writing this chapter, I could not find some material on anger I knew I had, and I became a bit frustrated and angry. Someone disappoints us and anger follows. Some situations are more likely to produce anger than are others. Minorities worldwide often have a more hostile environment than do majorities. It's hard in some situations not to get mad.

Perceptual

Our perceptions cause us to get mad. If I perceive that I am inadequate, I may get mad. If I perceive that a social situation is hostile to my well being, I will likely get mad. These perceptions serve as a filter through which I see the world. People don't make me mad; I allow myself to get mad. No one can make me mad unless I allow them to do so. The man whose wife knows how to push his button and make him mad needs to learn to adjust his button and stay in control. Anger is created by our will and our thoughts, which affect our emotions and our behavior. Unproductive reactions must be eliminated. It's hard but not impossible.

Righteous

God's anger as described in the Bible seems to be caused by injustice and sin. His wrath is revealed against all ungodliness (Romans 1:18). He is slow to anger (Psalm 86:15), but, as we have seen, His anger can be destructive (Isaiah 13:3-9; Jeremiah 50:13; Ezekiel 25:14; Numbers 18:5; 25:1-7). Of course, God never misdirects His anger.[4] He uses it for His righteous purposes. He even sent Jesus to deliver us from the wrath to come (1 Thessalonians 1:10). Our actions deserve His wrath, yet He delivers us from such wrath.

Jesus' anger was also caused by injustice and by people who misused doctrine and had no compassion. Two examples will suffice. When Jesus found religious leaders using the temple for their own gain, He made a whip out of cords and drove everyone out of the temple area. They had turned His Father's house into a market (John 2:12-16).

The other illustration is from Mark 3:1-6. Jesus went to the synagogue and healed a man who had a shriveled hand. Some, looking for a way to accuse Him, criticized Him for working on the Sabbath. Later, they wanted to kill Him on the Sabbath, which was definitely unlawful, and yet they criticized Him for doing good on the Sabbath. Jesus was angry and deeply distressed at their stubborn hearts. The Pharisees then went out and began to plot with the Herodians how they might kill Him.

Additional Causes

Other causes of anger might be listed as well: rejection or fear of rejection, lack of progress toward a goal, our assumptions and other reasons as well. You want something to happen, and it does not happen. You or someone you love is threatened. You or someone you love is ill or has been injured, and you get mad. One of my students said he became very angry when his young son was diagnosed with leukemia and died two years later. Another said he got mad when his self-esteem was threatened or when he felt powerless. Cain became angry when his brother's sacrifice was accepted and his was rejected (Genesis 4); Haman when Mordecai would not bow down to him (Esther 3); and Herod when he perceived that his position was threatened by Jesus' birth (Matthew 2).

So there are numerous causes of anger, which can be briefly summarized as biological, environmental or perceptual. Whatever the cause, anger usually harms others or ourselves. Its consequences are numerous.

Consequences of Anger

As I have implied previously, there are at least three consequences to anger, two of which are negative. Anger either drives us to hurt ourselves, hurt others or do something constructive.

Anger Hurts Others

Anger often drives us to lash out and hurt others. From my experience, this is by far the most common result of anger. We get hurt and get even. We get mad and say harmful words that devalue others and damage relationships. We talk behind people's back and do injustice to their name. Sometimes anger attacks physically – harms, rapes and kills others. So far I have mentioned Cain, Haman, Herod, Elihu, Jacob, Nuebuchadnezzar and Pharaoh who fit into this category. Their anger hurt others either emotionally or physically.

One horrible illustration of harmful consequences of anger is rape. Rapists describe their actions as acts of hatred meant to degrade and humiliate.[5] Moody says that rape is an act of control, violent overpowering and a desire for power. It is an angry act of aggression with sexual organs as violent weapons.[6] It is primarily violent – fulfilling non-sexual power, aggression and angry urges – and only secondarily sexual. It leaves the victim with the emotional reactions of fear, humiliation, shame, embarrassment, guilt, self-blame, anger, extreme mood swings, anxiety and distrust. She or he experiences blocked thoughts, disruptions in her or his lifestyle, bad dreams and nightmares, phobias, loneliness, a desire for control and grief.[7]

In my counseling experience, I have seen anger drive parents to beat their children, husbands and wives to beat each other and young men to lash out in violence toward others at school and on the streets. More often I have seen anger use cutting, degrading and belittling words that destroy others, often spouses and children. People don't seem even to be aware of how much words can hurt. Sometimes, however, anger is turned inward, and with it we hurt ourselves.

Anger Hurts Us

Freud said that anger turned inward causes depression. Instead of hurting others, we hurt ourselves. When I hate someone, I become his or her slave. He or she controls my thoughts. My resentment produces stress hormones, and I become fatigued. Work becomes drudgery, and nothing gives me pleasure.[8]

Anger can cause health problems including hypertension, cerebral arteriosclerosis and strokes.[9] Wright mentions problems swallowing, nausea, altered volition and diarrhea.[10] Depression, as I have said, sometimes includes an anger component. Anger is internalized and causes gloom and sadness. Life is not exciting any more.

I have noticed when I get mad that I often become quiet. I am afraid to say what I am thinking, so I bite my tongue and turn it on myself. The result is sadness and isolation from others. This may irritate people close to me and strain important relationships if I stay in this mode too long. Yet I would do more damage if I said everything I think when angry. I have learned how to overcome and will share this with you later. For now, let's just say that turning anger inward usually leads to negative consequences – repression and depression, low self-esteem, less brainpower and other health problems. Turning anger outward usually harms others, but it can lead to something constructive.

Constructive Anger

I'll admit that I haven't seen constructive anger very often. Constructive criticism does not usually seem constructive to me. God's anger would have to be thought of as constructive, since He as God determines right and wrong. His anger is directed at evil and is expressed under control in a way that does good. Anger then is a smoke alarm which alerts us to a problem that needs to be addressed. We are thus to be slow to anger and rule our spirit (Proverbs 16:32: James 1:19-20). Such anger is designed to heal and reconcile. Offenses can lead to relationship problems which need to be addressed (Matthew 5:23-24; 18:15-18).

The anger of Jesus was constructive and properly controlled. I don't trust myself to control my temper sufficiently to take action as He did in the temple (John 2), but perhaps I can at times rechannel my anger to do something constructive as He did when He healed the man's shriveled hand. He was mad. The religious leaders did not seem to care about the man's needs, just their distorted doctrinal agenda (Mark 3). That sometimes makes me mad too. I just try to keep my cool and focus on what needs to be done. Dr. W.B. West Jr. once told me under similar circumstances, "We must keep our shoulder to the wheel. Like Nehemiah of old, we have important work to do. We don't have time to come down and fuss."

If you are angry at your spouse, just don't say too much for a while. Do something constructive and think it through. You won't have so many words to take back later.

David Mace said that an angry person realistically has three options in the management of angry feelings: venting anger, suppressing anger and processing anger.[11] I want to turn our attention now to processing anger. How do we deal with anger objectively and express our inner thoughts and feelings constructively?

Processing Anger Constructively

Thus far you can see that conquering anger is very difficult. It wants to express itself often in destructive ways. One extreme of lashing out is stopped by the other extreme of clamming up. Constructive processing hits a middle ground and results in problem solutions and a healthier lifestyle.

Here are some suggestions that have worked for my clients and me:

• *Decide to control your anger and not let it control you.* Think of how important it is to be free from the domination of anger, to be more mature, not to lash out, to pout or to get even. The more mature you are, the less these motives will control you. When some driver speeds past you on the street, you won't have to speed up and pass him. When your husband neglects you, you won't have to give him the silent treatment or to cut him down verbally. It's liberating – to be free from anger's control, to be in control, to be able to decide objectively. It's hard but not impossible.

To help you make this decision, it might help you to look at the advantages and disadvantages of anger. Try the following exercise:

	Controlled by Anger	*Free from Anger*
Advantages	Can tell people off Can punish people Can get it off my chest	Can control speech Can be more constructive Can be more balanced Can succeed
Disadvantages	Will make enemies Will have lots to take back Can hurt innocent people Can leave you with regrets	Maybe being angry will cause me to take the action I need to take, to do something constructive as Jesus did.

This exercise can help you think through what anger usually does to you and others. Such reflection can help you set anger management goals which can pull you in a constructive direction.

• *Learn to monitor your anger signals.* Make a list of anger signs that could indicate to you that you are getting mad: hurt, frustration, fast heart beat, loud voice, clamming up, withdrawal, heated arguments, feelings of disgust and other signs. Monitor yourself for a week, put your list on a 4" x 6" card and carry it with you. Then, when you sense that you are getting mad, take out your card and check off the signs that you have. Then, analyze what it is that is making you mad.

• *Put an absolute ban on physical expression such as throwing things, striking, pushing or destroying objects.* This will make problems worse and will not help solve them.

• *Take time out.* Just as athletes do during games, call time. Prearrange this with those close to you. If either of you needs to call time out, you may do so. Just make the time out signal agreed upon ahead of time. You don't have to give the reason, just the signal. You may be too mad and out of control, too tired or too anything to discuss it at that time. Your reason is your own. Just call time out if you think it wise and then schedule another time to finish the conversation, usually within 24 hours.

• *Take responsibility for your own anger.* If your wife disagrees with you and you get mad, did she make you mad or did you get mad yourself? If a man hits his wife because she pushed his button, did she make him hit her? Unless you take responsibility for your own anger, you will not be able to conquer it. No one can make you mad unless you let them, and they do not determine how you respond, you do.

• *Take a deep breath, then exhale.* Continue to do that. Breathe in soothing, healing oxygen. Exhale anger. As you breathe in, say c-a-l-m to yourself or r-e-l-a-x. Just keep doing this until you break out of the anger spiral and are able to think more clearly. Then, you may need to take a time out before you proceed.

• *Learn not to be competitive.* Ask yourself such questions as these: Why do I have to win every argument? Why do I always have to be right? Why do I have to get even? Why do I have to set people straight? Why do I have to have my own way? Your answers may surprise you. It is liberating to realize that you don't always have to win, to convince people you are right or to get even. Respect other people's opinions, do not violate their boundaries, don't force your ideas on them and see what happens. Just try to be effective yourself, and don't worry if the world does not comply. To try to influence others is proper, but not winning at all costs, not forcing others to see it or do it your way.

• *Learn to communicate effectively.* Avoid pouting or aggressiveness. Neither is a mature or effective way to communicate. On this Jesus gives good advice. If you have differences with someone – you have something against them or they have something against you – go to them and state precisely but kindly what you need to say to facilitate a solution to the problem. This is not being aggressive; it is not ignoring the problem. It is addressing the problem in an assertive, non-offensive manner. If they respond appropriately, you have solved the problem. If they don't, you can feel good for trying (Matthew 5:23-24; 18:15-17). Constructive anger will express needs, end the denial process, energize you and help you negotiate and strengthen relationships. Learn to listen (Proverbs 18:13) and to say what needs to be said when it needs to be said (Proverbs 25:11). Be kind. Say only what builds others up and is helpful to those who listen (Ephesians 4:29). Such communication addresses issues in a Christlike manner and often leads to resolutions and good feelings.

• *Challenge your negative thinking.* Thinking affects anger, and anger affects behavior and other emotions. So when you change your thinking, you may free yourself from anger's control. As I said earlier, perceptions can cause anger. It's not just the situation; it is my perception of the situation. The driver who pulls in front of you or speeds past you does not require you to be angry. It depends on your thoughts. Events contribute to feelings, but they do not cause them. Anger is created by our perceptions of situations. We can't control most situations, but we can control our thoughts about them. Learning to communicate effectively will help you neither to clam up nor blow up but to finish conversations in healthy ways.

Our thinking patterns are influenced by our values and philosophies. What are your views and beliefs that influence your unhealthy anger reactions? What values need to change? What about cultural assumptions? One person told me that in his culture if someone looked at you, that was a sign of aggression.

Let me give you an illustration of cognitive restructuring as it relates to an anger experience of Brian.

SITUATION	EMOTIONS	NEGATIVE SELF-TALK	TALK BACK
A man in a car sped by me and pulled back over in front of me too quickly.	Mad Disgusted Put down Neck pain Moody	That idiot! He thinks he's king of the world. He could have killed me. I'll show him!	I wonder what is bothering him, why he needs to do that? What good will it do to get back at him? I don't need to do that. It might make it worse.

Brian said that a combination of deep breathing and talking back to himself helped him calm down and prevent further problems.

Michenbaum has a cognitive therapy technique he calls stress inoculation that can be used to help you deal with stressful situations. You can anticipate specific anger-causing situations and learn how to handle them ahead of time. The anticipation stimulus has to be strong enough to cause some stress, and then you overcome the stress. Look first at the possible causes of the anger, then at coping skills that will help (time out, looking for a way of escape, coping strategies and relaxation) and then look at ways to change your thinking in relationship to the situation. Is there another way to look at it? Perhaps the driver had just been fired from his job or he was in a hurry to get home to take care of an emergency. Who knows? You prepare for the provocation, confront it, cope with the arousal and agitation and then give yourself credit for a job well done.[12]

What has helped my clients the most with their anger? They consistently mention relaxation, talking back to themselves and spiritual principles. Taking deep breaths, telling themselves to be calm and reminding themselves of their need to live by the Spirit and not fulfill the lusts of the flesh calms and redirects their anger into something more constructive. Typical talking back phrases are: calm, cool it, relax, don't make it worse, be gentle, mercy, love and being angry, sin not. Such thoughts affect anger and what you do with it.

• *Keep an anger journal.* This is just another way to think through what bothers you, yet it is a specific technique that many have found to be very helpful. Writing about your anger helps you to process it constructively.

Here is the way that Erica did it. She used these categories: the situation, how angry I was (on a 1-5 scale), what I was thinking, what I did and how I should perhaps think and act differently. She used this to process past events and to anticipate future events that might provoke anger. It worked because it helped her control her anger with thoughts. Somehow, for healthy living, that has to happen. Why not get a blank notebook and try it? Many of my clients, especially women, have told me it helps them conquer their anger.

• *Learn to love, bless, do good to and pray for those who mistreat you.* What a challenge for me! I'm still working on this one, but it's a challenge from Jesus that I accept. Turn the other cheek. Go the second mile. When someone wants to sue you and take your tunic, let him have your coat as well. Love your enemies and pray for those who persecute you that you may be children of your Father in heaven. That's the way God is! If you only love those who love you, you are no different than the tax collectors. Even pagans are nice to those who are nice to them. Jesus says go beyond that. Do good even to those who mistreat you. When you do this, you are being Christlike and God-like, spiritually mature (Matthew 5:38-48).

• *Learn to forgive.* It is hard to stay mad at someone you love, pray for, do good to and forgive. One reason we do not forgive is that we do not believe people deserve forgiveness. Christy did not deserve forgiveness because she had betrayed her husband and broken their marital covenant by having an affair. Her husband Todd held on to his anger for three years – kept telling himself and his friends that she did not deserve forgiveness. He was right, yet that is the nature of grace. God forgives us by his grace, and we don't deserve it. It's hard, but we can learn to do likewise. Such love and grace are redemptive; it's not what people deserve, but it's what they need.

I keep thinking of two statements Jesus made relative to forgiveness. Be merciful as your heavenly Father is merciful (Matthew 5:7), and forgive us our debts as we have forgiven our debtors (Matthew 6:12-15). He continued this thought by saying that God will forgive us if we forgive others and that God will not forgive us if we do not forgive others. Remember the word forgiveness, and say it to yourself when you are mad. Some irritations can be laughed off; others need to be forgiven. Let not the sun go down on your wrath (Ephesians 4:26).

• *Learn to put anger away*. Release it, dismiss it, let it go by making a decision that it is no longer needed, that it will do more harm than good. God, in spite of His wrath and the fact that we were His enemies, reconciled us to Himself through the death of His son Jesus. Anger thus managed fulfills the objective of love (Romans 5:9-10). However, to follow this model you must look at the causes of your anger, challenge irrational beliefs and keep the goal of the restoration of relationships in mind.

• *Learn how others conquer anger*. We all know that we can learn from modeling. Others who handle anger well can become our models for conquering anger. Pick out people who handle anger well and observe them. If you continue to believe they handle anger constructively, interview them and find out how they do it. What are their strengths? What are their secrets of success? You'll probably find that they have more trouble with anger than you realize, but that they have learned to be disciplined, to persist in their efforts to overcome anger, to confront their thoughts and to talk it out in a slow, calm manner.

• *Pray for guidance and strength to overcome anger*. I hope you still pray. Most people do. My prayers are not always answered the way I want, but I still believe in God and in prayer. James tells us to pray for wisdom and it will be given us (James 1:5-7). But he says that we must ask in faith. John says, "This is the confidence we have in approaching God: that if we ask anything according to his will, he hears us. And if we know that he hears us - whatever we ask - we know that we have what we asked of him" (1 John 5:14-15). Jesus had said, "If you believe, you will receive whatever you ask for in prayer" (Matthew 21:22). James admonishes us to ask for what we want and then cautions us to ask with unselfish motives: "You want something but don't get it. You kill and covet, but you cannot have what you want. You quarrel and fight. You do not have, because you do not ask of God. When you ask, you do not receive, because you ask with wrong motives, that you may spend what you get on your pleasures" (James 4:2-3). This reminds me of Solomon's unselfish prayer, when, as a young man of about 20, he became king of Israel. He humbly asked for wisdom to govern his people and a discerning spirit to distinguish right from wrong. The text says that God was pleased with his prayer because he had not asked for a long life, wealth for himself or for the death of his enemies and that God gave him what he wanted. He also gave him riches and honor and promised him a long life if he would walk in God's ways and obey His statutes and commands as David his father had done (1 Kings 3:1-15).

What I suggest is for you to continually ask God for wisdom to conquer your anger and to discern between good and evil. Ask for His strength to help you find the discipline and persistence to overcome. I ask God every day to help me to be more Christlike in spirit. I want His spirit to permeate me and greatly influence what I do. I believe all of this helps me to conquer anger.

• *Learn to solve problems.* I believe that most problems can be either solved or that we can learn with God's help to live with them. I'll write more in Chapter 13 about God's strength to walk with us through the valleys, but now I want to say more about solving problems. Anger usually looks for a win-lose solution, which people resist with vengeance. I try to look for a win-win solution to problems. What do they want? What do I want? What can we live with?

With this in mind, let me share a problem-solving model I have often used. It proceeds as follows:

1. Define the problem. Be specific. Both you and they should offer definitions. See if you can agree.

2. Discuss the issues. Don't try at this point to solve differences but just to understand. If you are really mad, take turns and talk for three minutes each. I've found that when you do this twice each of you usually has calmed down considerably and understand each other's point of view. All conflicts don't have to be solved. You can learn to disagree on some issues and still get along. Try it. It's the truth. Love and tolerance can prevail. Other people have a right to be wrong if they wish, right? But some conflicts call for solutions. With these, proceed as follows.

3. Brainstorm various possible solutions. Amber and Landon were "stuck in a bad marriage." Their list included the following: get di-

vorced, kill him, keep fighting and sleeping in separate bedrooms, separate but don't divorce, continue in counseling and look for win-win solutions, start back to church, read the Bible and pray together, read Bible stories to the children and somehow put the past behind them.

4. Eliminate some of the suggested solutions. They eliminated divorce, separation and killing him and began to take counseling seriously. Within two weeks, they were sleeping in the same bed and going out on dates. Today, two years later, they are "having the time of our lives." They told me that my win-win suggestion was a breakthrough for them. They didn't have to have their way about every issue any more. In fact, they said that it is fun sometimes to be the one that gives in. What an idea! It's called maturity!

5. Choose a solution that is fair and that each of you can live with. Write it on two cards, keep the card with you, get it out as often as necessary and read it. Amber and Landon's card read as follows: "Landon agrees to talk with Amber without long periods of silence. If something is bothering him, he agrees to tell her in a slow, calm tone of voice. He agrees not to call her names she does not like. He agrees to help bathe the children at night and get them dressed for bed. He agrees to lead prayer at meals and to be patient with her sexually. Amber agrees not to point her finger in his face and yell at him, and not to tell her friends and family how bad he is. She agrees to tell him calmly what is bothering her and then listen to what he says. She agrees to be more attentive to his need for sex and love – try to be there when he wants me."

They carried these cards and read them often. They said it helped. I think the whole process helped them to talk through their issues, to understand each other better and to deal with their problems in a more objective, less passionate and angry way. That works.

• *Channel your anger into constructive activities.* Remember what Jesus did with the man's withered hand when he was mad? He healed it (Mark 3:1-6). Remember what we are to do for our enemies? Do good for them. Pray for them (Matthew 5:43-48). Don't repay evil for evil. Live peacefully if possible. Leave revenge to God. Paul said, "If your enemy is hungry, feed him; if he is thirsty, give him something to drink. In doing this, you will heap burning coals on his head. Do not be overcome by evil, but overcome evil with good" (Romans 12:17-21). Wow, what a challenge! It requires a lot of spirituality, but it works. A man who criticized Dr. West publicly later became his friend because Dr. West was a master at heaping burning coals on his head.

What I'm suggesting is to be nice to those who anger you. Calm down; go out of your way to look for something good to say about them. Don't be hypocritical, but you can usually find something if you listen and look long enough.

I have several other ideas I'd like to share with you before I end this chapter. Here they are. Just think about them and see if they can be used in your situation.

• *Be slow to anger*. Don't let so many things get under your skin. Solomon says, "Do not be quickly provoked in your spirit, for anger resides in the lap of fools" (Ecclesiastes 7:9). And in Proverbs 15:18, he added, "A hot-tempered man stirs up dissension, but a patient man calms a quarrel." James says for us to be slow to speak, quick to listen and slow to get angry (James 1:19). If you don't get mad so often, you won't have so much trouble controlling your anger.

• *Give a soft answer*. Yelling doesn't help. It just shows your lack of control. Solomon gives this advice, "A gentle answer turns away wrath, but a harsh word stirs up anger" (Proverbs 15:1). Just be calm, lower your voice, say what you need to say slowly. Then back off. Give them wiggle room. Let them save face if possible.

• *Meditate upon God's Word*. I can usually think of some message from the Bible to help me calm down. The psalmist said that he meditated on God's Word day and night (Psalm 1). He made it a part of him. He once expressed it this way, "I have hidden your word in my heart that I might not sin against you" (Psalm 119:11). Divine guidance helps conquer anger.

• *Overlook what people do*. You don't have to see everything, especially to look for offenses. They come often enough anyhow. Solomon said, "A man's wisdom gives him patience; it is to his glory to overlook an offense" (Proverbs 19:11).

• *Learn to love and respect others*. If we don't, we will say hurtful things and not really listen to what they say. Jesus teaches us to love one another, to love others as he loves us (John 15:12-17; 1 John 4). We love because God first loved us. Paul really challenges me when he says for us to count others better than ourselves. This means not to act out of selfish ambition or vain conceit, but in humility to consider others better than ourselves (Philippians 2:2-4). This is what Jesus did when He humbled himself and became obedient unto death, even death on a cross (Philippians 2:1-11). What a challenge!

Let me briefly summarize. I've defined anger and told of its consequences. I've talked about its causes and given you 22 ways to process it constructively. I don't expect you to memorize this list but to pick and choose the ideas that work for you in a given situation. That's the way it works for me. Think it through, talk it through, relax and channel what anger that is left into something constructive. That's the heart of the matter. Work on it. You'll be glad you did.

Reflections

1. How would you define anger?
2. What are its consequences?
3. What are its causes?
4. What are some constructive and destructive biblical examples of anger?
5. How can you be angry and sin not?
6. What words can you say to yourself to help you conquer anger?
7. Can you think of some examples of righteous anger you have right now?
8. How can you channel this anger into something constructive?
9. What scriptures help you most to conquer anger?
10. What does spiritual resilience – discipline, persistence and faith – have to do with conquering anger?

CHAPTER EIGHT

Overcoming Dysfunctional Family Patterns

F irst of all, let me define some key terms. To be *dysfunctional* is to interact, to live in unhealthy ways – to be non-productive, not constructive. Such people are not supportive of or helpful to each other although they may intend to be. *Patterns* refer to habitual ways people interact – he does this, she does that, in predictable ways. Some interaction patterns are functional, some dysfunctional; some constructive, some destructive; some healthy, some unhealthy.

In biblical times, family was synonymous with house or household. A household might include parents, children, other relatives, servants, travelers and anyone who might be under the protection of the head of the family. The family was a part of a larger clan and tribe. It took several forms including the extended family and sometimes polygamy during Old Testament times.

Wealthy Roman families might consist of the master, his wife, their children, other relatives, slaves, freedpersons and their families. The master had the power to punish the misdeeds of family members. The Christian family grew out of these family forms and altered them considerably. The family takes many forms today including extended family, nuclear family, single parent family, blended family and others. These different family forms can be functional or dysfunctional. The church itself is spoken of as the family of God, his household (1 Timothy 3:15). It can be functional or dysfunctional.

Many families today are in trouble. Some one-third of marriages end in divorce; reported percentages run from 12 to 70 percent. Many young people are so starved for love they fall in love quickly, marry and divorce.

Other signs of dysfunction include the following: 24 percent of all children in America are born out of wedlock; 13 percent to teenage girls, 96 percent of whom are single. Only 51 percent live with their mothers and fathers. Some 22 percent are abused. Every year about 3 million teens contract a sexually transmitted disease. More than 60 percent of males serving time in jail were born to adolescents.

Dysfunctional patterns seem to be increasing in the X generation, those born between 1963 and 1977. Thirty-eight million strong, they are typified by a backwards ball cap, high-top sneakers and baggy shorts. They sometimes describe themselves as a latchkey generation, throwaways, lost between doing something for themselves and doing nothing at all. Some 14 percent say they have attempted suicide – girls more than boys (statistics vary). Every day some 13 young people commit suicide; 16 are murdered; 1,000 become mothers; 1,000 begin drinking alcoholic beverages; 500 begin using other drugs; 650 are robbed; 3,500 commit assault; 80 are raped.

Howe, a good source for such statistics, says that the X generation will be incarcerated and executed at a higher rate than any previous generation in United States history.[1] Some 24 percent of this group thinks that anyone getting married should expect to get a divorce. Sixty percent believe that it is best to cohabit before marriage according to Barna.[2] Eis says that 60 percent of those who join the Navy do so to get away from their family of origin.[3]

Other statistics show further the extent of unhealthy patterns of living in America. Some 60 percent of men who are planning to marry do not plan to be faithful to their wife. About 65 percent have sex before marriage. Approximately 40 million babies have been aborted in the last 30 years. About 29 percent of all pregnancies end in abortion. Twenty-two percent of women in America have been forced to have sex with someone. Barna says that half of all adults under 30 will cohabit with someone before they marry although this has been proven to be a negative factor in marital adjustment.[4] Only about 30 percent say their religious beliefs guide them in their sexual lives.

Most families have been dysfunctional for a long time. This is not meant to criticize but rather to point to the challenge we face. Obviously, family structure, culture and values affect childrearing success or failure. All situations are not equally healthy. We become dysfunctional and then pass it on to future generations. Men impregnate women and then leave them with all of the parenting responsibilities. Sometimes it's the women who leave. Children have children and try to raise them without the necessary maturity or help needed. Family patterns are projected onto future generations; internalized, unresolved issues are acted out in the next generation. People look for and discover in relationships qualities that were present in their families of origin. There is an urge to work through these unresolved issues, but they often cause similar trouble in the next generation. Family commitment, devotion and loyalty cause one to hold on to functional and dysfunctional patterns in one's family of origin. Thus we often get stuck in dysfunctional patterns.

All of us have some dysfunctional patterns to overcome. It's a matter of degrees of dysfunctionality. Dysfunctional patterns, although well established, can be changed to a more healthy, functional way of living. It's hard but not impossible. It takes discipline, persistence and faith; but the effort is rewarding. By changing, you can create a new pattern of interacting that will influence you, individuals close to you, and your family to become more functional and less pathological.

Dysfunctional Family Patterns

Dysfunctional family patterns come in all shapes and sizes.

Adam and Eve, as described in the Bible, had a great environment. They lived in a beautiful garden. They were given what looks like a simple job to us, to work the garden and take care of it. They were free to eat from any tree in the garden except one – the Tree of the Knowledge of Good and Evil. They were to cleave to each other and become one flesh (Genesis 2).

Sounds simple enough, right? Wrong, not for them. They wanted more. They wanted to be like God. They listened to bad advice. They saw that the fruit of the tree was good for food, pleasing to the eye and desirable for gaining wisdom; and they ate it (Genesis 3:1-7).

When they heard the Lord walking in the garden, they hid from Him. They were afraid and made excuses; Adam blamed Eve, who blamed the serpent. Both received curses because of their disobedience. Pain during childbirth would be increased, and Eve's desire would be for her husband who would rule over her. The ground was cursed, and Adam would have to toil painfully to make a living. He would eat by the sweat of his brow until he returned to the ground from where he came. They became the parents of us all, were banished from the Garden of Eden, and were not able to eat of the Tree of Life (Genesis 3).

Wanting what we don't have, wanting to be like God, disobedience, blaming others, survival through pain and toil are patterns since that day. Their son Cain disobeyed God by not offering his gift according to faith. Abel his brother worshiped by faith, and his offering was approved by God. Cain became jealous and murdered Abel. Even in this first family, rejection, anger and jealousy are prime motivators and dysfunctional patterns. Cain then adds to these dysfunctions by feeling little remorse, if any, and became a fugitive and a vagabond – driven away from his family and punished for a lifetime (Genesis 4).

It doesn't sound as though the human race started out well. Selfish ambition, wanting to create God in their own image, disobedience, jealousy, anger and murder were all dysfunctional patterns in this first family.

Yet despite this unfortunate beginning, all of us came from them: Moses, Deborah, Elizabeth, John the Baptist, Mary, Jesus, Paul, John, Peter and all of the wonderful people you know. Dysfunctional patterns can be broken. Different attitudes and constructive action can create new, healthier ways to live.

Let's look at Abraham's family. He married his half-sister, Sarah. He lied about their marital status to protect himself and turned her over to the harem of Pharaoh (Genesis 12). He repeated this terrible mistake later by turning Sarah over to Abimelech, thus showing a lack of courage and respect for her (Genesis 20).

He and Sarah decided to have a child by Sarah's handmaiden Hagar. They named him Ishmael. Hagar was overly proud of her accomplishment, an attitude which agitated Sarah who then drove her and her son away from home (Genesis 16-20). Animosity has been between Ishmael and Isaac's descendants (Abraham's son by Sarah) ever since.

Isaac married his cousin, Rebekah, and repeated his father's mistake by lying to Abimelech about being married to her (Genesis 26). Isaac and Rebekah also had problems with their twins, Esau and Jacob. Isaac favored Esau, the older of the twins, and Rebekah favored Jacob. Rebekah and Jacob then deceived Isaac into giving Jacob Esau's birthright (Genesis 27). Esau was angry and wanted to kill Jacob who fled to another country and stayed there for 20 years. He never saw his mother again.

Jacob married his cousins Leah and Rachel who were sisters. Their father, Laban, deceived Jacob into marrying Leah (what a way to start a marriage). He had to work 14 instead of seven years for Laban to get Rachel. Jacob then naturally favored Rachel and her children, especially Joseph, over all of his other children causing animosity and dissension. There was great tension between Leah and Rachel. Jacob also had children by his mistresses, as did his grandfather Abraham.

This was Abraham's family. There were lots of dysfunctions: lying, deception, pride, resentment, jealousy, and greed. These caused problems that still exist among their descendants.

King David's family is another good example of dysfunction and re-

demption. He had several wives: Michal, Abigail, Bathsheba, Ahinoam
and perhaps his nurse Abishag as well as 10 concubines (1 Samuel 18:27;
25:42-43; 2 Samuel 2:2; 5:13-16; 11:27; 15:16; and 1 Kings 1:3-4). He
married Michal for political reasons. He committed adultery with
Bathsheba and arranged for her husband Uriah to be killed in battle before he married her (2 Samuel 11-12). His son Amnon deceived and
raped his sister Tamar (2 Samuel 13). Another son Absalom killed his
half-brother Amnon and then rebelled against his father by organizing
an army and trying to overthrow his father's kingdom. He was killed in
battle (2 Samuel 18). David's fourth son, Adonijah, was put to death by
his brother Solomon for aspiring to be king (1 Kings 1).

Solomon, another of David's sons, went against his religion and married many foreign wives (1 Kings 11). As his father had done before
him, he married most of his wives for political purposes. They led him
to worship their gods during his later years. In fact, he built a shrine of
worship for them so that they could worship their own god. As a result,
he lost the kingdom during the time of his son Rehoboam although God
let Rehoboam keep Judah, the southern part of the kingdom.

Rehoboam continued family dysfunctional patterns by being harder
on the people than was his father Solomon. He made them work harder
and punished them more. They rebelled and made Jereboam king of Israel
(1 Kings 12). They later were dispersed into Assyrian captivity.

David's line displayed many dysfunctions, some similar to those we
saw in the families of Adam and Eve; and of Abraham, Sarah, and Hagar
and their descendants. There were marriages for the wrong reasons:
aggression, lust for sex and power, murder, rebellion and abuse.

In spite of these dysfunctions, redemption, healing and a life of prolonged and productive service were still possible. We can learn from
the former generations who instruct us (Job 8:8-10).

The sins of Adam and Eve are reversed in Jesus Christ. One man,
Adam, brought sin; another man, Jesus, a descendant of Adam, brought
justification as the result of one act of righteousness that brings life to all
(Romans 8:1-17). Today, we can be in God's spiritual family, the church.
We are born into His family by the new birth process and are children of
God and His heirs (1 Timothy 3:15; John 3:5; Romans 8:16-17).

Abraham, who failed his wife miserably and his children as well, became the father of the faithful (Romans 4). If we today are in Christ,
we are blessed by Abraham; we are his seed, heirs according to the
promise (Galatians 3:26-29).

Isaac made mistakes as a husband and as a father. Yet he continued the line of descent that led to blessings for all nations in Christ.

Jacob, who deceived his father, cheated his brother, ran away from home to escape Esau's wrath, favored Rachel and Joseph and learned to get along with Laban who had deceived him. I think the real key to his reform came, however, when he encountered God and asked for his blessing. In doing this, he wrestled with himself as well as with God, took responsibility and began to act differently. He then returned home, reconciled with his brother Esau and became the father of the 12 tribes of Israel (Genesis 32-33). By the help of God and by his own volition, he overcame at least two dysfunctional patterns – passivity and family alienation. He learned that he did not have to be forever controlled by what his mother or Laban did or by anything in his past. He broke some dysfunctional patterns that had been going on for several generations.

Joseph, his son, was not ruined by Jacob's favoritism. He remained pure when tempted by Pharaoh's wife. He was a faithful prisoner and maintained a good attitude. He later rescued his family from their famine and forgave them for selling him into slavery. They meant it for evil; God meant it for good (Genesis 37-50). Joseph maintained good thoughts, which led to constructive action, causing him to overcome dysfunctional family patterns and to create a more healthy way to live.

King David, who committed adultery and murder, married for political reasons and failed in many ways as a father, was also the father of Solomon who built the temple and was an ancestor of Jesus Christ who changed the world. David, with all of his sins, turned it around and was later called a man after God's own heart (Acts 13:22). He also has blessed my life and that of millions by his authorship of some 75 of the psalms in our Bible.

Healing for You

As I studied all of this, I was encouraged. I know that I have made many mistakes. People who know me can still see much room for growth and improvement. Yet I am encouraged. I can see from the past that destructive dysfunctional patterns can be turned around. Disobedience, hatred, greed, rape, adultery, deception, betrayal, jealousy, favoritism of children, disloyalty, being our own God and other such dysfunctions can be and need to be broken in our own lives and not passed on to our children. Think what a difference that would make to correct the long list of problems I mentioned among various generations and families!

The point is, don't give up. Don't get sucked in for life to destructive patterns of behavior. God redeemed and used them, and he will do the same with you. He does not give up on you. Look at your pain, but don't get stuck in it and stay there forever. Your family dysfunctions are not as powerful as the grace of God and His kingdom. Such dysfunctions can be overcome by God's love and His reign in your heart. You can be a functional member of your family, your community and the family of God as well. What I've said before about spiritual growth applies here as well. It all starts in your heart. Jesus said, "But seek first his kingdom and his righteousness, and all these things will be given to you as well" (Matthew 6:33). "These things" refer to our needs. Jesus can make you a new creature, give you new life (John 3:5; 2 Corinthians 5:17). As Paul expressed it, "All this is from God, who reconciled us to himself through Christ and gave us the ministry of reconciliation: that God was reconciling the world to himself in Christ, not counting men's sins against them. And he has committed to us the message of reconciliation. Be reconciled to God" (2 Corinthians 5:18-20).

God has never given up on the human race with all its sin. Don't give up on yourself. Take action. Do something different. Carve out a new path, a new life. Patch up differences. Like Jacob, be reconciled to God and your family. Develop a vision for the future. This makes me think of Israel in Isaiah's day. God comforted their distress saying, "Forget the former things; do not dwell on the past. See, I am doing a new thing! Now it springs up; do you not perceive it? I am making a way in the desert and streams in the wasteland" (Isaiah 43:18-19). The same God who can make a stream in the desert can give life to you.

The key is responsibility – action you need to take. Like the prodigal son, sometimes we just need to come to ourselves and return home to our Father. When we try to be God, we mess up everything we touch (Luke 15).

Remember in all of your dysfunctional patterns and your pain that love is the most powerful force in the universe. Remember that God loves you and will give you the strength to do what is right.

Let me share some modern examples of people who have overcome dysfunctional interaction patterns along with some principles of communication they used to accomplish this.

Dysfunctional Communication Patterns

I mentioned Regina before. She felt put down by her father who often reminded her that "boys were smarter than girls." She also continued to remember that she was "only good for meeting the needs of men." After she hit the bottom emotionally, she was able to talk back to these irrational thoughts somewhat as follows:

> "Who says that boys are smarter than girls? Not true. In fact, girls score higher than boys on a lot of tests. It depends on the girl and the boy."

> "Dad was conditioned by his place in time, his family, and community. Girls have many more options today than he knew about. Times have changed, and I need to change with them. I just need to reach my full potential whatever that is."

> "If I find the right man and get married, that will be great. If I have a good career, that will be fulfilling; if not, that's okay too. I have options."

> "I don't think Dad meant to destroy me. At times, he would brag on me – tell others how competent I was. I need to hang on to this."

> "My Mom always believed in me. She thought I was something special."

Regina was able to turn the negative pattern of her life around. She began to think differently; and then act and feel differently. I think she was special too.

Candace described her marriage as terrible. "We are never able to talk things out," she said. "I yell; Michael gets quiet and pouts. The more I yell, the more he pouts. It's like he's shutting me out. He just sits there, arms folded, poker-faced, turns away from me and says nothing. Sometimes this goes on for days."

Michael had a different story. "I'm not going to talk to anyone who yells at me and points her finger in my face. She doesn't care what I am saying anyhow. So, why talk? She talks everything to death – makes a federal case out of everything. I don't talk because she hurts my feelings and won't listen. It just doesn't do any good to talk to her."

They both faced their interaction problem. They could see that it kept them from settling differences on any issue that needed to be addressed. Both came to accept the fact that it takes two to make a dysfunctional interaction pattern: she yells, he pouts; or maybe it's the other way around – he pouts, she yells. It's not so important to find out where it started. You can't anyway. You need only to see what is maintaining it and do something different. So what happened? Candace worked on one assignment – to catch herself yelling and pointing her finger at Michael; listen to him; then lower her voice; speak slowly, put her hands to her sides or behind her back and calmly say what she needs to say. Be assertive but not aggressive. Say it once but not twice. That took a lot of strength for her, but she was a strong woman and was able to do it.

Michael's assignment was to put his hands somewhere other than crossed across his chest, to listen carefully to what Candace said, to verbalize a response and then continue the conversation. He had to learn to force himself to talk even though he was sometimes hurt and angry. Both could call time out if they wished.

These changes began to have good effects. He said she didn't nag any more. She said he talked to her. Both said they were getting along better and were able to resolve conflicts more effectively than before. They still reverted to their old habits at times, but they caught themselves and went back to their assignments. They knew that if they continued to do what they had been doing they would continue to get what they had been getting. Both dysfunctional and functional patterns tend to perpetuate themselves. The simplest intervention is to do something different. They did, and it worked.

Brandi and Barry had a different problem but the same dysfunctional interaction pattern. Brandi had a headache just about every night when she went to bed. She would get into bed, give him a peck on the lips, a little pat on the back, then turn over and try to go to sleep.

Barry felt rejected, hurt and angry. He told her how cold and frigid she was and then wouldn't say anything. Brandi then felt shut out of his life and became colder. Barry called her a cold fish, which proved to become a negative self-fulfilling prophecy. She was cold. Barry became openly too affectionate with women at work; Brandi found out about it and became colder. Barry had an affair before things began to turn around.

Their interaction pattern had to change, and it did. Both took responsibility for what they had been doing and began doing something different. They could see that although they were doing what felt right at the time, it was not working. Smart people don't keep doing what is not working. It's like throwing gasoline on a burning house; it only makes matters worse.

So what did they do? They first could see the truth of what I have been saying. Both took appropriate responsibility for what they were doing and began to focus on doing something different.

Brandi began to consider Barry's sexual needs and reframe his wanting her every night to something more positive: "He still thinks I'm attractive after 10 years of marriage." She decided to get in bed, turn toward him, give him a big hug and kiss, talk to him and just be affectionate.

Barry quit calling her names. He quit demanding sex every night. He talked to her, was affectionate during the day, complimented her to their friend, and continued hugging her and talking to her even when she was not interested in sex. He learned that good sex less frequently is much better than what they had been doing. He loved her even more because "she forgave me and gave me a second chance," and he became a better partner. They still have problems like every other couple, but their marriage improved greatly because they learned healthy interaction patterns. I rejoice with them and respect them for their maturity. It took a lot of discipline, persistence and faith for them to turn it around.

Elaine, age 69, was an only child. She was married to Sherman, age 70. Both had significant stress-related health problems. He had just had surgery for cancer and she a heart attack. She was clinically depressed and anxious.

What was their problem? She had always been enmeshed with her family of origin who lived next door to them. When they moved, her parents would move, always buying the house next door to them. Her parents wanted a running report of everything Eaine and Sherman and their four children did. They made demands and, at age 90, were still in this enmeshed pattern. "It's still like I'm not a person on my own, just a part of them – their family. I don't have a family of my own: we're just an extension of their family," Elaine said.

The presenting issue was that her father's health was failing, and they expected her to "wait on them hand and foot." Neither she nor her husband was able to do this. They were barely surviving themselves. They wanted to help more but couldn't. When they tried to explain this to her parents, they "acted like they never heard a word we said." They would say that we didn't love them anymore, Elaine reported, "and that I was not a good daughter. My Mom wanted me to cancel a Christmas party with my children and grandchildren to be with them. I said I would check with them and get back to her. In the meantime, she told people at church that I refused her request and had abandoned my parents in their old age. She told me that she would never ask me for another favor. I feel guilty when she puts it like that. Even people at church are calling me and saying I should honor my father and mother like the

Bible says. What can I do?"

Here is what she decided.

"Don't let them make me feel guilty. No one can make me feel guilty unless I let them."

"Give myself credit for wanting to help and for the help I have given them over the years."

"Take care of myself. Our well-being is important too. God does not want my husband and me to break down either."

"Decide what I want to do and then do it. They can ask, but I have a right to decide what I can do and what I can't do."

"Discuss alternatives with them: assisted living, a nursing home or extra help. Explain to them that I love and honor them but that none of us can take care of all of their needs. We need help. Love does what is best, and I believe this is best. My health is a factor that I have to consider, and that's not being selfish. It's a fact that we have to consider."

"I will always be your daughter and will be there for you. I will never abandon you."

"I can accept the fact that they will not like me for saying all of this and doing what I have to do. I wish they felt differently, but I can't control that. I might feel the same way were I in their shoes. I just have to do what I think is right."

What happened? Elaine and Sherman had this talk with her parents and left a copy of their main points with them. The parents reacted as you would expect at first but then called in extra help. They have plans to move soon into an assisted living/nursing home facility. They even told their daughter recently that they knew she had done a lot for them. The people at church backed off when Elaine told them they did not have all the facts and that it was their problem. It's not an ideal solution, but it's better than before.

How did they turn it around? They could see the dysfunctional interaction patterns, did some clear thinking, did something different and then got different results. It worked for them, and it will work for you as well. Look for possible solutions. Look at family strengths and not just dysfunctional patterns. Think of what you need to do differently, and then do it.

Especially make an effort to communicate effectively. How?

• *Try to be a decent human being yourself: mature, with the right attitude.* Be willing to do unto others as you wish them to do to you (Matthew 7:12). Guard your heart for it is the wellspring of life (Proverbs 4:23). As Jesus said it, if you are evil, you can't speak good things (Matthew 12:34). As his brother James expressed it, good water can't come from a polluted spring (James 3:1-12). Clean up the spring, the heart, first.

• *Guard your mouth.* Don't say everything you think. Mull over it. Wait a while. Perhaps write it down. Solomon said, "He who guards his mouth and his tongue keeps himself from calamity" (Proverbs 21:23).

• *Listen empathically and carefully.* James tells us to be quick to listen, slow to speak and slow to become angry (James 1:19). My favorite proverb along these lines puts it like this: "He who answers before listening – that is his folly and his shame" (Proverbs 18:13).

• *Speak softly with a constructive message.* My two favorite proverbs on this are these: "A gentle answer turns away wrath, but a harsh word stirs up anger" (Proverbs 15:1), and "A word aptly spoken is like apples of gold in settings of silver" (Proverbs 25:11).

• *Learn how to cope with anger.* Solomon said, "A man's wisdom gives him patience; it is to his glory to overlook an offense" (Proverbs 19:11). Paul's advice has been on my heart for years: "In your anger do not sin. Do not let the sun go down while you are still angry" (Ephesians 4:26). The principles discussed in Chapter VII can be applied here as well.

• *Be kind to each other.* Paul admonishes us to be kind and compassionate to one another (Ephesians 4:32). A kind word will cheer someone up (Proverbs 12:25). Joseph was kind to his brothers after they had sold him into slavery (Genesis 37-50). Rahab was kind to the spies from Israel, and they were kind to her when they captured the land (Joshua 2). Jesus said that God is kind to the ungrateful and wicked (Luke 6:35).

• *Forgive each other.* Elaine forgave her parents because "they meant well." Jesus said for us to pray, "Forgive us our debts, as we also have forgiven our debtors" (Matthew 6:12). I pray that prayer every night before I go to sleep. Jesus reminds us, "Be merciful, just as your Father is merciful" (Luke 6:36). He practiced this Himself as He was dying on the cross with this prayer: "Father, forgive them, for they do not know what they are doing" (Luke 23:34).

• *Solve deep-seated foundational problems that cause dysfunctional communication problems.* It's hard but not impossible. Dig deeper to find the problem that is causing the communication problem. Solve it, and the communication problem will be solved. Remember Brandi and Barry? They weren't talking, but their problem was much bigger than that. It included a lack of affection and consideration, neglected sexual needs and other matters as well. When they solved these problems, they also solved their communications problems. In helping people solve problems, I often think of what Solomon said: "The first to present his case seems right, till another comes forward and questions him" (Proverbs 18:17).

• *Identify dysfunctional interaction patterns and do something more constructive.* Three of the more common ones are female pursues, male withdraws; escalation; and negative twisting of what each other says. These patterns are self-perpetuating. We looked at examples of these before: Candace yelled, Michael pouted; Brandi had headaches and turned away from Barry, he became hurt and called her names. They recognized the pattern and did something different, something more constructive. They learned to validate rather than invalidate each other, and the pattern stopped.

The key is to remember your strengths rather than your weaknesses. Look for solutions, not just problems.

Family Strengths

I have spent considerable time discussing family dysfunctions in order to show how to break those patterns and overcome them. I am more interested in family strengths than in family weaknesses. Upon reflection, I can't think of any family that I have known up close that did not have some strengths upon which to build. Many examples I have given of dysfunctional families also included strengths. So I want to close this chapter by looking at family strengths. They help us overcome our weaknesses or at least minimize them.

I have been fascinated by the research of several scholars on family strengths: Nick Stinnett, John DeFrain, David Olson, Herbert Otto, Froma Walsh and others. They all concentrated on what makes families strong rather than on what makes them weak. Stinnet and DeFrain found six characteristics always present in strong families: commitment, love, appreciation, communication, spiritual wellness, and coping ability.[5] Olsen and DeFrain listed cohesion, adaptability and communication.[6] Otto's strengths include the following: ability to provide for physical, emotional, and spiritual needs; sensitivity, communication; support, security and encouragement; growth-producing relationships, responsible community relationships, ability to grow with and from children, ability for self-help and to accept help, role flexibility; and unity, loyalty and cooperation.[7]

I benefited greatly from a workshop I had in Chicago with Froma Walsh who has written extensively on spiritual resilience. Her affirmative orientation includes a belief in strength through connection and collaboration, affirmation of the worth of the family and family members, focus on strength and potential, mutual trust and assumption of benign intention. She says that we need to make meaning of crises, to view crises as a shared challenge that is manageable and to maintain a positive outlook. Be active, persevere and seize the opportunity for growth out of a crisis. All of this is done in the context of transcendent values, or spirituality: larger values, purpose, faith, communion, rituals, solace and comfort. Envision new possibilities, live and love more fully and be socially responsible.[8] In a recent book she edited, 20 accomplished authors discussed such topics as Spirituality and Religion: Wellsprings for Healing and Resilience; Spirituality, Suffering and Beliefs: The Soul of Healing with Families; and Healing from Trauma: The Quest for Spirituality.[9] Walsh's philosophy is reflected in a quotation from Pierre Teilhard De Chardin who said, "We are not human beings having a spiritual experience; we are spiritual beings having a human experience.[10]

In my book on *Building a Healthy Family*, I identify 18 principles for building strong families. They are:[11]

1. Healthy families build on a solid foundation.
2. Healthy families are committed.
3. Healthy families are emotionally mature.
4. Healthy families develop spiritually.
5. Healthy families build on love and affection.
6. Healthy families build around a healthy family structure.
7. Healthy families are led by effective parents.
8. Healthy families communicate effectively and grow through difficulties.
9. Healthy families are able to grow and change from one stage of development to another.
10. Healthy families are able to cope successfully with anger and manage conflict well.

11. Healthy families somehow develop the ability to cope with crises.
12. Healthy families have a sense of humor.
13. Healthy families build self-esteem.
14. Healthy families make continuing efforts to prevent divorce.
15. Healthy families have realistic expectations.
16. Healthy families spend a significant amount of quality time with each other.
17. Healthy families learn to work and to assume appropriate responsibilities.
18. Healthy families seek help when they need it.

My context in growing up had some weaknesses, of course, as well as strengths. The fact that we were poor left its insecurity mark. Negative comments from those who had little hope of escaping the poverty, tenant-farming cycle helped write my script: "You'll never amount to anything, you'll mess it up, you should be ashamed and you're not good enough."

Yet I also learned that we were tough, that we "did things right," that I was a good worker, that I was strong physically and that I was from "good stock." Upon reflection, I learned the following from my parents: hard work, integrity, love, the great value of family, love for the Bible and the church, respect and concern for people, the value of being a peacemaker, "minding my own business," discipline, persistence and faith. I learned to love, obey, and respect my parents and others. They taught me to be kind, helpful, considerate and responsible.

All children probably have some feelings of inferiority and inadequacy at times just because they are children. They are smaller than others; they get pushed around; they have to subjugate their wishes to others. Yet most grow out of it. They learn some of these principles from family strengths. They thus learn to be mature, well-adjusted adults. You can too. Look for strengths in your significant others, practice some of the principles I have discussed in this chapter and you can overcome family dysfunctional patterns as well:

1. Respect what God has said and obey Him.
2. Don't always think that what you don't have is better.
3. Don't be jealous of the accomplishments of other family members. Rejoice – it's a good reflection on your family.
4. Be honest even if it gets you into trouble. Do it with kindness, but be honest.
5. Face your problems and take responsibility.

6. Reconcile with others. Be a peacemaker.
7. Seek God's favor, His direction and strength.
8. Learn to believe in the providence of God when times look dark.
9. Learn to resist temptation.
10. Don't try to cover up one sin by committing another.
11. Don't marry for the wrong reasons.
12. Value family. They will likely be with you when others won't.
13. Cleave to your spouse.
14. Express appreciation.
15. Learn to communicate effectively.
16. Nurture your spirituality: utilize your spiritual resources.
17. Live congruently with your values and beliefs.
18. Focus on strengths and potentials rather than on weaknesses and failures.
19. Learn to grow through difficulties.
20. If it doesn't work, do something different.

Breaking dysfunctional patterns is difficult but not impossible. You have to continually intervene into well-entrenched negative, non-productive patterns. If you do, you can turn it around.

Reflections

1. What sins did Adam and Eve commit?
2. What dysfunctional patterns do you see in Abraham and his descendants?
3. What about David and his descendants?
4. Do you see yourself in any of this?
5. What did they do to find redemption?
6. What are some common dysfunctional interaction patterns in marriages? What can be done to turn them around?
7. If you had to list five principles for building healthy families, what would they be?
8. What dysfunctional patterns do you see in your own life? What can you do to intervene?
9. What strengths do you see in your own family?
10. What do discipline, persistence and faith have to do with overcoming dysfunctional family patterns?

CHAPTER NINE

Resisting Sexual Temptations

Sexual temptations are almost universal. The sex drive is alive and well in most of us. It in itself is amoral. It creates sexual tensions that call for release. When not guided properly, it causes much pain: unwanted pregnancies, herpes, AIDS, genital warts and broken marriages to name a few. Temptation comes to heterosexuals and homosexuals, to marrieds and singles and to those who are single again. The sex drive must be guided by appropriate values.

We are living in a very sex-oriented, promiscuous society. So many stimuli from television to books, magazines, music and friends encourage sexual freedom. It requires persons strong in character and values to control their sexual impulses.

God created sexuality and pronounced that it was good (Genesis 1). The man is to rejoice in his wife, let her breasts satisfy him at all times and be ecstatic always with her love (Proverbs 5:18-19). Both the husband and the wife give and receive in the sexual embrace mentioned in the Song of Solomon. Both are active, both are loving, both give, both receive. This is joyous sex. There is the thrill of erotic touch and sight, excitement of conversation, passion, the wonder of exploration, joy, beauty, a sense of belonging and appreciation of friendship that endures.

Yet throughout the Christian era, all sexual feelings have at times been wrongfully condemned by religious leaders. Some thought that sex in itself was wrong and tried unsuccessfully to subdue their sexual feelings and impulses. They practiced sexual restraint and infrequent sexual intercourse though married. Couples were at times urged to refrain from sex for several days before communion at church. One problem for some was how the Holy Spirit could indwell Christian couples while they engaged in sex. Many men thought of women only in terms of harlotry or maternity. Sexual desires were thought of as an infirmity as late as the time of Martin Luther. Marriage was a hospital to cure the infirmity. During the Victorian period (1837-1901), good wives were expected to be virtually sexless. The modest woman was to submit to her husband sexually but only to please him. The Bible all along recognized that both the husband and the wife had sexual needs that can be fulfilled in marriage (1 Corinthians 7:3-5). They were to meet each other's needs sexually. This would bring joy and also prevent fornication.

At least four functions of sex are in marriage: procreation, recreation, communication – an exchange of affection, a non-verbal conversation of love – and sexual release. Sexual needs are difficult to bury, ignore or sublimate and channel into other activities.

People often give many reasons for promiscuous sex:

• *There is no good reason not to.* But there is.

• *Everyone else is doing it.* But they aren't and, if they were, it would not justify it.

• *I want to love and be loved.* Yet sex in itself is not love as many have discovered. Spiritually we are different from animals. We do not live by sex alone. Family, love, children, companionship, a permanent relationship, home, reputation, self-esteem and respectability are more worthwhile. Control is needed. Electricity is natural; but running wild is dangerous. Controlled and regulated, it is useful. Sex is good and healthy when properly controlled in a loving, committed, heterosexual marriage.

• *Sex is fun.* Yet not always. It can be painful if you are hurt emotionally. Sex under some conditions is a bad experience. The bed-hopping person is often too insensitive and superficial to be a good mate. The more sexual partners you have, the less meaning you find in such relationships. Wilt Chamberlain said he had experienced sex with 20,000 women, but that he could never commit to anyone. Such sex is very impersonal, shallow, loveless and meaningless.

• *Sexual restraint is unhealthy.* This is untrue, a Freudian interpretation gone wrong. You can develop more fully as a person if you sublimate some sexual energy into other worthwhile goals.

• *We love each other, so sex is okay.* Love does not give license for sex. Marriage does, and love and marriage go together. Extra-marital sex can lead to guilt, pain, a loss of respect and trust, disappointment, rejection and provide pressure sometimes to marry the wrong person. Falling in love does not require sex. Before you are married, express your love in other ways such as meaningful conversation, responsiveness, sharing and enjoying other activities together.

• *I want to try it before I buy it.* Yet in marriage compatibility as persons is important as well. I have read several reports recently of research showing that sex before marriage is a negative influence to marital happiness. An extra-marital affair is, for sure, a bad way to begin a new marriage.

• *I want to prove that I am grown up.* Yet there is so much more to growing up than sex. Promiscuity proves just the opposite – that you are too immature to control your sexual impulses.

• *We are really suited for each other.* Yet you may be suited sexually for perhaps 1 million people or more. Commitment and love in a permanent relationship lifts sex to a higher, yet no less enjoyable, level.

As you can see, these common reasons given for sex outside of marriage are inadequate. There are good moral reasons to keep sex in marriage, and there is a sense of security and integrity in maintaining your moral standards. Chastity, morality, and fidelity are virtues that have proven themselves to be valid over the years. Self-mastery and responsibility are signs of maturity. Responsible conduct is necessary for a happy marriage. Moral character and integrity are developed by doing what you know is right. The more mature you are, the more you will regulate your behavior by what you know is right.

Sex in the Bible

Dependable values can guide your sex life productively. Such values can be found in the Bible where God's plan for sex is given as well as examples of many deviations to that plan.

God's plan for sex has been overwhelmingly accepted in the Christian world for 2,000 years. God created people male and female thus providing sexual delineation and boundaries. He told them to be fruitful and to multiply, and they were to become one flesh (Genesis 1-2). Sex was meant to be between a man and his wife in a spiritual union created by God. It was meant to be wholesome, loving, beautiful and good. The joy of sex in such a relationship is seen in the Song of Solomon. Paul said that it would prevent fornication (1 Corinthians 7). Solomon said that whoever finds a wife finds a good thing (Proverbs 18:22). Both he and Jesus said that married people are to be faithful (Proverbs 5:15; Matthew 19:1-9). Paul said that our bodies were meant to be sexually pure so that we can glorify God in our bodies (1 Corinthians 6:12-

20); the Hebrew writer stated that the marriage bed is to be kept pure (Hebrews 13:4).

This is God's plan for sex from the beginning: one man with one woman in marriage. Anything different from this is unnatural and not the natural order God had in mind (Romans 1:18-32).

I have found eight deviations to this plan in the Bible, all of which were strongly disapproved. What struck me most in my studies was that it didn't take long for deviations to occur. Adam and Eve sinned by disobeying God. Many sexual deviations are reported as follows:

Adultery

God punished Pharaoh because he took Sarah, Abraham's wife, to be his wife (Genesis 12:10-20; 20:1-8). Potiphar's wife tried to seduce Joseph who resisted her advances and was imprisoned because of it (Genesis 39). King David had sex with Bathsheba, the wife of Uriah, and was punished for it (2 Samuel 11-12). Many biblical teachings show God's will regarding this matter. "You shall not commit adultery" is one of the Ten Commandments (Deuteronomy 5:18; Exodus 20:14). The Law said that if a man commits adultery with another man's wife both of them must be put to death (Leviticus 20:10). No wonder Solomon said that the adulteress lacked judgment. The man who follows such a woman is like an ox going to the slaughter, like a deer stepping into a noose, little knowing that it will cost him his life (Proverbs 7). Of course, the man is responsible too, but you get the idea here of how serious all of this was in Israel.

Incest

Lot's daughters got him drunk, had sex with him and became pregnant (Genesis 19:30-38). Reuben slept with his father Jacob's concubine, Bilhah (Genesis 35:22; 49:4). Judah was deceived into having sex with his daughter-in-law Tamar (Genesis 38). Later the Law of Moses prohibited sexual relations with your father's wife, your sister or half-sister, your granddaughter, your step-granddaughter, your aunt, your daughter-in-law, your sister-in-law, with both a woman and her daughter, or your wife's sister (Leviticus 18:6-18). A similar list is found in Leviticus 20:10-21.

Incest evidently was practiced in the early days of civilization. There was no one else to marry then. But it was later forbidden as a deviation from the norm.

Homosexual Sex

The men of Sodom tried to have sex with two angels who were Lot's guests. They were struck blind for their sin (Genesis 19:1-29). Jude 7 refers to this as sexual immorality and perversion. Other scriptures are also clear on this matter. Leviticus 18:22, a part of God's moral law for the family, says that sex between men is "detestable." Leviticus 20:13 adds that they must be put to death and that their blood would be on their heads. Paul says that some had left God out of their knowledge. One evidence of this was that men were having sex with men and women were having sex with women. This was unnatural, meaning that it was not God's plan from the time of creation (Romans 1:18-32). God then gave them over to shameful lusts, indecent acts and a depraved mind. He said that those who do such things deserve death.

Paul indicates that practicing homosexuals will not inherit the kingdom of God. Some of them had been homosexual but had changed; they had been washed, justified, and sanctified in the name of the Lord Jesus Christ and by God's Spirit (1 Corinthians 6:9-11). They had been saved!

One other passage specifically mentions homosexuality (1 Timothy 1:8-11). The law was made for such people who do not live according to the glorious gospel of the blessed God.

The emphasis is on behavior, not orientation, which is hard to change. Behavior, however, can be controlled.

Rape

Shechem raped Dinah, the daughter of Jacob, and lost his life because of it (Genesis 34). Amnon was killed by his half-brother, Absalom, because he raped his half-sister and Absalom's sister, Tamar (2 Samuel 13-14). I have read that as many as 25 percent of all women in America have been sexually abused to some extent.

Fornication

Women were expected to be virgins when they married (Deuteronomy 22:13-22). Men are to flee fornication, to call on the Lord out of a pure heart (2 Timothy 2:22). Fornicators have their part in the lake of fire (Revelation 21:8). I don't want to persecute you if you have had sex while not married. About half of all people have done so. Just consider it a deviation from God's plan and change your direction. God forgives. You can change. It's what happens in the future that's important.

Prostitution

No Israelite man or woman was to become a prostitute (Deuteronomy 23:17-18). Josiah tore down the quarters of the male shrine prostitutes that were in the temple of the Lord (2 Kings 23:7).

I counseled with a former prostitute who had been a Christian for a month. Needing money, she resumed her former way of life; old habits are hard to break. We prayed together, and her new Christian friends surrounded her with their support.

Bestiality

It was a perversion to have sex with an animal (Leviticus 18:23) and still is today. It is not according to God's plan.

Women as Status Symbols

Absalom had sex with his father's concubines in the sight of all Israel – to show his power (2 Samuel 16:22). Both King David and King Solomon discovered that it is folly to marry for status and power.

These eight examples are all deviations to God's plan as recorded in the Bible. They are all contrary to the natural order – one man for one woman in heterosexual marriage – that God set in motion at creation. He permitted polygamy for a while, but it is not his ideal plan.

His plan points to a stable, loving, intimate marriage between a man and his wife. Such marriages bring happiness and stability and help us overcome sexual temptations. How can this come about?

Keys to Marital Intimacy

What is marital intimacy? What prevents it? What makes it possible? Who wants it? Are there gender differences? Of what value is it? These are some of the seemingly simple yet complex questions to be addressed here.

First, I will review what numerous authors have said and then summarize my research with 180 Christian married people (164 white, 16 African-American, 86 males, 94 females) on this important topic as well as a follow-up survey of 155 additional married people (85 white, 70 African-American).

A Review of the Literature

Dandeneau and Johnson state that intimacy is an important predictor of psychological and physiological well-being, that well-being is likely to stem from contact with intimate partners, and that people who are married live longer than those who are single.[1] Reis[2] notes that the most frequent problem brought to psychotherapists relates to intimacy[3]

Scarf (1987) addresses some of the complicated personality issues that affect marital intimacy. In her chapter on "Autonomy and Intimacy,"[4] she discusses the need of everyone to be both intimate (close) and autonomous (distant).[5]

In a significant 1997 study of 386 couples, Rankin-Esquer and others found that autonomy and relatedness were significantly and positively related with marital adjustment for both genders. They concluded that autonomy and relatedness are important aspects of marriage that can exist together and are related to a satisfying marriage. Individual needs of spouses, they continued, are important as well as relationship needs.[6]

This corresponds with Bowen's model of emotional maturity and how emotional immaturity is unconsciously projected from one generation to another and from one partner to another.[7] He also says that the more emotionally immature people are, the more likely they are to fuse with and try to control others. On the other hand, the more emotionally healthy people are, the more likely they are to be intimate, to allow closeness with others.[8]

In Masters, Johnson, and Kolodny's book on heterosexuality, they concentrate upon sex yet often mention nonsexual intimacy as well. They say that it consists of certain "core" ingredients. "Although they are not always described in the same words, these are mutual caring and a willingness to translate that caring into commitment; sharing freely with each other; communicating with openness and depth; valuing a relationships enough to imbue it with vulnerability and trust; tenderness; and making a consistent effort to empathize with each other."[9] Women seem to be culturally conditioned to be more adept than males at self-disclosure and verbal expression of emotions which affect emotional closeness, they conclude.[10]

Certain conditions of intimacy seem to precede others. Trust precedes the willingness to be vulnerable with each other; caring, the expression of tenderness; and empathic listening and commitment, precede intimacy. It is difficult to be intimate with a person who is fundamentally hostile, bitter and defeatist.[11]

Schnarch's book is extremely helpful in putting all of this together. He gives an extensive review of the literature on intimacy and defines it as confiding in others, experiencing the essence of one's self in communion with another, the attempt to get close to another and to explore similarities and differences. It involves openness and mutual self-disclosure, and time thinking about and being with one's partner.[12]

Intimacy, therefore, is to be viewed as a relational and an individual process in which togetherness, differentiation (emotional maturity), family of origin and other experiences play a part. Intimacy depends upon the context, intended and perceived meanings, and not merely the knowledge that comes from mutual self-disclosure. Sharing with a loving intention usually produces greater intimacy; whereas, unloading in order to hurt another person results in greater distance in the relationship. Both result in an increased knowledge of each other. Congruent communication may lead to greater intimacy when the intention is loving.

Several contributions have been made by marriage and family therapists. Kerr and Bowen's concept of emotional maturity is a very useful paradigm in understanding individual mental health, relationships, differentiation and one's family of origin.[13] Beavers speaks of intimacy as the process of being open, vulnerable, able to share one's uttermost feelings and thoughts and as the joy of being known and accepted by another who is loved.[14] Wynne and Wynne state that the expectation and fulfillment of trust and communicated empathy are contributing factors to intimacy.[15] These and other concepts that have been mentioned previously are repeated by numerous authors.[16]

A person is more than just a part of a system. A person can stand alone, love when unloved and feel a sense of intimacy even when his or her mate does not (self-validated intimacy). This capacity to be separate is characteristic of both mature Christians who can turn the other cheek (Matthew 5) and emotionally mature persons described by Bowen.[17] Such people are not highly reactive to what others do. They can give even when not getting. They can remain calm even when being attacked. They can remain whole, caring persons when up close.

Though helpful, all of this leaves troubled marital partners as immature persons in a dysfunctional system with little if any ability to change. It is somewhat like being a defective engine without gasoline and with small chance of being repaired or fueled. There is no energy to push the dysfunctional system. The missing ingredients are *agape* love, strength and guidance that come from God which provide the energy and the maturity to stay, to struggle and to grow as a person and as a partner. Other words such as trust, commitment, tenderness and self-disclosure are also very important factors in marital intimacy. However, love (genuine, unselfish caring), gracious intention to be intimate and emotional maturity seem to be more foundational.[18] Trust, tenderness and commitment can grow out of love, which continues to give unselfishly even when not receiving as seen in the life of Jesus. This gets us past the often-practiced exchange theory of relationships that says, "I'll give if you will give. I'll be nice if you will be nice." Feuding couples tied up with this attitude cannot decide who will be nice first. Love provides the energy for the relationship; commitment and empowerment from God keep emotionally immature, anxious couples from doing an emotional cut-off which is a characteristic of immature people to reduce anxiety.

Love and commitment are central themes for marriage in the Bible (Genesis 2:24; Numbers 30:2; Ephesians 5:25-31). Such concepts are built upon the foundation of God's faithfulness and his love, which endure to the end. Such love and faithfulness are reliable, generous, empowering, kind and merciful. Being faithful to our identity as God's people, our relationships will reflect His character of love, holiness and faithfulness. As we focus on being close to Him, He empowers us to be transformed into the likeness of His son Jesus Christ from one degree of glory to another (Romans 8:29; 2 Corinthians 3:18). Commitment and love in marriage, empowered by such a relationship and foundation rooted in the character of God, provide both the energy and the glue for marriages to stay together and continue to grow. These are important factors in marital intimacy.

All of this requires a significant degree of spiritual maturity. For the Christian, spiritual maturity begins with God who is Spirit and the new birth into Christ and continues throughout life with growth in the grace and knowledge of our Lord and Savior Jesus Christ (John 3:5; 2 Peter 3:18). Love, patience, kindness, peace and discipline are fruit of the Spirit (Galatians 5:22-23). The sincere milk of the word (food for the soul) and spiritual exercise enable the Christian to continue toward Christian maturity throughout life. Such a person knows as did Christ who he or she is and is not overly threatened by being close in marital intimacy. God fills us with His love, transforms us by the renewing of our minds (Romans 12:1-2) and empowers us to model His relationships.

In *The Pleasure Bond*, Masters and Johnson conclude that the best sex is between people who have a sense of permanence and are intimate in their relationship. Intimacy then is said to be dependent upon their willingness to be vulnerable with each other, which is dependent upon trust. Love, trust, desire to be intimate, commitment and emotional maturity summarize key essential ingredients of marital intimacy.[19]

Survey of 335 Married People

With this information serving as a context, I designed a questionnaire to test some of the concepts derived from the literature and my counseling experience as a psychologist, marriage and family therapist and minister. In order to elicit different types of responses, nine true and false and seven open-ended questions were designed. In the last few years, I spoke 21 times in five Memphis-area churches to young married classes (ages 22-40) on intimacy in marriage. I administered this questionnaire to 180 married people with the following results.

First, they usually defined intimacy in much the same way as seen in the literature. They saw it as a close, satisfying relationship. There was little gender difference in their definitions. Although men usually mentioned sex first, they often did so after having mentioned such words as closeness, affection and sharing. Women acknowledged sexual needs as well.

The following is a summary in descending order of the true and false questions which identified hindrances to marital intimacy: relationship problems, too tired, lack of time for me, lack of romance, different desires, rushing into sex, husband too fast, lack of affection, wife too cold.

A summary of the open-ended questions is as follows. The first question asked for the main hindrance to sexual adjustment in marriage. Answers included lack of time, jobs, children, different moods, not sensing needs of spouse, lack of passion, man too fast, switching suddenly from no to yes after marriage, keeping up with spouse, sex not important to wife, he does not consider her needs, different needs, husband wants sex more often and wife wants more affection and romance.

There were some gender differences, but they were not extensive. Women were more likely to mention the children; rushing into sex; lack of romance; lack of affection; husband too fast; past sexual abuse; he wants sex, I want closeness; turned off when touched and focus mostly is on him. Men mentioned several of these as well but were more likely to list different desires: wife too cold, she thinks I just want sex, she misunderstands my desires, meeting my wife's needs and no variety. Both genders listed lack of time as being their main problem in achieving good sexual adjustment in marriage.

A question closely related was: I need my spouse to___. Mentioned more often were to be more attentive, to be more spontaneous and thoughtful in bed, to be more helpful, understanding, supportive and tender; to spend more time intimately, to be more affectionate, to talk to me, to listen to me more, to lead me closer to God and to be aware of how I feel. Wives were more likely to mention the need for affection, communication, being aware of how they feel and making time for them. Husbands did not seem to follow much of a pattern on this question. Their unique responses were as follows: I need her to overcome her sexual inhibitions, to respect me more, to love me for who I am, to put me above her friends, to be more forgiving, to understand my struggles and how hard I work to support our family and to enjoy sex.

Another open-ended question was: Real intimacy in marriage is___. Their response to this question was remarkably similar to our review of the literature on intimacy. Mentioned more often in descending order were love, mutual respect, closeness with each other, trust, openness, communication, caring, affection, sex, tenderness, being aware of each other's wants and needs, sharing and consideration for the spouse.

Another question was: The main strength of our marriage is___. Their answers in descending order of frequency were commitment to communication, love for and commitment to God and relationship with Him, trust, friendship, dedication to and respect for each other, honesty and being Christian in our home. The most noticeable gender difference here was that wives were more likely to mention commitment to each other than were husbands. For both genders, marital strengths were almost identical to their definition of marital intimacy.

A follow-up questionnaire was designed to check out the validity of what had been learned already and to discover additional information. Twelve keys to marital intimacy were incorporated into the questionnaire (Likert-type questions) along with three open-ended questions and one Likert-type question rating marital intimacy. This questionnaire on "Hindrances to Marital Intimacy" was administered to 155 married individuals in six Mid-South churches of Christ: 85 individuals were white, 70 African-American; 59 were men, 96, women. Their average age was 46 (range 21-80), average time married 23 years.

The open-ended questions produced similar results to those previously reported. Intimacy was defined by such words in descending order of frequency as closeness, holding-touching-hugging, communication, sharing, love, time together, caring, attention, understanding, kindness, affection and sex. Primary hindrances to marital intimacy in descending order of frequency were lack of time, tiredness, lack of communication, children, age, lack of commitment, dishonesty, TV, relationship problems, health problems, other commitments, different needs, needs not considered, selfishness, lack of privacy, lack of affection, lack of time and financial fights. They thought that more time alone, better communication, kindness, love, understanding needs, better health, honesty, rest and relaxation, less TV, working on problems, being open, youth, pleasing each other, being Christian and more tenderness and romance would increase intimacy.

Some gender differences were detected. Women were more likely to mention holding hands, touching, hugging, romance, affection, sharing feelings, tenderness, communication, TV, meeting needs and being Christian. Men were a little more likely to mention sex, rest and relaxation, age, kindness and health problems.

Here is a summary of my findings. The main hindrances to marital intimacy in descending order were ineffective sharing and communication; lack of tenderness, non-sexual touching, lack of affection and warmth; sexual frequency disagreements, emotional immaturity, different sexual desires, lack of loving sex, inadequate *agape* love; fear of closeness, mutuality, communion and reciprocity; lack of mutual respect and support, lack of mutual attraction, lack of commitment and lack of mutual trust. When these are missing, so is marital intimacy.

There were some racial and gender differences but not as many as I had guessed. What everyone was saying was that marital intimacy was another way of defining a healthy marriage and that a healthy marriage usually led to good sexual adjustment in marriage.

With this in mind, I offer the following observations and conclusions: Intimacy in marriage is desired though feared by most people. It is defined by using such words as closeness, mutuality, sex, togetherness, tenderness, caring and sharing. The more important causative factors producing intimacy seem to be emotional maturity, unselfish caring, desire to be close, trust and commitment.

Agape love provides the energy to grow through emotional immaturity and become a more healthy personality. Commitment to God and to each other provides the sticking power to prevent emotional cut-off and to work through personal inadequacies that arise from being up close, permitting each to become more mature emotionally.

Closeness without good intentions is not real intimacy in marriage or in other relationships.[20] Fusion and control by manipulation is not healthy intimacy. Distancing to the point of little emotional contact is not intimacy. Marital intimacy should be pursued patiently. Personality patterns are hard to change. Such healthy intimacy, however, may lead to greater individual maturity and increased joy and a better, more satisfying marriage.

Marital intimacy is a key to overcoming sexual temptations. Some other ideas help as well.

Reasons for Marital Unfaithfulness

There are many reasons for marital unfaithfulness, one of which is sexual temptation – to have an affair. To overcome this common temptation, husbands and wives need to ask themselves why they want to have an affair.

Men's Reasons for an Affair

Some reasons given by men who have had such affairs include: to avoid intimacy, to act out my fantasy, narcissism, to make a conquest, away from home too much, intimacy with an outside person, low self-esteem, nourishment and acceptance, wife has changed, sexual addiction, anger, inability to resolve conflicts, family pattern, alcohol and other drugs, pushy wife, dissatisfied with sex at home, additional recreation, emotional immaturity, and seeing nothing wrong with it. Some 60 percent of all men who get married today expect to have an affair. Then, of course, they do.

Women's Reasons for an Affair

Women say they have affairs because they have a bad relationship with their husbands; are seeking a meaningful relationship and love; want approval, nourishment and acceptance; were sexually abused as children; low self-esteem and distant fathers. They have husbands who are not concerned with their sexual needs, do not communicate well, do little or no non-sexual touching, are away from home a lot and are not affectionate.

They often are women who have changed, but their husbands have not. They may be compulsive sex addicts and emotionally immature. Some, like men, want additional sex as recreation and see nothing wrong with it. Some are overly dependent and will do whatever men want in order to please them. Some drift into affairs out of long and meaningful conversation and sharing with other men. They build a relationship; the sex then just happens as a byproduct of the relationship. They get emotionally close, then have sex; whereas, men are more likely to have sex just for fun and avoid closeness, entanglement or real intimacy.

Thus, women's affairs take longer to get over. They are often still in love with the man with whom they had an affair and have difficulty resuming sex with their husband. It's as though they are stepping out on the one they love and having sex with someone they don't love any more.

Crystal overcame this hurdle by making a decision that she did not want to get a divorce and by just acting better than she felt. She said, "I knew that sex goes along with marriage, and I wanted to keep my marriage together. I did what I needed to do and finally learned to enjoy it again. I felt good about keeping my family together, and I knew my husband still loved me. It helped me to remember that I need mercy as well. God has been merciful to me."

Principles for Overcoming Temptations

The first step in overcoming temptations whether you are married or single is the desire to do so. If you have read this far, I believe you have such desire. Please read on for some specific suggestions that will help you meet your goal of overcoming sexual temptations.

The Bible teaches us that we all will be tempted. Abraham (Genesis 22), the people of Israel (Exodus 20:20), Job and Jesus (Matthew 4) are familiar examples.

One way of conceptualizing problems is to think of them in terms of temptations to do wrong. We need to learn how to overcome temptations and to help others to do likewise. James gives us a model for doing this in his first chapter, verses 2 through 18. He does this by answering three questions:

What Temptations Will We Face?

Before we are tempted, it often helps to contemplate the temptations we are likely to face. James says that we will face both internal and external temptations. Internally, there are lusts or evil desires crying out for satisfaction. Paul recognizes such internal inclinations when he admonishes Timothy not to have an unhealthy interest in controversies nor in love of money (1 Timothy 6:3-10). Such inclinations result in constant squabbling and in all kinds of evil. Externally, insults and harassments arise from others because of poverty (James 2:1-7); innocent men may be murdered (James 5:6). Pressures and temptations to do wrong come from every angle, and the Christian fight is on.

Why Should We Overcome Temptations?

An answer to this question will motivate us to overcome, and James gives us a good answer, a three-pronged answer. First, overcoming temptation leads to happiness. Blessed or happy (James 1:12) are those who overcome temptations. They are peaceful, pure, refined and joyful. This word for "blessed" is used by the Greeks to denote the kind of life the "immortal gods" lived. It is used of the "blessed God" (1 Timothy 1:11), of "God, the blessed and only Ruler, the King of kings and Lord of lords" (1 Timothy 6:15). It denotes depth beyond outward circumstances. In Daniel 12:9-13, the "blessed" are those who are purified, made spotless and refined, those who understand, those who made it through the many trials of persecution. They suffer, yet remain faithful. Peter said that trials are to be expected because we are of Christ who suffered and because we are to share in his glory and rejoice with exceeding joy (1 Peter 4:12-13)!

Second, overcoming temptation leads to a more refined Christian character, to Christian growth and maturity (James 1:2-3). We can "count it all joy" when we fall into every kind of temptation because of this. Testing develops perseverance; perseverance finishes its work so that "you may be mature and complete, not lacking anything." Peter says that our faith must be proved by fire in manifold trials that the proof of our faith may lead to praise, glory and honor at the revelation of Jesus Christ, and in this we are to greatly rejoice (1 Peter 1:6-7). Persecution may lead upward. A person endures a painful operation to obtain better health, and we endure trials because of Jesus and Christian growth.

Third, overcoming temptation leads to the crown of life (James 1:12). It is interesting that the Greek word here for crown is the word *stephanos*, and Stephen (*Stephanos*) was the first recorded Christian martyr (Acts 7). Jesus said, "Blessed are those who are persecuted because of righteousness, for theirs is the kingdom of heaven" (Matthew 5:10,), and "By standing firm you will gain life" (Luke 21:19). Paul said that we compete in life to get a crown that will last forever (1 Corinthians 9:25). He also speaks of the crown of righteousness which the righteous judge will award on that day to all who have longed for his appearance (2 Timothy 4:8). The contemplation of this crown is motivation enough to spur Christians on toward the overcoming of temptation.

How Do We Overcome Temptations?

We know that temptations of every sort are coming, and we are motivated to overcome them, but how? James and other biblical writers give us help in this fight.

• *We are to remember.* The words by James in our text are helpful as are many others. The psalmist laid up the word of God in his heart "that I might not sin against you" (Psalm 119:11). Jesus knew the word of God and quoted it to the devil as He overcame temptation (Matthew 4:1-11). We are to remember relevant examples from the past (1 Corinthians 10:1-13). Some gave in to temptation and died; whereas others overcame temptation and lived. We are to remember our commitment to Christ (1 Timothy 6:11-14). Thus we flee all evil; pursue righteousness, godliness, faith, love, endurance, and gentleness; fight the good fight of faith; keep His commandments and take hold of eternal life to which we were called when we made the good confession.

• *We are to think clearly,* not with a double-mind or a "bi-souled" attitude (James 1:7). We cannot even pray for help as we ought when we are double-minded but are rather unstable in all that we do. This should not surprise us. Thinking affects behavior (Philippians 4:8-9; Romans 12:1-2). To overcome temptations, we must think with one mind and then act according to God's righteousness.

• *We should pray in faith* (James 1:5-6). Such prayer brings wisdom from God, and we need wisdom to overcome temptations. Jesus said for His disciples to watch and pray "so that you will not fall into temptation" (Matthew 26:41). We need to "Look to the Lord and his strength; seek his face always" (1 Chronicles 16:11). When we do, He will come through. King Solomon is a good example of one who received wisdom from the Lord. His good judgments as king reflect this wisdom (1 Kings 3:4-15).

• *We should put on the whole armor of God* (Ephesians 6:10-11): truth, righteousness, the gospel of peace, faith, salvation, the sword of the Spirit which is the word of God. Then we can stand against the devil's schemes!

• *We must take responsibility for our own behavior* (James 1:13). Do not blame God. He is not evil and has no inclination toward evil; thus He cannot be tempted with evil; and He, Himself, does not tempt anyone. But we are tempted because of our lusts or evil desires. We give in and die. Adam blamed Eve (Genesis 3:13); we blame God, the church, our mates, our associates and many others. People who have affairs say, "They made us do it." While others influence us, they cannot control us without our consent. Take responsibility for your own thoughts, feelings and actions, and you will be in a position with God's help to overcome temptations!

• *Shun evil companions.* Many temptations are external, so we are to avoid certain situations. Jesus taught His disciples to pray, "And lead us not into temptation, but deliver us from evil" (Matthew 6:13). We will "fall into temptations" without looking for them. "If sinners entice you, do not give in to them" (Proverbs 1:10). Paul said, "Do not be misled: 'Bad company corrupts good character'" (1 Corinthians 15:33). "And do not give the devil a foothold" (Ephesians 4:27). Build a fence around your temptation. Don't put yourself into certain situations.

• *Look for God's way of escape.* God is faithful. "He will not let you be tempted beyond what you can bear. But when you are tempted, he will also provide a way out so that you can stand up under it" (1 Corinthians 10:13). Some responsibility is yours: you must look for God's way of escape and remember that God will help you to overcome. It may not be easy, but it is possible. And life does not have to be easy to be meaningful and victorious!

• *Substitute good activity for bad activity.* This is often easier to do than is merely the cessation of evil. Put something in the place of evil or something will move back into its place. Other evil spirits are looking for a home, and an empty house is so inviting (Luke 11:24-26)! Isaiah and Paul gave good illustrations.

Isaiah said, "Stop doing wrong, learn to do right! Seek justice, encourage the oppressed. Defend the cause of the fatherless, plead the case of the widow" (Isaiah 1:16-17).

Paul admonished us not to let sin reign in our mortal bodies but to let God reign. Do not obey evil desires; obey God. Do not offer yourselves to sin, as instruments of wickedness, "but rather offer yourselves to God, as those who have been brought from death to life; and offer the parts of your body to him as instruments of righteousness" (Romans 6:12-13).

Stop drinking alcohol; drink more water. Stop going with the wrong crowd; go with the right crowd. Stop eating certain kinds of food; eat a healthier list of foods. Stop going to topless bars and pornographic stores; start praying and going to church. Stop giving too much attention to those other than your spouse; start giving more attention to your spouse. Stop wasting time; start filling your time with profitable pursuits. And on and on we could go. It is a sound principle; substitute good activity for bad activity.

• *Rejoice in the Lord whatever your circumstances.* "Count it" all joy (James 1:2-3). You can make something good out of your life. Both the rich and poor should rejoice that they are in Christ (James 1:9-11). Paul said, "I am not saying this because I am in need, for I have learned to be content whatever the circumstances. I know what it is to be in need, and I know what it is to have plenty. I have learned the secret of being content in any and every situation, whether well fed or hungry, whether living in plenty or in want" (Philippians 4:11-12).

Make a good life where you are. The grass in not always greener across the fence. Someone else's mate may bring you more problems than you have now. Satan may call, but he does not tell you the whole story. Do not give in to evil temptations; it only makes life more difficult. Rejoice in the Lord in all circumstances.

• *Love God with all your heart, soul and mind* (Matthew 22:37-40). This is the great commandment. This kind of love leads to obedience and the overcoming of temptations (1 John 5:3). Love of neighbor follows love of God. So when tempted, draw upon your love for God. He will help you to overcome.

James said, "Blessed is the man that endures temptation; for when he has been approved, he will receive the crown of life which the Lord has promised to those who love Him" (James 1:12 NKJV). Just as muscles are hardened and enlarged by strenuous labor, genuine Christians are strengthened by trials endured. Just as runners train and punish themselves in order to win, Christians win by the grace of God, hard work and endurance. We live with him in order to reign with him (2 Timothy 2:11). The crown of life motivates us to be faithful even in the face of death (Revelation 2:10). While the Judgment Day will be our final test, we are being tested now. By the power of God, we must endure temptation and we must overcome the trials of life. God will give us the strength to do what he wants us to do!

These principles have helped me overcome temptations. Many of my clients have told me the same. Nolan said that the woman he had an affair with recently came into his office. He called a colleague to come in for a consultation. He thus caught himself and rebuilt the fence around his temptation. Damon, wanting to cease his homosexual lifestyle, caught himself going to a meeting place for pickups, turned around and came home. He did not put himself into that situation again.

He started back to church, became very devout spiritually and is now living a celibate Christian life. He felt genuine, better because he did what he thought was right.

Let me share some instruction from Paul (1 Corinthians 6:12-20) that has helped many. In this passage, he gives seven reasons not to be sexually immoral:

1. Sex is not morally neutral like food.
2. You may be mastered (addicted) by it.
3. Your body is not created for sexual immorality.
4. Your body as well as your spirit is important: God raised Jesus' body from the dead.
5. Your body, not just your spirit, is a member of Christ.
6. Your body is a temple of the Holy Spirit. We are not to desecrate that which is holy.
7. You are bought with a price and are to glorify God in your body.

Ashley and Alex both had affairs; yet they wanted to keep their marriage together and "redeem their lives." As a part of this process, they resolved to recommit to each other for life. They cried as they spoke of their behavior and their guilt. Three years later they are still together and feel much better about their marriage. "It's better than ever," they reported. What helped them do this? Here is the list they gave me:

1. Our genuine re-conversion to God (John 3:5; Acts 8:9-24).
2. Our covenant of love with God and with each other (Matthew 19; 1 Corinthians 7:34).
3. Building a good relationship with each other and a healthy sexual relationship (1 Corinthians 7:1-5).
4. A meaningful church membership (1 Corinthians 12).
5. An accountability group at church (James 5:16).
6. The spiritual disciplines of scripture reading and prayer (1 Thessalonians 5:17; James 1:19).
7. Living in accord with our spiritual identity (1 Peter 1:17-2:3).
8. Practicing the Golden Rule (Matthew 7:12).
9. Building a fence around our temptations (1 Corinthians 15:33; 1 Thessalonians 5:22).
10. Learning to honor God with our bodies as well as with our spirits. We are total persons who want to honor God completely (1 Corinthians 6:12-20).

Your list might look a little different. That's all right. But let me ask you to consider the principles they used to overcome temptations, to rebuild their spiritual lives and their marriage. These are proven values rooted in eternity.

All of us have sinned and have fallen short. Yet these principles can help us overcome temptations and turn into constructive channels of healthy, godly living. Values must give direction to sexual desires in order for this to happen. Just feeling a certain way does not determine values. We must turn to God for values and principles that will stand the test of time.

What he says, as revealed in the Bible, is that sex as he created it is good, that it is to be enjoyed in a heterosexual loving, committed, intimate marriage, that we are to take responsibility for our thoughts and behavior and that he will help us find a way of escape from our sexual temptations (1 Corinthians 10:13). The first step is for you to look for that way. When you find it, you will grow spiritually. By overcoming temptations, you are living by discipline, persistence and faith. God bless.

Reflections

1. What is God's plan for sex as given in the Bible?
2. Why have some people historically gone to extremes in making all sex evil?
3. Why does our society today justify all sex?
4. Why do men have affairs?
5. What about women?
6. What is your definition of marital intimacy?
7. What to you are the most important factors that cause marital intimacy?
8. What helps you overcome sexual temptations?
9. Discuss 1 Corinthians 6:12-20 as it relates to sexual temptations?
10. How do discipline, persistence and faith help you overcome such temptations?

Growing
Through Grief

I wrote a book on grief titled *Growing Through Grief*. I decided to
use this as a title to this chapter because of its optimism and its double meaning. "Growing through" implies progression through and
denotes an optimistic spirit – people can become stronger emotionally and spiritually as they progress through grief. They are not the same,
but they may be more autonomous and more mature.

I want to give you some illustrations of how certain biblical characters handled their grief, look at some common stages of grief, examine children's grief, give some suggestions on adjusting to grief, offer some conclusions and ask for your reflections. I will share some of
my grief experiences with you as well.

Personal Grief Experiences

From my old homeplace, every funeral conducted in the Flatt/Union
Hill Cemetery was in full view. Add to that the rural practice of min-
istering to each other in times of grief and you can see that I was fully exposed to death and grief very early in life. Dad and Mom would
take us to the house of the deceased; the casket would be there, and we
would sit around and sing a lot of good old songs about heaven and
God's care for us. That has stuck with me.

The death of children bothered me the most. I remember a 2-year-
old boy who died. We sang "Gathering Flowers for the Master's
Bouquet." The family was devastated. My Uncle Leo's son, L.A., died
as an infant. Charlie C. Medlin, a friend Leamon and I hunted with at
night, was accidentally electrocuted at age 17. I still remember the
preacher's remarks: "It rains on the just and the unjust."

My grandfather, Hiram Way, who lived next door, died when I was
15. He was a farmer, preacher and schoolteacher. They buried him with

an open Bible in his hands. His faith carried him through the deaths of four of his children and helped him to look forward to heaven. He could talk about dying as calmly as about going shopping. He looked forward to being with his 9-year-old son Jesse, who had been killed when he fell off a mule.

Ma Way died when I was in the Air Force in Germany. She had told me before I left that she would never see me again. She finally found the peace that she seldom had in this life.

The deaths of my first cousins, Layton and Litton, bothered me for a long time. I dreamed for years about them – they would return and we would be together. I grew up with them and was in the same grade as they from primer (kindergarten) through high school.

My paternal grandparents died in the 1970s: first Ma Flatt, then Pa Flatt. The night before Ma died, she told Pa to fix supper for them – that she wanted to eat one more time at the family dining table. He did, and during dinner she said, "Henry, I won't be with you by tomorrow at this time. I'm going home. I want you to tell the children to follow me." Pa died about four years later.

I miss my uncles – Leo, Noah, Harold, Russell, Hubert, Tom B., J.D., Mitchell – and others as well. I could also list aunts: Lillie, Ina, Helen, Clennie, Eunice, Rebeccah and others. I have lost 19 uncles and aunts during the last 10 years. They were all a close part of my network.

Flora Dyer, my mother-in-law, was almost like a mother to me. We lost her suddenly when she was 68. Her husband, equally precious to me, died some 10 years later. They were an important extension of my family and a blessing to me. They always gave us food from their farm when we left, even after we had more than they did. They wanted to take care of their children.

Mom died when she was 74. A great woman of faith, she left her imprint on all of us. While she was in a coma, she would sometimes raise her arms and say several times, "Preach it from the mountain tops." She had heard her father say that, and she was passing it on to her boys. I grieved for her many times during her life because she had significant health problems. Dad died some 14 years later. He had the same kind of trusting faith that his mother and Pa Way had as expressed in his last words to us: "Don't worry. Everything is all right."

Other significant losses to me included Dr. W.B. West Jr. He was a dear friend and encourager. I still think about him almost every day. When I think of personal grief, I also think of how I felt when a grandchild died in the womb.

We grieve over anything of value that we lose or anticipate losing. It hurts. A client of mine grieved when two of her boys were unable to get jobs for a long time. She could see what it was doing to them, and it hurt a great deal. Some of you have had few grief experiences, some many; and they may have been much more severe and intense than what I have mentioned.

How Biblical Characters Handled Grief

Perhaps it would help to see how certain biblical characters handled grief. Losses came to them, and they hurt just as we do.

Adam and Eve lost their son Abel who was murdered by his brother Cain (Genesis 4). We don't know much about how they handled their grief except that they went on with their lives – had Seth and perhaps other children as well.

Abraham's family worked through a great deal of grief. Sarah, his wife, died at age 127. Abraham mourned for her and wept over her. He then bought a field from the Hittites and buried her (Genesis 23).

Abraham left everything he had to his son, Isaac; but while he was still living, he gave gifts to his other sons and sent them away. At age 175, he breathed his last and was gathered to his people. His sons, Isaac and Ishmael, buried him in the cave with his wife Sarah (Genesis 25:5-11). There was a sense of peace and comfort after his death. He made serious mistakes, but he turned from them and became the father of the faithful. His was a life well lived.

Isaac lived to be 180, breathed his last and was gathered to his people, old and full of years. His sons, Esau and Jacob, buried him (Genesis 35:27-29). Mourners were not shielded from the reality of death.

One of the more intensive examples of grief found in the Bible is that of Jacob when he thought his favorite son Joseph had been killed by a ferocious animal (Genesis 37). His other sons, jealous of Joseph, sold him into Egyptian slavery. They then stripped him of his special coat, slaughtered a goat and dipped the coat in the goat's blood. They took the coat back to their father and let him incorrectly conclude that some ferocious animal had devoured him – that he had surely been torn to pieces. Then Jacob tore his clothes, put on sackcloth and mourned for his son many days. His children came to comfort him, but he refused to be comforted. "No," he said, "in mourning will I go down to the grave to my son." He wept for him – didn't think he would ever adjust to his son's death.

You perhaps know the wonderful ending to this grief story. Joseph, though imprisoned for a while because of Potiphar's wife, did well in Egypt – became second in command to Pharaoh. He saved grain during years of famine and was able to provide grain for his family when they were in need. And the highlight of this story is that Jacob got to see his son again and that Joseph was mature enough to forgive his brothers (Genesis 37-50). You will not get to see your deceased loved ones again in this life, but there is that life to come.

Before Jacob died, he gathered his sons around him and blessed them. He gave them instructions, much as Daddy did us, drew his feet up into his bed, breathed his last and was gathered to his people (Genesis 49).

Genesis 50 gives us another glimpse of how they mourned. Joseph threw himself upon his father, wept over him and kissed him. He then had him embalmed, and the Egyptians mourned over him for 70 days. When these days of mourning had passed, Joseph, along with a large group of family and Pharaoh's officials, took his father's body back to the Promised Land for burial. There they observed another seven-day period of mourning. They buried him in the cave with his parents and grandparents.

After the burial, Joseph returned to Egypt along with his brothers and all the others who had gone with him to bury his father. After the burial, instead of carrying on the family feud as his brothers expected, Joseph forgave them saying, "Don't be afraid. Am I in the place of God? You intended to harm me, but God intended it for good to accomplish what is now being done, the saving of many lives. So then, don't be afraid. I will provide for you and your children" (Genesis 50:19-21). He reassured them and spoke kindly to them.

When there are hard feelings in a family, someone needs to be big enough to give wiggle room, back off and forgive. Usually, it's the most emotionally and spiritually mature person in the group. Such people mend fences.

When Moses died, the whole nation of Israel mourned. He lived a great life but did not get to go into the Promised Land. Evidently God himself buried Moses, his servant, who had lived 120 productive years. The Israelites grieved for Moses for 30 days, until the time of weeping and mourning was over (Deuteronomy 34:5-8).

Israel wept over not having meat to eat and wanted to go back to Egypt (Numbers 11). The Lord provided quail and manna for them to eat.

The Jewish people grieved over their anticipated deaths. King Xerxes had issued an order through Haman to destroy, kill and annihilate the

Jews in one day. Haman had greatly influenced the passing of this law because Mordecai would not kneel down and pay honor to him. When Mordecai learned of this law, he tore his clothes, put on sackcloth and ashes and went out into the city wailing loudly and bitterly. In every province that heard of this edict, there was great mourning among the Jews with fasting, weeping and wailing. Many lay in sackcloth and ashes – a sign of sorrow and humility (Esther 3-4).

Queen Esther then entered the picture. First, she sent clothes to Mordecai, but he refused to wear them, preferring to continue wearing his sack clothes to express his humility and sorrow. Next, he urged the queen to go into the king and beg for mercy and plead with him for her people. She was understandably reluctant since such action could result in her death. Mordecai challenged her by saying that she and her father's house would perish also and "who knows but that you have come to royal position for such a time as this?" (Esther 4:14.)

This story has a good ending. Xerxes canceled the law, and Haman was hanged on his own gallows that he had prepared for Mordecai, who was honored instead of Haman (Esther 4-7). The point here is that they grieved and did what they could to work through their grief.

Hezekiah grieved over the prospects of his own death. He was ill and at the point of death. The Lord through Isaiah told him to put his house in order because he was going to die. Hezekiah turned his face to the wall and prayed to the Lord, reminding him of his faithfulness and whole-hearted devotion. Then he wept bitterly. God saw his tears, heard his prayer, extended his life 15 years and delivered the city from the hand of the king of Assyria (2 Kings 20:1-11).

Nehemiah, in exile, heard that his people back home were in great distress. The walls of Jerusalem had been broken down, and the gates to the city had been burned. He then sat down and wept: he mourned, fasted, and prayed before the God of Israel (Nehemiah 1).

The Grief and Faithfulness of Job

Job is a good example of cumulative grief. He suffered great loss "without cause." He lost his property, his servants, his 10 children and his wife's support and understanding (Job 1-2). He suffered from sore boils from the soles of his feet to the top of his head. He sat among the ashes and scraped himself with a piece of broken pottery (Job 2:7-8).

Job suffered from misunderstanding, which he verbalized to himself and others. He cursed the day he was born (Job 3). He told himself, that there is no peace, no rest, no hope (Job 7); the night dragged on and he tossed until dawn (Job 7:4). He wondered why God made him his target, why God did not forgive him of his sins (Job 7). He wished he were dead. He despised his life.

In his answer to Bildad, Job wondered how a man can be just with God. He cannot answer God; God's ways are past finding out. Job cannot perceive him even when he passes by. God will not withdraw his anger but multiplies Job's wounds without cause. Job was bitter because he thought that God destroyed the perfect and the wicked and mocked the despair of the innocent. Job labored in vain and was afraid (Job 9). He thought he had no way to defend himself against God. He was full of shame and drowned in his afflictions.

In answering Zophar, Job said that he was a laughingstock to his neighbor. He had called upon God, and he answered with punishment. Robbers prosper, but he was punished. Who can fight God (Job 12)? Job thought that he had no hope. He continued by stating that man born of a woman is of few days and full of trouble. He wished to hide in the grave until God's anger passed (Job 14).

In a second response to Eliphaz, Job mentioned that people had jeered at him and struck his cheek in scorn. God, he thought, had broken him, taken him by the neck and dashed him to pieces and made him his target (Job 16). His spirit and purposes were broken (Job 17).

To Bildad, Job said that he cried out for help but was not heard, was not given justice. God, he said, had stripped him of his glory, had counted him as his enemy and turned his brethren, friends and family against him. His bones cleaved to his skin and to his flesh (Job 19).

To Zophar, Job asked why the wicked live and prosper. God did not punish them though they rejected him (Job 21). To Eliphaz, Job wondered where he might find God, though terrified before him to "set his cause before him" (Job 23). He seemed to hide which made Job's heart faint (Job 23)!

Job asked Bildad who could understand the thunder of God's power (Job 26)? He wished he were in the days of old when God watched over him and his children were about him; when the rock poured out streams of oil; when the aged, the princes and the nobles respected him and he helped the poor, the needy and those who mourned (Job 29). Job grieved that they spat in his face, they abhorred him, he hurt constantly, his body burned with fever, and he thought God was persecuting him (Job 30).

Job not only suffered from the loss of his property and his children and from his own misunderstanding, but he also suffered from bad advice and false explanations from his friends Eliphaz, Bildad and Zophar. Eliphaz said that Job was getting what he deserved (Job 4:6-9; 5). In his second speech, Eliphaz accused Job of being crafty and condemning himself. "What is man, that he could be pure?" You are not pure and cannot stand against God, he said (Job 15:14). In his third speech, Eliphaz said that there is no end to Job's iniquities. He even listed several sins that Job had omitted and admonished him to receive God's word in his heart and to put away unrighteousness. Then the Almighty would be his treasure, and he would be lifted up (Job 22).

Bildad agreed that God would not punish Job without cause (Job 8). Job must still be impure and unrighteous, or God would answer him with prosperity. God would not cast away a perfect man but would fill Job's mouth with laughter and his lips with shouts of joy, said Bildad. In his second speech, Bildad told Job that he expected too much. The light of the wicked shall be snuffed out. He shall have neither sons nor grandsons, said Bildad (Job 18). In his third speech, Bildad made two points: God is extremely powerful and just, and man cannot be pure in His sight (Job 25). So Job should repent.

Zophar piled on the criticism by saying that God had forgotten some of Job's sins. He admonished Job to put away his sin and then he could lift up his hands without shame and fear and his misery would be behind him (Job 11; 20).

Some harmful advice also came from Elihu, a younger man, because he thought Job justified himself rather than God. Angry at Job for what he had said, Elihu pointed out that God is greater than man, a fact Job already knew, and that God gives to a man what he deserves, that Job spoke without wisdom and was rebellious against God (Job 33-34).

After all this, Jehovah answered Job by asking him a number of unanswerable questions: Where was Job when God laid the foundations of the earth? Who shut up the seas with doors? Had Job ever commanded the morning or shown the dawn its place? Who causes it to rain or gives understanding to the mind (Job 38)? Had Job given the horse his strength or clothed his neck with a flowing mane? Was it by Job's command that the eagle soars and builds a nest on high (Job 39)? Let him who accuses God answer Him (Job 40:2)! Who has first given unto God that he should repay him? Can Job pull in the leviathan (possibly a crocodile) with a fishhook? Can he then stand against God (Job 41)?

The pondering of these questions brought Job a solution (Job 40-42).

He recognized God's place: that He can do all things, that His plans cannot be thwarted! He also came to see that God had spoken of things he did not understand. Job concluded his answer with these words: "My ears had heard of you but now my eyes have seen you. Therefore I despise myself and repent in dust and ashes" (Job 42:5-6).

The result was that Job prayed for his three friends, and God then gave Job twice as much as he had before along with seven sons and three daughters. His family and friends came and rejoiced with him. He lived 140 years and then died being "old and full of years" (Job 42).

Job did not know why he was having to suffer. Neither do we. This makes it more difficult. Yet we can know by faith that God does not intend that our losses result in evil. He wants us to trust Him no matter what and to serve Him faithfully. This Job did although he often did it with great pain, anger and complaining. He was human; so are we.

David's Grief

King David was a man after God's own heart (Acts 13:22), yet he suffered more losses and grieved more than most. He grieved at the loss of King Saul and his sons, especially his friend Jonathan. David and all his men tore their clothes (an expression of protest and horror), mourned, wept and fasted until evening because his friends and their army had fallen by the sword. He then wrote a lament including these lines: "How the mighty have fallen! Saul and Jonathan were loved and gracious, swifter than eagles, and stronger than lions. I grieve for you, Jonathan my brother; you were very dear to me" (2 Samuel 1:19, 23, 16).

David also grieved when Abner was murdered by Joab. He declared that he was innocent of Abner's murder and told Joab and all the people to tear their clothes, put on sackcloth and mourn before Abner. He walked behind the casket and wept aloud as they buried him. All the people also wept (2 Samuel 3). The king then sang this lament:

> Should Abner have died as the lawless die?
> Your hands were not bound,
> your feet were not fettered.
> You fell as one falls before wicked men.
>   (2 Samuel 3:33-34)

All the people wept over him again, and the king praised Abner by saying: "Do you not realize that a prince and a great man has fallen in Israel this day? And today, though I am the anointed king, I am weak" (2 Samuel 3:38-39).

At a later date, David grieved over the death of his baby boy born to Bathsheba. As he anticipated the death, he pleaded with God for the child. He fasted and lay on the ground. The elders of his household tried to get him up from the ground, but he refused either to get up or to eat. On the seventh day of his illness, the boy died. David then got up, washed, put on lotions, changed his clothes and went into the house of the Lord and worshiped. He went to his own house and ate food.

When asked why the difference in his actions, he answered that while the child was alive, he fasted and wept, thinking that the Lord might be gracious to him and let the boy live. But after the child died, there was no need to fast because that would not bring him back. He continued, "I will go to him, but he will not return to me" (2 Samuel 12:23). He then comforted his wife and had sex with her. She gave birth to Solomon, whom the Lord loved (2 Samuel 12).

David was furious when he heard that his son Amnon had raped his daughter Tamar. Absalom, Tamar's brother, waited to get even and then killed his half-brother Amnon. The king and all his servants wept very bitterly. He mourned every day. After three years, he was consoled concerning Amnon's death and longed to go to Absalom (2 Samuel 13).

Later Absalom rebelled against his father, organized an army and tried to overthrow him (2 Samuel 18). David's army caught and killed him. When the king heard of his son's death, he grieved deeply:

> The king was shaken. He went up to the room over
>   the gateway and wept.
> As he went, he said: "O my son Absalom! My son,
>   my son Absalom!
> If only I had died instead of you –
> O Absalom, my son, my son."
>   (2 Samuel 18:33)

As David continued to grieve, he evidently was neglecting his work, and Joab confronted him about it. David had turned victory into mourning, he said. You wish that your army had been defeated and Absalom were still alive, he charged. He then told David that he would lose his army if he continued in such withdrawal and mourning. At first, David continued to cry aloud: "O my son Absalom! O Absalom, my son, my son!" (2 Samuel 19:4). Then, he could see his military commander's point. He went out, encouraged his men, took his seat in the gateway and the people all came before him (2 Samuel 19:1-8). I'm sure he did not feel like going back to work, but he did.

How Jesus Handled Grief

Several illustrations of grief appear in the life of Jesus. He withdrew to a deserted place after hearing that His cousin John the Baptist had been wrongfully executed by Herod (Matthew 14:13). Later that day He fed the crowd and then withdrew a second time to pray (Matthew 14:23).

Centuries before Jesus was born, the prophet Isaiah described Him:

> He was despised and rejected by men,
>   a man of sorrows, and familiar with suffering.
> Like one from whom men hide their faces
>   he was despised, and we esteemed him not.
>
> Surely he took up our infirmities and carried our sorrows,
>   yet we considered him stricken by God,
>   smitten by him, and afflicted.
>
> But he was pierced for our transgressions,
>   he was crushed for our iniquities;
>   the punishment that brought us peace was upon him,
>   and by his wounds we are healed.
>
>   (Isaiah 53:3-5)

Indeed this was the case. Even before Jesus died, He knew what He was to endure. As He faced death, His soul was very sorrowful, even unto death as He asked His Father if it were possible to remove the cup from Him (Mark 14:34-36). During this time, He prayed earnestly, and His sweat became like great drops of blood falling to the ground (Luke 22:44). Yet He did many things to help others to adjust to His death.

• *Jesus talked.* Jesus began to teach His disciples that He must suffer many things, be rejected and killed, and after three days He must rise again from the dead (Mark 8:31). He explained to them that some would mock Him, spit upon Him, scourge Him and finally take His life. But after three days, He would rise again (Mark 10:32-34). Jesus talked, and it is very difficult today to adjust to grief without talking.

• *Jesus cried.* During His life, Jesus offered up prayers of supplications with loud cries and tears to God who was able to save (Hebrews 5:7). Crying today is thought of as positive behavior for those who are grieving. We are to rejoice with those who rejoice, weep with those who weep (Romans 12:15).

• *Jesus lamented.* Jesus said, "My God, my God, why have you forsaken me?" (Matthew 27:46). He was human; He protested; He questioned.

• *Jesus experienced physical symptoms of grief.* When Jesus was in the Garden of Gethsemane, just before His death, His sweat became like great drops of blood falling upon the ground. Yet even during this period of grief, Jesus expressed His faith to God. God heard His prayer and sent an angel to strengthen Him (Luke 22:43-44).

• *Jesus surrendered.* When He was on the cross, when He was overwhelmed, when He questioned, Jesus said, "Father, into your hands I commit my spirit!" (Luke 23:46).

• *Jesus forgave others.* Even on the cross, Jesus said of those who put Him there: "Father, forgive them, for they do not know what they are doing" (Luke 23:34). When people are grieving and feel a sense of guilt, they need to remember that forgiveness is possible. If God could forgive those who took the life of Jesus, He can forgive you.

• *Jesus accepted hostile feelings.* When Mary and Martha were upset because Jesus did not come in time to save their brother Lazarus, He did not get upset with them but responded with gentleness and kindness. He understood their emotional state of mind and was able to comfort them (John 11:11-37). He encouraged them by telling them that their brother would rise again.

• *Jesus continued to work.* Even after He knew He was going to die, Jesus continued His activities: praying, teaching, giving hope. When one grieves, a natural inclination is to cease activity. This may be best for a while, but eventually resumption of work is usually the best therapy for us. Jesus is our example in continuing to work.

The apostles returned to their normal activities after the death of Jesus. Simon Peter and the others returned to their fishing (John 21:3). This may be a sign of their giving up the hope of resurrection; yet with the state of their minds at that point, that was the only thing they knew to do. They could not just continue to grieve over the death of Jesus and remain completely inactive. They went back to their activities. In light of the death and resurrection, Paul admonishes us to be steadfast, immovable, always abounding in the work of the Lord, knowing that in the Lord our labor is not in vain (1 Corinthians 15:58).

• *Jesus offered hope.* When people are grieving, they often go through long periods of despair with little hope. We need hope. Every grief group I have conducted has mentioned something about the resurrection from the dead and life beyond the grave. Jesus knew of this need, and He told Mary and Martha that their brother would rise again (John 11:23). Many such passages give hope in the New Testament:

Blessed are those who mourn, for they will be comforted (Matthew 5:4).

Jesus answered, "Everyone who drinks this water will be thirsty again, but whoever drinks the water I give him will never thirst. Indeed, the water I give him will become in him a spring of water welling up to eternal life" (John 4:13-14).

I have told you these things, so that in me you may have peace. In this world you will have trouble. But take heart! I have overcome the world"(John 16:33).

Peace I leave with you; my peace I give you. I do not give to you as the world gives. Do not let your hearts be troubled and do not be afraid"(John 14:27).

• *Jesus adjusted to reality.* Jesus was willing to accept God's will for His life. He placed His life into the hands of God.

Jesus not only grieved Himself, but He also comforted those who were grieving. Perhaps the best illustration of this is His work with Mary and Martha, sisters of Lazarus (John 11). They had called for Jesus because Lazarus was sick. He deliberately waited so He would arrive after Lazarus died. He could then demonstrate the power of God at work in Him. However, the effect upon Mary and Martha was that they were upset with Him when He arrived. If He had been there, they believed that their brother would not have died. Why did He take so long? He accepted their apparent anger and cried with them. "Jesus wept" is not only the shortest verse in the Bible but one of the most meaningful (John 11:35). We know by this verse that Jesus cares. Jesus saw Mary and Martha weeping and was deeply moved in spirit and troubled (John 11:33-34). He knew their sorrow. He cared. He cried with them.

When we summarize what Jesus did, we see His great concern for us. He tried to minister to the needs of those who grieved. He visited His friends during their grief. He told them that their brother would rise again. Martha understood this in terms of the resurrection on the last day. However, Jesus meant something different because He was the resurrection and the life. Although a person dies, he or she will live again (John 11:25-26). Jesus responded to the sisters' tears by going to the grave of Lazarus. He groaned in Himself as He came to the tomb, a cave. He saw a stone lying against the cave and ordered it to be removed. Martha protested because their brother had been dead for four days. But Jesus lifted up His voice and cried out with a loud voice, "Lazarus, come out!" and he came back to life (John 11:41-44).

Jesus knows our sorrows. Because He has experienced what we experience, He is in touch with our feelings and understands us. It is comforting for me to know that Jesus understands me even when I do not. He cares. He is with us (Matthew 28:20). This is meaningful even when the pain will not go away.

Some Stages of Grief

The biblical examples from Adam and Eve to Jesus give us an insight into how certain biblical characters handled grief. They also give some indication of different stages of grief that are common to most people who lose someone or something they love.

Notice that there were certain periods of grief. The Egyptians mourned over Jacob for 70 days (Genesis 50:3), then Joseph observed a seven-day period of mourning for his father (Genesis 50:10). Israel grieved over the loss of Moses for 30 days, "until the time of weeping and mourning was over" (Deuteronomy 34:8). A few years ago, a widow from Syria in one of my grief recovery groups told us that "in the old country" they observed a 40-day period of intense mourning after the loss of a loved one. This included fasting and refusing to bathe. It's like the whole world stops when we lose someone we love.

Most people experience certain stages of grief to some extent, depending upon their personalities and the nature of their loss. The stages aren't experienced in an exact linear sequence going neatly from one stage to another never to return to a former stage. People often instead experience several stages at once, move forward a little, then regress, then move forward again. Special times and occasions resurface issues and feelings that have to be worked through again. Yet progress usually happens, and life continues in a meaningful, though painful, way.

Several years ago, I attended a workshop by Elizabeth Kübler-Ross on grief. In this workshop and in her writings, she outlined five stages of grief that are experienced by those who are facing their own death: denial and isolation, anger, bargaining, depression and acceptance.[1] These can be applied also to the grief of survivors.

Each author has his or her own interpretation of the stages of grief. Judy Tatelbaum lists three stages: shock, suffering and disorganization, and aftershocks and reorganization.[2] Harold Bauman lists six: shock, numbness, fantasy and guilt, release of grief, painful memories and learning.[3] Catherine Sanders mentions shock, awareness of loss, withdrawal, healing and renewal.[4] Robert Bailey adds such stages as expressed emotions, hope, and readjustment;[5] Robert St. Clair, such stages as bodily distress, guilt, hostility, resistance to life as usual and reality.[6] Granger Westberg lists these 10 stages: shock, emotional release, depression and loneliness, physical symptoms of distress, panic, guilt, anger and resentment, resistance of the norm, hope and affirmation of reality.[7] In my previous book, I mention 10 stages of grief: shock, lamentation, withdrawal, frustration, panic, depression, detachment, adaptation, reinvestment and growth.[8] In an earlier work, I used a shorter list of three: shock, suffering and recovery.[9]

Remember when you think of stages not to think of any one emotion as experienced alone but rather as a dominant part of a theme. No stage is sufficiently comprehensive to contain the complexity of human emotions that are interacting at any given moment. Remember also that stages often happen simultaneously and out of order. I have never seen a list of stages, including my own list, that adequately describes the grief process for all individuals. Such lists indicate the approximate path of many who grieve, and it may help some to know that their similar grief is normal and there is life beyond grief. With this in mind, let me share my latest thinking about stages of grief.

Shock and Denial

I remember Larry, a 7-year-old boy who was told that his dad had been killed in an accident. He took off running and went into the woods. He refused to believe it and would not go to the funeral home nor to the funeral. Lori's husband, age 28, was killed in a motorcycle accident. She was "stunned" for weeks and "could not believe it even after the funeral." Once, she told me, when she approached a motorcycle, she speeded up in her car, caught up with him and looked over to see if he was her husband.

During this stage you feel numb, and your actions are mechanical. You put things up and forget where you put them. You find it hard to focus, to concentrate or to make decisions. Clara told me that she did not remember a word the minister said at her son's funeral. "I was just in a daze." When I asked my friend Willene, who had lost her only child in a car accident at age 20, what helped her, she replied, "Nothing, at first. I couldn't remember anything I had read. I just couldn't focus. It was like there was a big hole in my heart and nobody right then could fill it."

This stage seems to have a survival function. You hurt so much that your system is overloaded and can't stand the pain; so God gives you numbness and denial that puts the pain on hold for a while. Twenty years later, for example, Willene said that time does help as well as strength from God and from friends at church. When she was at her worst moments, she said that she remembered a little poem about Jesus being by her side "every live long day" that helped as she continually said it to herself.

Anger and Guilt

In the last grief support group I led, eight of 10 were stuck in their anger. The anger spreads all over the place to doctors, nurses, hospitals, family who were inattentive to needs, others who still have their loved ones, sometimes even to the deceased and to God as well. The laments in the Bible in the psalms and in the book of Job are full of anger and resentment. Tom, who had lost his father to cancer, stayed angry at his closest friend for more than a year because he did not call him and offer emotional support. His friend said that he was very supportive in his heart but didn't call because he didn't know what to say and was afraid he would make it worse.

Anger is closely related to jealousy, a word that I have heard often lately from those who grieve. Jennie was jealous of her friend because she still had her mother after Jennie's mother had died. Sherry had lost her baby at birth and was jealous and angry at other mothers with babies, often bursting into tears and running out of church, restaurants or other locations when a mother with a baby walked in.

I felt some sense of guilt because I was the only child of eight to be absent when my mother died. She had been in a coma for some nine days. I left to go back to work in Memphis. They called me that night to say that Mom had died. I wished I had stayed there another day, but I know now that Mom would have understood. She would have wanted me to take care of my responsibilities; and, of course, there was no way we could have known when she would die. I said goodbye before I left. I'm not sure she heard me because she was in a coma. Perhaps she did.

Shirley felt guilty because she did not take her daughter to another hospital. The doctors had all told her there was nothing anyone could do. Shirley asked if there was another test that could be given. The doctor told her that there was such a test at another hospital but that it would do no good for her daughter to be examined further. Shirley left her 12-year-old daughter at the hospital, and she died that night. She kept saying to herself that she should have taken her to the other hospital. She was a bad mother. I asked her how she would have felt if she had taken her daughter to the other hospital and she had died. She replied that she would be saying that she should not have moved her and that she was a bad

Mom. That's not being fair to yourself, but that's how we feel sometimes in the depths of our grief. We're angry, we're jealous and we're guilty. Other emotions are also present, but these predominate at times.

Suffering and Withdrawal

Of course, one suffers and may withdraw when grieving. You hurt, feel dejected and sad, yet it gets worse before it gets better. You lose interest in just about everything; you are inactive; you cry; you feel about as low as you can get. There may be a change in self-image, in work and social habits and in your identity. Even your sex life is affected. You may avoid referring to your deceased loved one and stay very much in control, yet grief cannot be controlled. It brings on additional illnesses, personality changes and social maladjustments. To control anger, you may repress it, and then it controls you.[10]

You may also experience hallucinations, a loss of warmth toward other people, a concentration on your relationship with the deceased, personal aggression toward specific persons, simplification of complex facts, attempts to resurrect the deceased and going to pieces in order to stay together. You may realize that you can't bring them back; so you'll die yourself.

Mainly I think of this stage as the center of the grief process – just hurting. There is pain, and it seems to never go away. Beverly, who lost her 18-year-old son a week before he was to graduate from high school, told me that her heart actually hurt. She thought she was going to have a heart attack. "There was a hole in my heart," she said, "that no one could fill in." She told me later that God filled the hole.

When suffering, you don't feel like being around people. April, a friend of mine, lost her sister at age 26. She was in severe pain from the start and would not participate in visitation with friends and relatives at the funeral home. She said she had rather be alone. She had to cry it out and to reflect in order for additional progress to be made.

Panic

Anxiety and panicky feelings may come at any time during the grief process. They often come early on or a few weeks or months later. Everyone is then gone, and you are alone with your frustrations and fears, responsibilities and feelings of vulnerability and inadequacy. The whole world seems to be on your shoulders, and you can't carry the load. You have such questions as these: How can I go on alone? Who is going to take care of me? How am I going to support myself? Will my other loved ones leave me too? What if I die? Who is going to protect me from the world, which seems to be even more hostile now? What is going to happen to me? There is a sense of vulnerability and despair. This leads to many of the anxiety and panic psychophysiological symptoms I mentioned in Chapter 3 such as difficult respiration, heart palpitations, chest pain, choking sensations, dizziness, feelings of unreality, tightening in the hands or feet, perspiring and trembling or shaking. Such pain is intense and continuing. It is often felt near the heart, yet it may be felt throughout the body. It is difficult to return to normal.

Depression
  If you have lost a beloved child, you will probably not be able to turn the grief around until you are depressed. The same is true if you lose a parent or a spouse in an untimely manner and perhaps other losses as well. When my cousin Litton lost his twin brother, Layton, in a car accident, he hit the bottom. I don't think he came out of his depression completely before he died of a heart attack four years later at age 35. He was sad, he cried often, he hurt deeply, and he felt as though he had died also. He and Layton were almost the same person.
  In grief, there is a going down and a coming up. There is disorganization and reorganization, disequilibrium and equilibrium, deconstruction and reconstruction. There is disintegration and a return to wholeness. There are feelings of sadness, dejection, hopelessness, helplessness, restlessness, dejection, uselessness, loneliness, emptiness, a sense of great loss, passivity, tiredness, agitated sleep, inattention and usually a diminished appetite for all pleasure including sex and food. When depressed, you feel guilty if you catch a glimpse of happiness. You think you are not supposed to be happy.
  When depressed, you relive the past, put your deceased loved one on a pedestal and finally realize that he or she will never return. You have difficulty in accepting this and incorporating it into your cognitive structure and in dealing with the cares of everyday life. Like Elijah, you may feel threatened, withdraw, give up on your purpose for living and may want to die yourself (1 Kings 19).
  During depression, major decisions should usually be postponed until more rational thought is possible. Give yourself time to reflect on where you have been, where you are, and where you are going in the future. Take time to think of others who need you as well. Elijah began to come out of his depression when he realized that God loved

him, that he was not alone in his mission and that he still had important work to do. You do as well.

Remember, when you reach the bottom of depression, there is no way to go but up. Paul was strengthened in his weakness. He realized that God's grace was sufficient for him (2 Corinthians 12). God will help you cope as well.

Adaptation

Nathan, an only child, had lost his father, with whom he had been closely associated all of his life. He lived next door, and they were in business together. At his dad's grave, he said, "I felt like they were lowering me into that grave." He was preoccupied continually for months with his loss. He lived in the past and "had no present or future." "Then," he said, "I'd begun to detach to some extent emotionally from my dad. I realized that I was a different person from him, that I was not in the grave but was still alive. I further realized that my dad wanted me to go on with my life, to keep the business prospering and to be happy. I'd begun to adapt and to turn it around."

Nathan began to talk more freely, to go back to church, even to laugh again. He took care of the business, checking accounts, funeral bills and probated the will. His energy that had been all tied up with his deceased loved one was now released, and he was able to use it to adapt to the present – to move on to the next task. He overcame the negative, accepted reality and began to live again.

This stage is somewhat like Kübler-Ross's stage of acceptance. At this point, you are at peace with yourself and the world and not simply resigned to a state of hopelessness. You reflect on deeper meanings of life and death – reorientation is in process. You are making emotional, cognitive and behavioral adjustments. You begin to fit in again. You don't feel the same as before, but you are okay – doing what you need to do. Actions are not mechanical any more, less forced than they were during suffering, panic and depression and more normal. You are not the same but a different person. You have fully accepted the loss and are affirming your own life again. You can express your feelings, think rationally, communicate effectively and be patient. You realize that God has given you additional life, and you want to live it abundantly.

Growth

I mentioned Tom earlier. He had lost his dad, age 50, to lung cancer. He had shunned his closest friend for over a year because "he never called once to offer sympathy. So I don't want him in my house."

Tom had many negative thoughts about Jim while he was angry and depressed. He, however, began to talk back to these thoughts with such thoughts as these:

TALK BACK

"He cares about me and has for a long time."

"He may not be able to nurture me the way I want, but that does not mean he does not care for me."

"He was always nice to me and to my children."

"He was afraid he would make me feel worse."

"He thought I did not want to talk."

"In the future, he will be there for me."

"I'll look for other signs of friendship."

When you seek, you find; and Tom did find that caring in Jim again. He realized that part of the problem was his anger which he directed at Jim. Because of their maturity and their efforts, they re-established a meaningful friendship. So can you.

At this stage of growth, you begin to reinvest in life, to initiate the positive. You have adjusted to the loss and are ready to return to a meaningful style of life again. You begin to rebuild, to express your feelings, to re-establish old friendships and to make new ones as well. Memories become more friend than foe. You have learned how to say goodbye.

You begin to reinvest in others and to participate in life comfortably and patiently. Grief runs its slow course, and you begin to rebuild. Grief's walls are gradually penetrated, and they begin to crumble. You are now able to affirm life and to reinvest socially and emotionally in other people, in your work and in other activities. Roles are shifted in the family to adjust to the loved one's death. Thoughts and habits change. You find new meaning and new purpose for living as did Elijah many years ago. Your broken world is reconstructed and renewed. God cares. You are still needed. You are able to incorporate death into an ongoing, vibrant faith. You persist.

Growth is a painful process. It's hard to believe that it can come from grief experiences. Of those who finished our grief support groups, 93 percent of the 500 widows and widowers in my research said that they had grown because of their grief experiences. They felt closer to God and more autonomous and capable as persons. They did not let as many little things bother them any more. They had a long-range perspective on life.

Perhaps some illustrations will help you understand the growth stage. A welder welds a broken piece of metal together, and it holds even when other parts of the piece break. Muscle building may result from weight lifting which breaks down muscles. They grow back stronger from being torn down. As I mentioned before, Paul became strong when he was weak (2 Corinthians 12:9). People who grieve often become stronger as well. They are torn down by the loss of loved ones, but they grow stronger in the grief process as they become more mature and more complete. This can happen to you as well.

Factors Affecting Grief Adjustment

Numerous factors affect grief. Some that I have frequently noticed are as follows: the nature of the relationship, the nature of the death, the age of the loved one at the time of death, the emotional and mental health of the griever and the way grief was previously handled. These principles are generally true: the more you love the more you hurt; tragic deaths are more painful;untimely deaths intensify the grief; good emotional and mental health help with the grief process and a history of successful grieving aids the grieving process. However, cumulative grief can be a negative for anyone.

In my follow-up study of our GROW (grief recovery of widowed) groups, I sent questionnaires to 500 widows and widowers an average of five years after their recovery sessions to determine factors that affected their grief recovery. There were 13 statistically significant correlations as follows:

1. More church activities and less grief.
2. More church activities and more social relationships.
3. Losing additional relatives by death and fewer social relationships.
4. Beginning "other activities" and more social relationships.
5. Coming to GROW groups earlier in the grief process and actions that are more normal.
6. Earlier GROW groups and increased level of happiness.
7. Better health and increased happiness.
8. Increased age and decreased sexual problems.
9. Consideration of remarriage and increased sexual adjustment problems.

10. Becoming less religious and fewer sexual adjustment problems.
11. Earlier GROW groups and better feelings about the future.
12. Months widowed with negative feelings about the future.
13. Better finances with positive feelings about the future.[11]

Many factors affect the intensity of grief as well as the grief process. The more you have going against you, the more difficult the grief. Yet most work through their grief slowly and painfully and are able to restructure their lives successfully. You can too.

Abnormal Grief

What I described under stages of grief is considered normal by most grief counselors today. Some strange experiences such as hearing voices of the deceased, seeing deceased relatives, smelling their aftershave lotion or perfume, setting an extra plate for them, talking to them, writing them a letter, or expecting them to return may seem abnormal to you, but they are not. The best definition of abnormal grief is grief that does not progress – grief that is intense and stuck for a prolonged period of time at any stage prior to adaptation. The more common stages of abnormal grief are prolonged anger, guilt, suffering, withdrawal and depression. Other signs are prolonged overactivity, the acquisition of symptoms identical to those of the deceased, a psychosomatic medical illness, prolonged alteration of relationships and work habits and engaging in activities detrimental to self.

Normal grief affects us physically, emotionally, cognitively, behaviorally and spiritually. It cannot be effectively dealt with by the use of drugs, by lashing out at others or by trying to avoid the pain of grief.

If such symptoms persist, I encourage you to seek professional counseling. However, give yourself time. As you know, you can't rush yourself through such pain. Most people take at least a year to work through their grief and adapt. Some take longer.

According to William Rogers, most who grieve have needs such as the following: support from others; emotional emancipation (detachment) from the deceased; acceptance of the pain of bereavement; expression of sorrow and a sense of loss; verbalization of hostility, guilt feelings and memories; formation of new relationships and cultivation of old ones and finding meaning in life.[12] The biblical characters we studied worked through their grief by weeping and mourning, fasting, writing down feelings, dealing with guilt, dressing to express powerful feelings, arranging and attending the funeral, verbally expressing feelings, praying and lying prostrate on the ground. Other grief work included washing and changing clothes, worship, seeking forgiveness, associating with friends, going back to work and expressing hope. Some of these, including fasting or lying on the ground, may not be appropriate for you, but perhaps other activities will be helpful. All of this indicates that it's okay to grieve. Some of God's favorite people did.

Children and Grief

I'd like to make two points concerning children and grief. First, children grieve differently than do adults. They often feel abandoned when a parent dies and wonder if the other parent will leave them as well. They are affected by the change in family structure. They need an outlet for their grief such as play therapy or drawing. They appear normal, then change suddenly, often displaying anger, sadness or irritability. They may be stoic, depressed, do poorly or get into fights at school. They may run away, have difficulty with teachers, stammer, have bad dreams, bite nails, wet the bed, rebel, withdraw or experience role shift difficulties. They usually have questions that need to be answered. They need to be hugged and reassured that their needs will be met. They need to be given honest answers. They cannot be shielded from grief.

Children grieve differently depending on their age. Pre-school children tend to adjust better than older children if their needs are met – a caring parent, security, food and love. They usually forget more readily and bounce back faster.

Elementary school age children probably have the most difficulty with their grief. Concretistic in their thinking, they experience more difficulty with abstract, philosophical, theological ideas. What they see is what they know. It's hard for them to process the idea that their loved one is "in heaven."

Adolescents tend to process grief similar to adults if their needs are adequately met. They are capable of abstract philosophical and theological thinking and can believe that their loved one is "in a better place." This, of course, does not take grief away, but it may help.

You can help children work through their grief by helping than with their grief process rather than trying to protect them from it. Communicate honestly, allow them to mourn, reassure, support, explain death to them as best you can and give attention to their needs even though it's hard to do this since you are grieving also. Explain the funeral service to them and encourage them to say goodbye. Reestablish family structure and help them continue their daily routines. Encourage meaningful rituals such as the following: write messages if they wish to their loved one and attach these messages to balloons and release them at the cemetery. Try to live a meaningful, fulfilling and happy life in front of your children. The most important factor for successful grief work for children is a stable and strong parent. Don't lean on children, but let them lean on you as you lean on God and special friends.

Second, I want to say something to parents who have lost a child. I haven't. I don't know how you feel. Yet I care very much. I've listened to many such parents, and my heart has gone out to them. It must be very difficult for several reasons.

It's unnatural. Children are "not supposed" to die before you do. You may feel helpless and have many "why" questions that no one can answer. You may need to cry or just to sit in silence. You may be physically and emotionally drained. You may "see or hear" your deceased child. It's your way of processing your grief and keeping the memory of your child alive. You may make erratic decisions, change jobs, refuse to visit the child's grave, keep his or her room exactly as it was for years or try to have other children. It's all a normal part of your grief process.

However, if you see your health deteriorating, experience sudden weight change or a change in sleeping habits, please see a medical doctor. Other signs of a need for help include substance abuse, becoming absorbed in your work to avoid grief or regression to an earlier time in your life that inhibits you in your daily functioning. Please rush to a psychiatrist, psychologist or some other qualified professional counselor if you have lost meaning in life and are suicidal. If such feelings persist, you need to reach out for help. Such professionals can help you get through your crisis and give you a chance to regain a meaningful life.

Perhaps in all of this, it will help to remember these two ideas from the Bible. God knows how you feel: He lost His son (John 3:16). I know it doesn't take the pain away, but He knows how you feel. Another thing I thought of when we lost our grandchild early on in the womb was that Jesus loves little children. He took children in His arms and put His hands on them and blessed them (Mark 10:16). Perhaps with King David, you can get some comfort in knowing that although they cannot come to you, you can go to them. That's my hope.

Let me share a thought with married parents who have lost a child. Chances are you will have marital problems during the next year after the death of your child. You may blame yourself or your spouse for being a bad parent, for bad genes or for not seeking proper medical care for the child. There are also gender differences in the way parents grieve which may cause you to blame your spouse for not caring, not understanding or not being there for you. Please be patient. Give it time. You need each other more now than ever.

Working Through Grief

When I am with people who are hurting deeply in their grief, I am reluctant to give suggestions at all. I remember a mother in Booneville, Miss., who had just lost her 22-year-old son to suicide; a 2-year-old boy in Jackson, Tenn., who kept telling me about the big roar of a tornado that blew their house away while they were in a closet, and speaking at the peak-of-the-week service in Searcy, Ark., to over 1,000 university students right after a fellow student had been killed in a car accident. I remember how difficult it was to talk to David and Kevin, our grandsons, about the severe illness and death of their other grandfather. I especially felt challenged when conducting a grief seminar as a follow-up to the school shootings in Jonesboro, Ark., with some 150 persons present. No amount of experience or education prepares me to feel completely adequate in such moments. Yet there must be some helpful wisdom that we can learn and share. Please consider these suggestions.

• If you have just lost a loved one, plan a meaningful funeral – pay tribute, seek comfort from scriptures, and arrange for testimonials from friends and relatives. I wrote a poem about each of my parents and read it at their funerals. My brothers who preach also spoke meaningful messages. Women sometimes participate in such tributes as well as men.

Thank God for His blessings; call upon Him for strength. Think of hope, trust and God's plan for your life. Some funerals include display tables representing the life of the deceased – pictures of different stages of the person's life, awards, samples of their work. A funeral is very private. Do it to meet your needs and provide for an appropriate memorial to your loved one. This is an important part of your grief process including visitation at the funeral home. Try to appreciate the community's efforts to pay tribute and to support you.

• Cry if you wish. Crying is a gift from God to help you work through your grief. Jesus wept (John 11:35). Jesus thus refuted by His tears the idea that big boys don't cry. People who don't cry often have more difficulty working through their grief.

• Talk it out. It usually helps to process your guilt feelings, your anger, and your memories – pleasant as well as unpleasant. It's hard, but it's a way to work through your grief and to move on – and it gets easier.

• Here is an example of talk back to your negative, irrational thinking:

NEGATIVE SELF-TALK	TALK BACK
"I killed my husband."	"Not really. I tried to get him to go to the doctor, but he wouldn't go."
"The doctors killed my wife."	"Not true. She died on the operating table, but she probably would have died anyway. They knew that."
"I was a bad son."	"Not true. I wasn't perfect, but I loved my Dad and did many nice things for him. He knew I loved him."
"I don't think I told my husband I loved him the night he died."	"He knew I loved him. I took care of him in a loving way for 12 years while he was sick."
"God doesn't love me any more.	"Not true. He will never leave me nor forsake me."

• Try to learn from biblical and other examples of grief. The way they handled it may help you hang on and work through your grief.

• Learn typical stages of grief. This may help you to realize that your craziness is normal and to have hope for a new day.

• Force yourself to act better than you feel. Get up. Go back to work, school and church. Cook. Socialize. This is especially important during early stages of your grief. You don't feel like doing anything, but you don't need to sink into that hole.

• Focus on the future – your family, your work, your friends – without your loved one in your life. Don't stay focused on the past, live in the present as best you can and look toward the future.

• If you have lost a child or a spouse, put off major decisions such as where to live for a while. Give yourself time to reflect and to think.

• Consider going to a well-qualified minister for spiritual guidance. This is especially important if the assumptions underlying your faith have been disproven by experience. Discuss your doubts and fears. Pray together.

- See a psychologist or some other well-qualified counselor if you are experiencing prolonged symptoms of abnormal grief.
- Accept help from friends. Remember that Jacob's children tried to comfort him, the Egyptians mourned with Joseph; David's friends tried to comfort him, get him to eat (2 Samuel 3; 12) and to go back to work (2 Samuel 19). Esther sent clothes to Mordecai and talked to King Xerxes (Esther 4-7). Job's friends tried to help. Mary and Martha accepted comforting words and hope from Jesus (John 11). God comforts us that we might comfort others (2 Corinthians 1:3-10).
- Do something constructive in memory of your loved one. I know people who have put out a memorial garden, planted a tree and given money to a good cause. Willene and Earl Priest left a significant amount of money in their will to establish a ministerial scholarship in honor of their only child, a son who was killed in a car accident at age 20. They had thought they would preach the gospel through him but had to change their plan when he died. What a meaningful thing to do!
- Try to overlook insensitive things people say to you. They probably mean well.
- Save some of your favorite sympathy cards and read them again and again. The poetry as well as the notes from friends can be uplifting for months.
- Develop a plan for holidays. Invite someone over, go to someone's house, discuss pleasant memories and reflect on the theological meaning of the holiday. Focus on what you need to do right now.
- Read a good book. Several I have mentioned in this book might be a good starting place.
- Realize that a significant loss changes you. That's why I have tried to avoid the word recovery. You recover, but you never return to the way you were. You change. You learn. You may even grow. Yet you will still miss your loved ones, even yearn for them, feel lonely and grieve at times even years later. That's okay. It's your way of working through your grief toward a new life.
- Serve others. Try to get your mind off the past, off yourself and do something to help someone else. Many grievers have told me that this helped them.
- Make a list of meaningful scriptures. Here are a few psalms that comfort and strengthen me: Psalms 62:1-2; 63:7-8; 68:19; 71:20-21; 73:26; 86:7; 86:15; 91:4; 94:18-19; 100:5.
- Lean on God. Paige, who lost her teenage sister, said these words helped her when she felt stuck and helpless in her pain.

When your nights are filled with loneliness,
    And your days are dark with discouragement –
When you can't seem to read or pray or do anything else –
    Just sit still and let God love you.

A poem by Maxwell N. Cornelius, which we sometimes sing, has uplifted my friend Betty who lost her son to an unusual disease.

God knows the way, he holds the key,
    He guides us with unerring hand;
Sometimes with tearless eyes we'll see;
    Yes, there, up there, we'll understand.

Reflections

1. Recount some of your grief experiences. What helped you work through your grief?
2. How did various biblical characters deal with their grief?
3. Which do you identify with the most? Why?
4. What are the seven stages of grief I mentioned? Do you see yourself in any of them?
5. What are some common factors that affect grief?
6. What is different about children's grief?
7. How can we help them?
8. Why do grieving parents often have marital problems? What can they do about it?
9. What suggestions for working through grief help you the most?
10. What do discipline, persistence and faith have to do with growing through grief?

CHAPTER ELEVEN

Finding Alternatives to Suicide

The first time I remember anything about suicide was when I was a small boy. Our neighbor had terminal facial cancer that was very painful and disfiguring. He wanted to die but did not want to commit suicide. Instead he begged my Dad to take a brick and hit him over the head and take his life. Dad empathized with him but could not do what he wanted.

I have had suicidal attempts in my extended family; Louise has suicides in her extended family. We had a close friend from church to commit suicide several years ago. She had severe migraine headaches and some hints of paranoia but gave no major signs of suicide to those close to her. She was friendly, unselfish and very affectionate and encouraging to everyone. I always looked forward to seeing her. I enjoyed her warm smile, affectionate hugs and words of encouragement. She shot herself during one of her migraine attacks, leaving a bereaved husband, two boys and a suffering and bewildered extended family.

I have counseled with hundreds of suicidal people both in person and over the phone. I only know of three former clients who committed suicide. Frances, age 35, was very depressed, felt worthless, guilty, and helpless. She grew up "on the wrong side of the tracks." The merchants in town never wanted her family to come into their stores because they never had any money to buy anything and their clothes were always shabby. People like that, she reasoned, "could never amount to anything." Although she was attractive, was married to a good man, had two small children, and was well provided for, she still felt ugly and a "nobody." She quit counseling after five sessions because her husband did not believe in shrinks and thought it was a waste of money. She took poison, which slowly and painfully killed her in four days.

Her husband told me at the funeral that she called him the day she killed herself and told him she could not take it anymore, but he did not think she really meant it. Death to her seemed to be a solution to a miserable life. "I'm just a burden to everyone," she said.

Sarah, age 60, came to see me one time. It was a Friday night and she was miserable. She had embezzled $1 million from the small-town factory where she was a trusted employee and had spent some $200,000 of it. She was depressed, felt extremely guilty and was ashamed of what she had done – just couldn't believe it. She could not face her children, grandchildren and fellow workers with the truth of what she had done. She was extremely depressed and had lost 40 pounds. We talked about a plan: she would call a lawyer and give him the remaining money to return to the company which had gone bankrupt because of her actions. She would talk to her minister about what she had done, seek his spiritual guidance and then face whatever happened. I called her husband in and told him the whole story. He agreed on what had to be done. I recommended that she be admitted to a hospital, telling him that she was suicidal. She refused saying that just being in a hospital would not help and promised us she would not kill herself. He said he would watch her closely.

She followed up on seeing her lawyer and giving him the money. She saw her minister and confessed what she had done at church on Sunday. The church embraced her with hugs and forgiveness. She felt better than she had in months. She went to church again the following Wednesday night with hugs and loving words continuing from everyone.

That night, she stayed awake until her husband dropped off to sleep, got their car and drove to a river bridge. She left the motor running, got out and jumped to her death. The sheriff called me when they recovered her body the next morning. The guilt and shame seemed to be more than she could bear.

Paul, age 65, had just divorced for the fourth time. Each time the pain of rejection and the sense of abandonment increased. When he was 8 years old, his mother divorced his father and abandoned them. His father tried but could not give the children the nourishment they needed. Although he experienced a great deal of success in his career, he felt unlovable and not really worthwhile. The last divorce felt as though "I had fallen down one time too many and could not get back up again," he said. He also had chronic severe back pain and migraine headaches. His son and a few close friends were loving and supportive; he was treated by me for a while and then by two psychiatrists; yet he just did not seem to "have the will to live." Life just seemed too much for him. I genuinely liked all three of these clients and was hurt by their actions. I understand why families of suicidal victims feel guilty and helpless when suicide occurs. Rationally, there should be some way that suicide could be prevented, but suicide is not controlled by rationality. Suicidal people are not thinking straight when they do it. Various problems and severe depression are almost always involved.

I do feel good about being a part of the treatment of several hundred suicidal persons who somehow survived their crises and went on to live happy and productive lives. Dozens attempted suicide but someone got to them in time and their lives were saved. I called the police one time and had them break into an apartment and take a woman who had overdosed to the hospital; they pumped her stomach, she received treatment and is still alive today.

Michelle was 24 and had just lost her boyfriend. She overdosed and was taken to the hospital. I saw her after that. Her reason: "No man will ever love me on a permanent basis. They all dump you." One reason she did it was to hurt him. She said that as she overdosed she was thinking, "When he comes by my casket, he'll be sorry." My reply was, "Yes, but you wouldn't be there to enjoy it." All kinds of irrational thoughts take over when one is suicidal.

Karla was 40 when she took rat poison. She had stolen a large sum of money from her employer and had been arrested when I saw her in counseling. She overdosed three months later and went to a hospital while awaiting sentence for her crime. She was ashamed that she had let her children down as had their father who had abandoned them much earlier. She said that she stole the money "to give my children what other children have."

When I visited her in the hospital, I told her I felt as though I had let her down – that I had not been able to help her. She responded: "You have helped a lot. I have decided I want to live. I'll go to jail and do my time. I'll level with my children and be there for them when I get out of jail. Getting to the bottom of it," she continued, "is the main thing. I'm not worthless as my mother always told me I was. It's not your fault. You did all you could. I guess there are no magical words anybody can say to help. There just didn't seem to be any other way out at the time. You always treated me as though I was worthwhile. I think that helped the most. I've changed my mind now and won't try again."

Suicide is about the eighth leading cause of death in America, depending upon the statistics you check. Official statistics say that one person dies from suicide every 18 minutes, 30,000 people every year, and probably even twice as many as are officially reported. There are some 20 non-fatal attempts for each completed suicide. Of some 30 people who have jumped off the Golden Gate Bridge, the seven who survived said they wished to live as soon as they jumped; they knew immediately that they had made a mistake.

People of all ages are affected. Suicide is the fourth leading cause of death for teenagers: 18 take their own lives each day, 100 each week, 6,500 each year. Yet older people are more likely to commit suicide than younger people. Men succeed about three times more often than women, although women attempt suicide more often than men. Caucasian people are more likely to commit suicide than African-Americans or Asians; Americans more likely than most others in the world.

According to Lukas and Seiden,[1] for every person who commits suicide, seven to 10 people are intimately affected: parents, siblings, children, aunts, uncles, grandparents, grandchildren and close friends. This means that from 200,000 to 600,000 become suicide survivors each year. If those people live another 20 years, it is staggering to imagine that there are some 6 million survivors of suicide in America.

The first and most difficult question we all ask is: Why? What causes people to take their own lives?

Some Causes of Suicide

It's hard to determine the causes of suicide because people and situations are different, and we cannot talk to those who succeed. We don't really know their thinking. The closest we can get is to read suicide notes, remember what they said before they did it and interview people who attempted suicide but survived.

From the friends I mentioned earlier, I would list guilt and shame, trapped feelings, physical illness and pain along with a perceived bleak future, severe depression and a lack of will to live. Previous experiences in the family may contribute as well.

Weisharr lists several cognitive (thinking) risk factors such as hopelessness, problem-solving deficits and few reasons for living. These and other cognitive features may interact with other factors such as stressful life events to pose a more proximate risk.[2]

Other factors include talking about it, giving away property, trouble eating and sleeping, drastic changes in behavior, withdrawal and loss of interest in hobbies and pleasure in general. Some make detailed plans for death including their funeral. Others have attempted suicide before, take unnecessary risks such as drug abuse and high-speed and reckless driving and are preoccupied with death. Some just have numerous things going against them such as recent losses, lack of a support system and an inability to interact meaningfully with others. Pathological grief, chronic illness, anxiety, low self-esteem, anger and a get-even feeling, legal troubles and models of others who have committed suicide may also be causative factors. Such examples seem to plant the idea and also perhaps give permission to do it. That's why highly publicized suicides seem to be followed by other such events.

Nick, age 15, had found his sister Tammy in her bedroom when he came home from school. She had shot herself and there was blood all over the place. She was his best friend and he could not imagine why she could abandon them this way – why she would do such a thing. He and his parents knew that her boyfriend had just broken off with her and that she was depressed, but they still could not understand why she would kill herself.

When I first saw Rick, he had bought a shotgun and kept it loaded in his room. He was depressed, slept very little and had no reason to go on living. He wanted to be with his sister, and the only way he knew to do that was to kill himself. I'm glad to say that he changed his mind and is now happily married.

Biblical Examples

Six examples of suicide are mentioned in the Bible:

• King Saul and his armor-bearer fell on their swords in a trapped situation in battle with the Philistines (1 Samuel 31:4-5).

• Zimri, king in Israel, having plotted against the former king and murdering him, went into the citadel of the royal palace, set it on fire around him, and died "because of the sins he had committed" (1 Kings 16:15-20).

• Ahithophel, entrapped after his advice to David had been rejected, put his house in order and hanged himself (2 Samuel 17:20-23).

• Samson's suicide was unusual. Though a man of God and fighting for a cause, his sins had led him to marry the wrong woman. She betrayed him into the hands of the Philistines, who gouged out his eyes, put him in bronze shackles and set him to grinding in the prison. He regained his strength and pulled down the pillars of the temple, killing himself along with many of his enemies (Judges 16:20-30).

• Judas betrayed Jesus, felt a sense of shame, and went out and hanged himself (Matthew 27).

Five of these had to do with battle, sin and being entrapped. Judas faced shame because he had betrayed Jesus. All of them probably felt, as had countless others, that suicide was the best solution although it wasn't.

Main Causes

To summarize, here is a list of the main causes of suicide:

1. Chronic physical illness.
2. Emotional and mental illness, especially depression and bipolar disorder.
3. Recent losses and pathological grief.
4. A perceived lack of a support system.
5. Guilt and shame.
6. Legal problems.
7. A trapped feeling – suicide is perceived as a solution.
8. An attempt to get even.
9. Doing something dramatic to be noticed, to be somebody.
10. A specific plan to commit suicide along with the means to carry it out.

Whatever reasons are given, they are not good enough to justify the loss of life and the enormous grief and pain that follow. Thus, if you have thoughts of suicide, please consider the following reasons not to do it.

Reasons Not to Commit Suicide

I've seen the pain and the wasted lives caused by suicide. I've also seen hundreds of suicidal people get through their crises and go on to happier, more productive days and years.

• *Suicide is not God's will.* He gave you life for a purpose, and He wants you to live it, not take it. The end of your life will come in due time. When that happens is not your decision. As Job said, "The Lord gives, and the Lord takes away. Praise the name of the Lord" (Job 1:21 EASY-TO-READ VERSION).

• *Suicide hurts so many people.* Your relatives and friends will be devastated if you commit suicide. They may even blame themselves, get depressed and follow in your steps. Suicide is not a solution; it is a cause of additional pain and distress. That's not the best way to leave this world.

• *Suicide is really a cop-out on living.* Life can be a challenge, but it is yours to live in the best way you can. Your life does not have to be easy to be meaningful. You want to encourage others to face their problems and cope with them rather than to give up. The life of Paul was hard, but we are still influenced by his fighting the good fight in the face of persecutions and laying hold on eternal life. That's the example you want to leave (2 Timothy 4:6-8; 2 Corinthians 11).

• *You are God's servant* (Romans 14:4). You do not have the right to take the life of God's servant. Life and death are issues that are in His hands.

• *You are the temple of the Holy Spirit.* You have been bought with a price; therefore, glorify God in your body. Don't destroy it (1 Corinthians 6:18-20).

• *It is unhealthy and abnormal not to care for your own body* (Ephesians 5:29). It is normal and healthy to feed and care for it.

• *Difficulties may make you stronger.* The dove might consider air resistance a problem, but without it the dove can't fly. Paul's thorn in the flesh helped him to grow stronger (2 Corinthians 12:1-9). He ran the race of life with great persistence and faith because he was running for a crown (1 Corinthians 9:24-27). Like James said, you can become more mature as you grow through difficulties (James 1:2-4).

• *God loves you.* He will give you strength to overcome. There is always a way of escape that you might be able to bear your burdens (1 Corinthians 10:13). You can find meaningful fellowship and security in Him and with His people. Hope for a better tomorrow is found in Jesus. You are a person of value, and your life is important. You have a responsibility to live the life that God meant for you to live. Just do the best you can with what you have and where you are. You can feel good about that.

• *There are people who care for you and will help you.* Call someone. You are not alone. Survival is possible though difficult.

• *You are special.* You have a unique contribution that only you can make in life. Make that contribution. Fulfill your role, hold up your head, go on. You'll be glad you did.

I hope these reasons to live will challenge you to go forward. Focus on what you need to do right now, and do it. To accomplish something is very meaningful and good for your self-esteem – and you can feel good about not creating additional grief for those who love you.

Stages of Grief for Survivors of Suicide

I know that some of you have lost friends and loved ones to suicide and that your grief is more complicated and more intense than typical grief at the loss of loved ones. In fact, it's hard to predict what form grief for suicide survivors will take. Some do not have funerals, most do. Some keep it secret to avoid the shame that comes with suicide. Some get angry and feel betrayed. Others are just sad and crushed. My friend Jeanette told me about her favorite nephew, age 22, who killed himself. He had been mentally ill for several years, yet they were shocked to hear that he had shot himself. When Jeanette arrived at her mother's house, she was sad and crushed; her mother was overwhelmed with depression and suffering; her sister was very angry at Brett, this nephew, for doing this to them. Her brother did not come to the funeral. He did not want to be associated with the shameful family event. His father blamed himself for giving him the defective genes that caused the mental illness, and another brother blamed himself for not being there when his brother needed him. As Jeanette related all of this to me 15 years after the funeral, she cried. "It was the most awful thing," she said, that ever happened to them.

I'd like to walk you through the stages of grief I mentioned previously and show you how it often plays out with suicidal survivors. Here is the common trail it follows.

Shock, Denial and Shame

More shock, more denial and more shame are connected with suicide. Even when there has been mental illness for a while and several suicidal attempts, it still is a shock to hear that a loved one has killed himself or herself. It just doesn't make sense. How could they choose to leave those who love them so much? It's irrational and hard to believe. So this sets them up for denial as well as the possibility of shame for the family. Denial in such cases takes the form of denying that the death was a suicide. It was an accident. They didn't intend to do it. Suicide causes cognitive dissonance, and denial is our way out of the dilemma. They didn't deliberately choose to abandon us.

Anger, Guilt and Blame

More anger, guilt and blame are connected with suicide. Anger is sometimes directed at the loved one who committed suicide. How could they do this to us! It's a cruel, non-caring thing to do! Guilt takes the form of things we should have done to prevent the suicide. I was a bad mother, a negligent son or daughter or a thoughtless friend who did not show enough concern. I came up short. I said the wrong thing. It was my fault. Then, when that is not a good solution for us, we blame others: the suicide victim, this parent or that parent, the medical profession, professional counselors when they are involved, even God himself. Each side of the family may blame the other side of the family for defective genes. The blame game goes on and on with no real solution. We are still left with the dilemma of how could such an unloving, irrational thing happen. There must be some rational explanation.

Suffering, Withdrawal and Silence

When all of our efforts to divert attention away from our pain fail, we suffer. We cry and are in intense stress. We continue to demand an answer, which just doesn't seem to be there. We withdraw because of our shame and guilt, and we are silent. In fact, silence is one of the unique enemies of working through grief for suicide survivors. We don't want to play the blame game and feel the guilt and shame, so we remain silent. Suicide survivors sometimes go for years with the understood agreement that "we just don't talk about that." Progress is thus impeded.

Panic and Fears

The silence increases the load that we carry and makes it more likely that our bodies will react in a panicky way – fast heartbeat, headaches, choking sensations and other psychophysiological reactions that I mentioned previously. We fear facing people with our shame and especially on the possibility that someone else in the family will also commit suicide. Maybe it runs in the family because of genetics. Or maybe since one did it that such an act will give permission for others to follow in their steps. All of this increases our anxiety symptoms.

Depression and Suicidal Ideation

Depression for suicide survivors is usually more intense and more prolonged than in the case of ordinary grief. Suicide adds to the feelings of sadness, hopelessness and helplessness. You feel abandoned and extremely sad. The worst scenario is that you may feel suicidal yourself. It may seem like a solution to all of your pain, but it isn't. It has a snowball effect on your family's grief.

Adaptation

When you have hit the bottom, you need to turn it around. Learn to think differently, feel differently, and act differently. It is wrong but not shameful. It was not your fault. There are so many possible causes that you do not need to blame anyone. Depression and a chemical imbalance, for example, are often connected with suicide. Those who commit suicide were not thinking straight – were not themselves. Try to get past the guilt, the anger and the blame and begin to turn it around for yourself and your family. Don't add to the pain – bring solutions.

Helping Survivors of Suicide

These suggestions have helped other survivors of suicide:

• *Reach out to others for help.* Call a friend. Go see a well-qualified minister. Talk to a professional grief counselor. Get a medical checkup. Process your pain.

• *Break the silence agreement in the family.* That inhibits the processing of guilt, blame and fears, which can cause so many problems. Talk it out. Be gentle with yourself and others. Don't blame anybody. It's not that simple.

• *Have a meaningful funeral.* Express your pain and confusion. Admit that you can't answer the why question. Accept the love and support of your family and community. They are sad too.

• *Learn to lean upon God.* Fear no evil because He is with you (Psalm 23:4). Remember that Jesus is with you always, and He lost one of His apostles to suicide (Matthew 27-28). Let your requests be made known to God and His peace will guard your heart (Philippians 4:6-7). Remember that you may be perplexed but not unto despair, pursued but not forsaken, struck down, but not destroyed (2 Corinthians 4:8-9). With God, you can be renewed day by day (2 Corinthians 4:16-17).

• *Learn to accept pain and disappointment.* This is difficult; but with God's help, you can do it. Moses learned to suffer ill-treatment with the people of God rather than to enjoy the pleasures of sin for a season (Hebrews 11:24-27). Life does not have to be easy to be meaningful.

• *Learn to take one day at a time.* Don't let yesterday or tomorrow ruin your life today. Each day has enough trouble of its own. So don't worry about tomorrow (Matthew 6:34).

• *Live for a purpose and your life will be meaningful.* Victor Frankl said that the ones who survived the Nazi concentration camps were the ones who had a purpose that enabled them to keep their sanity in a crazy world.[3] What God made was and still is good. Life is worth living.

• *Clarify problems that you have.* Do you have medical problems, psychiatric, situational or other problems that need to be addressed? If so, get help and work on them one at a time.

• *When you feel stuck, think outside of the box.* Look at alternatives. Make good decisions and then carry them out. Look at solutions you have made in the past and do it again.

• *Learn to talk back to your negative self-talk.* Play lawyer with yourself. Here is an example of what Betty, whose son committed suicide at age 23, did.

NEGATIVE SELF TALK	TALK BACK
"I must have done something wrong."	"Not true. Nobody is perfect, but I was a good mother."
"I gave him defective genes."	"I don't know this. And, if I did, I couldn't help it."
"I must have said something that triggered it."	"I don't think so. It's not that simple. He had been ill for some time."
"I should have known that he was in danger. I should have taken him to the hospital."	"I did take him for medical treatment many times. I did what I could. We did what they suggested."
"We were very close. How could he do this to me?"	"He didn't do it to hurt me; he was ill."
"My family must be crazy."	"We're not crazy. What people think is their problem. It's out of my hands."
"My love wasn't enough. I failed my son."	"Love can't make someone mentally healthy. I loved him deeply and I feel good about that."
"This will happen to my other children too."	"Why borrow trouble? They seem to be doing okay."
"Everything is out of control."	"Not true. I'll control what I can, and leave the rest to God."
"I wish I could just die, too."	"That would be no real solution. My son would not want that."
"He didn't really mean to do it."	"I'd like to think that, but the evidence shows that he did. He was ill – not thinking straight."
"I can't go on living."	"Not true. It will be painful, but it's my lot in life. I'll do the best I can with whatever life God gives me. He'll help me cope" (Philippians 4:13).

• *Learn to help others.* Because of your experiences, you can be of help to others who are suffering in similar ways.

• *Learn to enjoy the little things around you.* I look for the sun, God's light, through my bathroom window every morning. It reminds me that He is still there: still warming, energizing and giving life to us all. Then, I think along with the psalmist: "This is the day the Lord has made; let us rejoice and be glad in it" (Psalm 118:24).

If you are suicidal, please consider what I have said. I care about you. Please reach out for help. If you are grieving because of a suicide (see Appendix A), please let go of your guilt, your anger and blame. Please learn to talk about it and cry about it. It may take a while, but you can successfully work through your grief and live a useful life.

Reflections

1. What are some common causes of suicide? What do you think is the most common cause?

2. List the common signs of suicide. Which would scare you the most?

3. What are some good reasons not to commit suicide?

4. What scriptures would you use to encourage someone not to commit suicide but to live life to the fullest?

5. What are some typical reactions to suicide?

6. What are some stages of grief for suicide survivors?

7. What is different about these stages and normal grief?

8. If you are grieving right now, what is the next step you need to take?

9. What is the difference between passive euthanasia (letting nature take its course) and active euthanasia (doctor-assisted suicide)?

10. What do discipline, persistence and faith have to do with suicide and grieving as a suicide survivor?

CHAPTER TWELVE

Overcoming Divorce

Some of you are in troubled marriages and are considering divorce.
I hope to say something in this chapter to help you try harder. Some
of you have already divorced. I hope to encourage you to overcome divorce and rebuild your life into something meaningful. I want
to give special emphasis to children of divorce so that they don't get
lost in the shuffle.

Statistics on divorce in America are alarming. Over 1 million couples divorce every year – two divorces each minute. About 77 percent of all divorces happen before age 45. About 80 percent of those
who divorce remarry. An alarming 1 million children experience the
divorce of their parents each year. Children born today probably have
a 50 percent chance of living in a single-parent home before they reach
age 18. Why is all of this happening? What can we do to help prevent
divorce and to overcome its devastating effects once it happens?

Some Causes of Divorce

What are some of the causes of divorce? We probably do not know
all of the causes but here are some possibilities:

Marrying the Wrong Person

People marry the wrong person. So many high risk-people get married: people with personality disorders and/or mental illnesses, alcoholics and drug addicts, people who are emotionally immature and people from dysfunctional families. This is not to say that such people
should not seek a marriage partner, but it is to emphasize that they will
need to make greater effort to achieve adequate adjustment in marriage.
Often such effort is not made.

We pick the wrong person to marry because we use an inadequate method in selecting a mate. In our society, choosing a mate is a matter almost completely of romance, good looks and passion. Find an attractive person, go out on a date, park the car, kiss and pet, perhaps "make out" for a while and see what you think. While physical attraction is a vital element in marital love, it is not a complete definition of such love. Sacrificial love, friendship, partnership and affection also help round out the picture. Our method of selecting a mate majors in passion and minors in real love and friendship, in what the Bible says and what the family of origin thinks. Taking such factors into consideration could result in better mate selection. God's will, compatibility, romance, passion, friendship and caring are all important factors in a good marriage.

Dating patterns based on this expanded approach to choosing a mate would start off with a biblical concept of what marriage is all about, with proper guidance from church and family. Thought would be given to physical and spiritual attraction and lead to a gradual buildup in intimacy by dating in many situations over a considerable amount of time. This allows the couple to get to know each other before the center of emotionality completely fuses with and blocks out cognitive and reflective functions when guidance is taken over by the glands. Some expression of physical affection is appropriate at different stages of the dating process leading up to marriage; its full expression is best reserved for marriage itself.

Passion should thus not dominate dating patterns. Learning to communicate about various important considerations, getting acquainted with families of origin, developing social skills in interaction with peer groups, growing spiritually and getting an education are important developmental tasks that can be short-circuited by an early emphasis on passion. Passion is so intense and all-consuming that it usually overrides and short-circuits all other considerations when engaged in prematurely. Sex without love is a modern emphasis - not a biblical one. A total expression of passion with total commitment in marriage is a biblical idea (Genesis 2:24; Proverbs 5:18-19; 1 Corinthians 7:1-5).

It would seem to follow that no love should lead to no expression of passion outside of marriage; some love, some expression of affection; and as affection and love increase, expression of love would increase to a certain appropriate level of such expression before marriage. But such expression of affection should stop far short of intercourse. To get too close to the fire is dangerous. Build relationships in dating. Get into healthy interaction patterns. Respect each other's feelings. Get into habits that will please God and leave you with a clear conscience. Talk about many topics. Discuss numerous questions. Do not marry the wrong person. It is extremely difficult for some people to adjust to each other. Take your time. Find out a great deal about each other before you get too emotionally and romantically involved. Otherwise, you will discover that although love is blind in dating, it recovers its ability to see in marriage; thus, the result may be divorce. Look for someone with similar backgrounds and interests who seems interested in your life, your needs – someone interested in a permanent relationship with you. Christianity is a very important factor to consider. Being of the same convictions gives you a good start.

Both Mates Working

The phenomenon of both mates working outside the home[1] received a big push in World War II as women took jobs in factories to help in the war effort. After the war, many never returned home. Most of us would agree that working outside the home is not sinful for women (Proverbs 31), yet we can see that it brought married people together more and that romance, passion and divorce sometimes followed.

Most Christians do not start out with a plan to commit adultery or to have an affair. Rather, they start out talking to each other, developing friendships, becoming increasingly affectionate and committing emotional adultery with more and more time spent together. Thus, limits are moved a little at a time (talking, holding hands, hugging, a little kiss, passionate kissing, petting and adultery).

Once the process goes all the way, they try to rationalize it away. Husbands are accused of being aloof. Wives are thought to be cold, and it all seems to make so much sense. They say, "I'm happier than I have ever been, and surely God is not against my being happy, is He? If He is, I can't serve a God like that." So they "hide" the affair and leave God out until their conscience gnaws for correction, and it all finally comes out in the open. When it does – when it has to be confessed at church and explained to mates, children, other relatives and friends – it looks ugly. Reality finally must be faced – and it is not easy to do. That is often the scenario.

Women Gaining Financial Independence

Women make their own money and are not as dependent on men as before. A woman's financial dependence upon her husband is not an adequate basis for a happy marriage. There must be more to their relationship than that. This sociological change in women's careers, however, is positively correlated with a sharp increase in divorce rates in America since World War II. Having one's own money makes it easier to leave. Thus, a woman or a man may leave too readily. In fact, the norm for many by the 1980s was to leave if you did not have a good marriage. After all, "He's not the only man in the world! If he doesn't appreciate me, someone else will." Both genders sometimes think this way. So divorce has become commonplace.

Making Money a Priority

More emphasis is placed on money today than on persons, relationships, and spiritual realities. Money takes over. One's worth is measured in terms of money and commodities. Two-career couples face additional stresses and strains on their relationship. They work harder and harder and want more and more. They both work all day long and then have other duties at home that both are too tired to do. Their relationship is strained. Neither spouse has enough time to make a home for them. They spend less and less time together. The family meal all but disappears. They get irritated at each other and may grow apart. Little time and effort may be spent on building the relationship or on spiritual concerns. Other factors become divisive and they often divorce.

Adjusting to Children

Couples do not adjust well after their children are born. It is common knowledge among professional marriage and family therapists that anxiety from a dyad (a couple) often "gets solved" by diverting it into a third party (triangulation into a child). The child then becomes an ally of the parent who drew him or her into the parental struggle. Yet the dyad problem is still unsolved although anxiety from it is diverted into a child. This usually hurts the child and keeps the problem from being solved.

This process often proceeds as follows: Marital problems begin, a child is born, the mother concentrates on the child, the father concentrates on his job, they grow apart, the child or children grow up and leave home, and the parents divorce. One way to look at the situation is that they no longer have anyone to triangle, their problems remain unsolved and they divorce.

Religious and Cultural Changes

Theological and sociological liberalism is a causative factor in the divorce puzzle. Divorce is no longer a significant stigma as it once was. So many are doing it that few are shocked by a divorce announcement. Up close a few people are always shocked, hurt and embarrassed but not the whole community as once was the case. Divorced people no longer wear a big D on their foreheads, and to some extent this is good. No one wants to cause hurting people undue pain. But the lack of a stigma for divorce loosens up divorce possibilities. The restraining social stigma is all but gone.

While sociological changes have diminished the stigma of divorce, theological liberalism has "all but removed its sin." There is not only no-fault divorce but no-guilt divorce as well. As a psychology colleague said to me once, "If you are in a job that doesn't fit you any more, change jobs. If you are in a marriage that doesn't meet your needs, get a new partner."

While counseling with Jane Doe on one occasion, she said that she no longer loved her husband of three months and that she knew one thing for sure, "I will not live with anyone whom I don't love." When I asked her if she could think of any reasons to continue the marriage she said no. I said, "What about the Bible and your vows of 'until death do we part,' isn't that reason to stay together?" She replied, "No. That doesn't bother me at all." A lack of biblical conviction leads to more divorces. Liberalism denies the inspiration of the Bible, makes the text seem irrelevant or explains the text away, thus, paving the way for divorce.

Narcissism

Narcissism (self-centeredness, preoccupation with personal needs and less emphasis on the relationship) leads to divorce. In psychology professions, the 1980s were known as the decade of narcissism. A person with a narcissistic personality disorder exhibits characteristics such as the following: a grandiose sense of self-importance or uniqueness, preoccupation with fantasies of unlimited success, power, brilliance, beauty or ideal love; exhibitionism which requires constant attention and admiration, cool indifference or marked feelings of rage, inferiority, shame, humiliation or emptiness in response to criticism, indifference of others or defect. In addition, such a person would display at least two of the following characteristics of disturbances in interpersonal relationships: entitlement (expectation of special favors without assuming reciprocal responsibilities), interpersonal exploitativeness (taking advantage of others to indulge self), over-idealization and devaluation extremes in relationships and lack of empathy (unable to recognize how others feel).[2]

Few want to nurture anymore. Most seek nurturing and getting "my needs" met. John Doe, for example, had been married for six years and had experienced seven affairs, including a current one in which he was engaged when he and his wife came for marital therapy. Although he was a member of the church, he refused to give up his girlfriend. "She meets my needs better than my wife does," he stated. And as far as commitment to his wife and the possibility of additional affairs in the future were concerned, he said only that he did not know for sure. "You never know what will happen in the future." His needs were paramount, not God's will and not his marital relationship. God owns us: we were bought with a price. Our body was not made for fornication but for God's glorification (1 Corinthian 6:13-20). His wife sued for divorce.

Stress

Excessive stress on marital partners may lead to divorce. The extra work involved in dual careers, preschool, the Scouts, Little League, church, entertainment and social obligations leave both marital partners exhausted. Fatigue takes over, irritations are numerous, tempers flare, someone may be unfaithful and cruel, nobody's needs are being met and divorce often results. With working women, roles need to be renegotiated and proper adjustments made. Schedules need to be simplified with some time left for leisure, rest and the building of the marital bond. Otherwise, in the rat race, people suffer and sometimes break.

In conclusion, none of these reasons have to lead to divorce as many good couples have demonstrated, but they often do. Put them and other such reasons together, and the divorce rate doubles several times as has been the case since the 1940s. Something needs to be done. Divorce causes so much pain for so many people!

Some Consequences of Divorce

Divorce hurts people: the marital partners who divorce, grandparents, the church, friends and especially children. No one escapes unscathed. What evidence is there for such a conclusion? Much from many sources. I have spoken to some five retreats for divorced Christians with an average attendance of more than 100 at each retreat. We never went to bed before midnight. So much pain led to much discussion in small informal groups as well as in formal program situations. Even those who initiated the divorces often expressed deep sorrow over the loss of what could have been. Divorced persons who were put away by their spouses were almost always more devastated than were their mates by divorce. And this was often true years after the divorce; anger, guilt, panic, depression, fatigue, confusion, low self-esteem, feelings of rejection, shame and a sense of failure were still present. Some were still preoccupied with such grief years after the divorce.

These seminar experiences have been reinforced by my counseling experiences as a psychologist, marriage and family therapist, minister and elder for many years. Divorce hurts not only spouses but also children and others. They often feel rejected by the church and sometimes stay in therapy for several years working through their grief, pain and disappointment, as they try to readjust in their single and/or blended family situations following the divorce. Their family structure is broken – a new structure must emerge. Everyone feels the chaos. There are conflicts over roles, anarchy and confusion over new boundaries around and within the nuclear and extended family. And when children are involved, in one sense, no divorce really occurs. Parenting issues, visitation rights and family rituals (graduations, weddings, funerals, socials) keep the divided family in some degree of contact over the years.

The pain continues. Even when the divorce is carried out in a relatively friendly way, when parents do not triangle their children into their adult problems, and when children are not used as weapons against one's ex-spouse, pain is still there. Ex-spouses and children of divorce are often insecure, lonely and empty. One child of divorce described it as "a hole in my heart." Such a hole is hard to fill. Such pain continues for years.

To put it into a more personal perspective, let me give you a few examples. John Doe, age 40, was divorced by his wife who "ran off" with another man. The whole community noticed that "he never smiled again." A 28-year-old woman, Jane Doe, was divorced because her husband "didn't want to be married any more." She became despondent, cried for years, blamed herself, attempted suicide, lost her job and continued to punish herself for 12 years after the divorce. Many children are shuttled back and forth, sometimes on airplanes, between parents. They lose a sense of having a home, a real base of operation. The look on their faces as their parents leave them tells the whole story.

Jim Doe, a client of mine, age 35, brought a tape recording of a telephone conversation between himself and his 3-year-old son to a counseling session. The boy's mother had taken the boy and run off, not leaving a forwarding address. The boy told his dad over the phone, "I miss you. I want to see you." His dad replied, "I want to see you, too, but I don't know where you are." The boy replied, "But I want to see you. I miss you." Something like this sequence was repeated several times, and by that time, I felt the pain of both of them and reached to get my handkerchief. How sad! And this scene is multiplied thousands of times each year throughout our country.

Second Chances, published in 1989, emphasizing the effects of divorce, has shocked the world of psychologists and marriage and family therapists. Authored by two psychologists, Judith Wallerstein and Sandra Blakeslee,[3] it is the most extensive longitudinal study of the consequences of divorce ever published. Its impact has been powerful!

The authors of this extensive study began with a commonly-held assumption of mental health professionals that the effects of divorce are relatively minor and of short duration. They thought that everyone would be relieved of a bad situation, feel better and be well-adjusted by the one-year follow-up time. False! They secured more research money and followed up the 60 divorced couples and their 131 children after five years. They would surely be fully recovered by then! False! More research money and five more years brought similar results! The researchers had difficulty believing what they found. But they reported it, and their book is wet with tears although several stories of good adjustment are a part of the report.[4]

Marital partners suffer from divorce. Research indicates that there are still painful scars from divorce five and 10 years after the breakup – wounds that will not heal. Someone said that obtaining a divorce is like being hit by a big truck. Remarried persons and single again persons often suffer because of the same problems they had in their marriages: depression, irritations with people, passive-aggressive or narcissistic tendencies, low self-esteem and other problems. Women and children are usually drastically poorer after divorce, and men are better off financially.

Wallerstein and Blakeslee found that:
1. Some divorced spouses report a greater degree of happiness in second marriages.
2. Many grow in competence and self-esteem.
3. Recovery is not guaranteed. Feelings such as anger, hurt and humiliation often remain for many years after divorce.

4. Women with young children are especially at risk. Single parenting, financial problems, career pressures and other concerns take their toll. Many feel dead inside.
5. Older men and women feel alone and unhappy. Opportunities for work, play and marriage decline rapidly with age, especially for women.
6. Younger men are often adrift, arrested in their normal development into adult roles as husbands and fathers.
7. Those who remarry often are divorced again, and such failure is often even more devastating because it powerfully reinforces their first failure.[5]

Wallerstein and Blakeslee also found that there were serious consequences for parents and children of divorced families. "Evidently," they said, "the relationship between parents and children grows best in the rich soil of a happy, intact family."[6] Without this nurturing family situation, parent/child relationships can become very fragile and may be easily broken. Specifically, they found that:

• Continued parenting is necessary but much more difficult following divorce. Fathers often become more distant, and about half of them disappear after one year.

• Most divorced parents experience a diminished capacity to parent: less time, less will to discipline, less sensitivity to children and more preoccupation with personal issues of divorce and its aftermath.

• Some children of divorced parents who did well were helped by the example of parents who were able to rebuild their lives after divorce while others were able to turn away from bad examples set by their parents. Those who seemed to do best had parents who were able to cooperate in the task of childrearing. Cooperating grandparents and step-parents also made important contributions.

• Almost half of these children of divorce entered adulthood worried, underachieving, self-deprecating, deprived, troubled, depleted, neglected and sometimes angry.

• Boys had difficulties in school achievements, peer relationships, in handling aggression and in maturing.

• Girls struggled with anxiety and guilt in efforts to seek commitment with young men, which led to multiple relationships, impulsive marriages and early divorces.

• Adolescents reported a strong need for family structure, family protection, clear guidelines and more encouragement from parents. They

felt abandoned and were haunted by inner doubts and uncertainties.
• The divorce experience affected the way children of divorce viewed
themselves and society. Their negative experiences in families in con-
flict were not erased by divorce. Divorce does not rescue the children.
• Half of these children saw their mother or father obtain a second
divorce in the 10-year period after the divorce.
• Half saw their parents remain angry at each other.
• Sixty percent felt rejected by at least one of their parents.
• Very few were helped financially with their college educations,
even though they stayed in contact with their fathers who could afford
to provide such help.
• Many turned out well: compassionate, courageous and competent
young adults.
• Divorce is more devastating for children than for their parents.
• It is very difficult for fathers who move out of the home to sus-
tain a close, meaningful, loving relationship with their children, es-
pecially if one or both parents remarry.
• Some children of divorce are overburdened by the parentification
of children or by serving as a pawn in continued parental battle.
• All children suffer from divorce.[7]
"All families are not alike in the protection they extend children.
Moreover, the voices of our children are not represented in the political arena. Although men and women talk about children, it is hard
for me to believe that they are necessarily talking for children,"
Wallerstein and Blakeslee concluded.[8] Children of divorce often grow
up thinking that love can be transient and commitment temporary. Most
children today live with the fear that their families may come apart as
so many others have.
     Divorce hurts teenagers even more than it hurts young children.
Divorce changes the image they have of their role model at a crucial
time of their emotional and sexual development. These effects are long-
lasting and powerful. Teens may act casual about it, keep busy at school
and in other activities, but this denial as a defense will last only a short
time. They often feel shame, embarrassment, anger, hurt and resentment – deprived of what they thought was theirs to keep. They may act
out their frustrations at school, defy teachers, make cutting remarks to
parents, become grouchy, destroy property or fight and yell at peers.
     They may play the role of peacemaker in order to reunite their par-
ents: cause trouble, get sick or disobey both parents in order to force
them to be together. They may experience pain, sadness and depres-

sion before they see hope at the end of the tunnel. They feel powerless and daydream and are torn in their loyalty between Mom and Dad. They lose interest in everything and may attempt suicide. They work through the stages of shock, denial, bargaining, depression and acceptance of the divorce before they adapt and see hope for the future again. They then may begin to accept their new roles, improve family relations, form new friendships and come to a sense of peace. They no longer blame themselves but adjust to their new financial, social, emotional, community and family situation. Hopefully, they will be loved and supported by both parents and by their extended families.

Children from birth to 4 may regress to a time of greater security. For example, children who have learned to feed themselves may regress and prefer being fed instead.

Children from 5 to 7 may harbor resentment, blame themselves and fear abandonment. They may be sad, have a poor appetite and show signs of muscle weakness and physical exhaustion.

Children 8 to 12 are aware of their parents' tension. They experience anger, confusion, discouragement, pain and resentment. Unresolved issues are carried forward to their teen years.

The only conclusion we can make with all of this data is that divorce hurts – spouses, children and others. Divorce is seldom the answer! Most couples with whom I have counseled were not divorced for physical abuse or adultery, although some were. Most list such problems as lack of communication and intimacy, a lack of affection, financial problems, sexual adjustment problems, family of origin intrusions, religious differences, problems with parenting, personality differences, incompatibility, "power struggles" and dysfunctional family patterns. Such problems are difficult but not impossible to solve. Most marriages are worth saving. Most divorced spouses I have counseled have told me that they wished they had tried harder to preserve their marriage, feeling they moved too fast to get their divorce.

Remember the consequences of divorce. Divorce hurts. Try hard to prevent it.

Saving Your Marriage

Since there are many contributing factors to divorce and many painful consequences, what can be done for those of you who are still married to stop divorce? The following are suggestions designed to help:

Emphasize Strengths

Look for solutions, not just problems; look for strengths, not just weaknesses; look for possibilities, not just impossibilities. Most couples can work out their difficulties. But we must emphasize strengths rather than weaknesses, for we tend to find what we are looking for, and the couple tends to be influenced in their thinking by the questions we ask. Look at the good years you have had together and try for more good years. Look at the hundreds of problems you have solved and solve others. Look at what is different about the times when you were getting along well and repeat what you were doing.

Emphasize what you have going for you and what you like about each other and continue to try. Look for healthy patterns of interaction and repeat them over and over again. A good snowball effect can be self-perpetuating. Quit thinking of divorce as a solution. Usually, it is not. It becomes a part of the problem. Look for alternatives. Seek help. A well-trained professional can sometimes see things more clearly than you can. You may be too emotionally involved to be objective.

Be Faithful

Be loyal to your mate; be faithful. Do not commit adultery (Deuteronomy 5:18; 1 Corinthians 6:9-11). Keep your vows even when it hurts (Psalm 15:1-4). Do what you said you would (Numbers 30:2). Think in terms of a permanent covenant of love, grace, intimacy and empowerment. You cannot sustain a good marriage while having an affair. If you do not want a divorce, be faithful to your mate. Flee youthful lusts (2 Timothy 2:22).

Respect God's Word

Take all of the Bible seriously. Just to stay married isn't enough. Build a good marriage! One Christian man refrained from having affairs but "did not speak to his wife for a whole year." How cruel! John Doe desperately encouraged me to prove to his wife that she could not divorce him after he had hit her in the stomach area causing her to have a miscarriage. He admitted he had not taken the total biblical message seriously and had neglected the weightier matters of the Bible – love, kindness and consideration.

Jesus says to do unto others as we would have them do unto us (Matthew 7:12). Paul says to follow after righteousness, faith, love, peace and purity (2 Timothy 2:22). Walking the walk of Jesus will help you to be a good spouse and help prevent divorce. It will not always stop divorce, but it will usually help. Real conversion to Christ (John 3:5) – letting Jesus live in you (Galatians 2:20) – will make a difference.

Accept what the Bible says about divorce and remarriage: God hates divorce (Malachi 2:16). Divorce was never His wish (Deuteronomy 24:1-4; Genesis 2:24). He allowed it because of the hardness of their hearts, their rebellious nature (Deuteronomy 24:1-4; Matthew 5:32; 19:1-9; Mark 10:2-12; Luke 16:18). He does not authorize the Christian to divorce the non-Christian (1 Corinthians 7:15). Paul does not authorize the non-Christian to leave the Christian. It is wrong for him to do so (Genesis 2:24). He merely speaks to the situation in case the unbeliever leaves.

Love Your Mate

Love needs to be singled out as a biblical principle in marriage. Husbands are to love (sacrificially care for) their wives (Ephesians 5:25). Older women are to teach younger women to love their husbands (Titus 2:2-5). They are to be friends, partners, companions. They are to be romantic, passionate, one flesh (Genesis 2:24; Proverbs 5:18-19). Paul recognized that both husbands and wives have sexual needs. The husband's body belongs to his wife, and her body belongs to him (1 Corinthians 7:1-5). The idea that women have no sexual needs was a Victorian idea and is not biblical.

As God loves us, love your spouse even when he or she does not deserve it. God gradually won Israel over by practicing such covenant love. It's the right thing to do, and it may bring good results for you as well.

Encourage One Another

So many people in troubled marriages are in dysfunctional patterns of criticism. We need to break such patterns and encourage one another. Pat one another on the back. Show appreciation. One day faithful Christians will hear Jesus say, "Well done" (Matthew 25:21). Paul often complimented people to whom he wrote such as Phoebe and others (Romans 16). One man told me that his wife had never expressed any appreciation for him and what he did in their 20 years of marriage. Many wives have expressed similar sentiments about their husbands. How sad. Encourage one another.

Divorce Is Seldom a Solution

Realize that divorce will not solve all of your problems: personality disorders, a bad temper, moodiness, low self-esteem, depression, a lack of interpersonal skills and other problems. If you have such problems, you would probably have them if you were married to someone else. So divorce will not solve them. They will remain, and divorce will create additional problems such as loneliness, guilt, a sense of failure, financial problems, damage to children and others. Let marriage reveal personal weaknesses you need to grow through and proceed toward such confrontation and growth. Otherwise, you may be running from your own problems for the rest of your life. Problems tend to repeat themselves.

Examine Yourself

Try to become a better marital partner yourself. Be more responsive, cooperative, committed, loving, submissive, sharing, complimentary and fun to be with. It will be harder for your mate to leave in such cases. And if he does leave, he will know what he is missing. Jane Doe serves as an example. Her husband complained of her coldness and dominance for 25 years of marriage. She concentrated on the children and was always too tired for him. Finally, he decided to divorce her. She then realized that the marriage was extremely important to her and changed her attitude toward him immediately. She began to cook his favorite food, massage his back and be very passionate. He pushed her back at first but then was gradually won over. I have also seen it work the other way around. Neglectful, abusive and aloof husbands became responsive and attentive and recultivated their wives. It will not always work, but it is worth a try.

There are many causes and consequences of divorce. Divorce is painful. It is wrong. It can be stopped. The key is submission to the reign of God and to the lordship of Jesus Christ in every aspect of our lives. Preventing divorce will not be easy at times even then, but it will be possible and very rewarding.

Yet I know that many of you tried hard to pick the right mate and to stay married but for numerous reasons were not able to do so. This does not mean that you are an outcast and that your life is ruined forever. Your life has been shattered; you have been severely wounded, but you still have a lot of important living to do. You have a mission in life that will pull you forward, but it will require discipline, persistence and faith. Hold your head up and move forward.

When Divorce Happens

Divorce does not happen all at once; it usually happens after years of unhappiness, misery, unmet needs, coldness, separate bedrooms, deteriorating friendship, sharp words, decreased trust, poor communication, different goals, discontinued marital intimacy, physical and psychological abuse and various dysfunctional patterns.

Stages of divorce look somewhat as follows: at least one spouse notices that something is wrong (usually the wife) but does not want to believe it. When blaming something, such as finances or depression or somebody else, does not bring a solution, others also notice the marital problem – both spouses, family and friends. At some point, they may read books or go for counseling. When no improvement comes, one of them moves out (usually the husband). This brings on a disruption in the family system which affects everyone. Co-parenting and custody issues must be solved. A couple who can't get along with each other must get along enough to co-parent and to decide important family issues. Then, new families are formed which frequently include remarriage and step-parents.

It's complicated, but many have been able to regroup and form healthy family units after divorce. Conflicts can cease, and people can learn how to get along, to learn from their experiences and to function well. Neither divorced adults nor their children need be forever crushed by divorce. God still loves you; he is gracious, and you have a lot of living yet to do.

Adjusting to Divorce

By following these suggestions, you can better adjust to living with divorce.

• If you are getting divorced, both of you tell the children ahead of time. Reassure them that it is not their fault and that their needs will be met as well as you can meet them given this marital breakup which you have been unable to avoid.

• Reflect on what happened. What led to the divorce? What part did you play? What did you do right? Wrong?

• Get in touch with your feelings. Are you hurt, dejected, ashamed, depressed, angry, ambivalent, overwhelmed, disillusioned, empty, still enmeshed or completely disengaged? You may also feel sad, lonely or relieved. There may be feelings of optimism, resignation, excitement, curiosity, regret, acceptance, self-confidence, self-worth, wholeness, exhilaration, independence and autonomy. How you feel is influenced by personality variables, time, reasons for the divorce and many other factors.

• Focus on issues you need to address one at a time and questions such as these: finances, child custody, parental visitation, co-parenting without hostility, forgiveness, guilt, love mingled with hate, sexual desires, remarriage, property settlements and adjusting to church and your new family arrangement.

• Try to learn from your mistakes. What did you do to hinder the marriage? How did you fail to be a good partner? What are some personal inadequacies that you need to work on to grow and to keep you from repeating your mistakes?

• Consider counseling. Talk it out. Work through your grief. Process your pain.

• Take an anger management and co-parenting class. Learn how to put your children's needs first. Learn how to be civil when dealing with your former spouse – he or she is still your partner in parenting your children. Formulate a co-parenting plan – include living arrangements and visitation rights.

• Don't use your child to get at your ex-spouse. Don't pump them for information on your ex-spouse. Don't tell them they look just like your ex. They will see this as rejection, which they don't need. This point is extremely important. Consider what is best for your children. Share your hostility with another adult; don't dump your emotional problems on your children. It's not fair to them. They don't need to have to deal with all of that. Those are adult problems that adults, not children, should solve.[9]

• If at all possible, support your children through a good education including college or trade school. Help them prepare for a career. Statistics I have seen indicate that only about 25 percent of fathers contribute to college expenses of their children after a divorce. It's as though they don't need a college education since they are children of divorce. Such fathers tell me that their ex-spouse turns their children against them so much that they get hurt and mad and then distance themselves to maintain sanity. Something needs to change. Somebody needs to mature emotionally and take care of their children's needs.

• Proceed cautiously before you remarry. Work through your grief, your depression and your anger before you get serious with someone else. Otherwise, it's not fair to either of you, and you are likely to repeat your mistakes. If you were attracted to an abusive husband before, you may be so again. If you were attracted to an extremely dependent wife before, you may repeat the mistake. This is where effective counseling can help – you may gain insight into the dynamics of what is going on.

Before you remarry, ask such questions as these: Have I given myself enough time? Have I learned from my former marriage? Do I have
a scriptural right to be remarried (study Deuteronomy 24; Matthew
5:32; 19:1-12; Romans 7; and 1 Corinthians 7, and perhaps talk to a
well-qualified minister)?[10] It is far better to remain single than to be in
a marriage and feel guilty about it or to be married to the wrong person. A person may have a scriptural right to remarry but not be a good
candidate for marriage because of various reasons: personality disorders, emotional/mental illness, previous traumatic experiences, venereal diseases, AIDS, children, finances, poor health, prison, homosexual orientation, emotional immaturity or other reasons. Jesus recognized the fact that not everyone should be married (Matthew 19:12).

• Read some good books on divorce recovery and co-parenting. A
Christian bookstore is a good starting place. Some churches now have
good collections of videos as well as books on these subjects.

• Provide good role models for your children. Effective parents are
vital. Children of divorce who adjust well often give credit not only to
their parents, but also to their grandparents, extended family, sometimes step-parents, Sunday school teachers, ministers, schoolteachers,
coaches and others.

• Give special attention to the self-esteem of your children. The divorce of parents affects children socially, financially, emotionally
and in other ways as well. The children's status may be affected which
affects how they feel about themselves. Let them know that they are
important to you and help them adjust and achieve. Give them shape
and stability. Be the adult in the situation that they desperately need.
Help them deal with loneliness, guilt and responsibilities. Be honest,
firm and kind; set appropriate standards, communicate love, value what
your child can do, help them compensate for their weaknesses, correct
misconceptions, emphasize their strengths, give recognition when they
succeed, encourage peer group activities and teach them the inner beauty of real spirituality.

• Introduce your children to a well-qualified youth minister. They
often have a special interest in children of divorce and develop pro-
grams that are helpful.

• Give yourself time to mourn over the dead marriage, the mistakes,
the loneliness, the isolation, the anxiety and hostility, the sense of failure and the deprivation and loss.

• Give attention to the various aspects of divorce: economic, legal,
co-parental, community, emotional and psychic.[11] Divorce is multi-

faceted. With each area there are unique questions to consider. Under the area of economics, for example, there are issues about finances, debts, child support, houses and other topics as well. Legally, insurance and wills need to be discussed.

• Help build your congregation into a supportive extended family to help support hurting people. The church can encourage meaningful, in-depth relationships, provide spiritual strength and guidance, as well as good role models, and perhaps baby-sitters and other helpers as well. Sixty percent of the women in one study said that support groups were instrumental in obtaining information, emotional support and gauging where they were in the recovery process. They were buoyed by their faith and by their observance of religious practices. The process of letting go and the pursuit of spirituality go hand in hand.[12]

• Plan for an interesting and productive future. Look at the past, learn from mistakes, think things through and plan for your future. Ask such questions as these: Why get stuck in the past? Am I interested in another romance? Am I ready yet? What is my financial situation? Do I need to get a job? What about childcare? What about my children's education? Should I go back to school? There is no reason why a divorced person cannot be happy and productive and live a useful life. Joy and the peace that passes understanding are not limited to married people. Set worthy goals, focus and press forward.

Kaslow lists several "requisite actions and tasks" for divorced people. In the pre-divorce stage, these include confronting one's partner, quarreling, seeking therapy, denial, withdrawal, pretending that all is okay and attempting to win. During divorce, he lists bargaining, screaming, threatening, possibly attempting suicide, separating, filing for legal divorce, considering economic and custody arrangements, grieving and mourning and telling relatives and friends. In the post-divorce stage, his list includes finalizing the divorce, reaching out for new friends, undertaking new activities, stabilizing new lifestyle and daily routine, re-synthesis of identity, completing psychic divorce, seeking a new love object and making commitment to some permanency, becoming comfortable with new lifestyle and friends and helping children accept the finality of their parents' divorce and their continuing relationship with both parents.[13] All of these actions and tasks point to many items that may need to be discussed. Apply God's will in every situation of your lives. This will point you in a wholesome direction.

Illustrations from Families of Divorce

Perhaps it will help you to see some specific illustrations of how all of this plays out in real life. Consider these cases.

Sherman was a church leader who never thought he would consider divorce. He complained that his wife was cold and always whining about something. She let herself go and became more and more unattractive. He became depressed and confided in a female friend at work. She was very empathetic and nurturing as well as attractive. They eventually had an affair; his wife divorced him, and he married the other woman. After some struggle with guilt, they "adjusted and went on" with their lives. His ex-wife is still letting herself go and is depressed. Their son went with his father, and their daughter with her mother. Each child turned against the other parent, and the ex-wife is still bitter 15 years after the divorce. Surely this is not the best way to handle marital problems and divorce! Apply the suggestions in this chapter, and you will likely not end up as they did. Perhaps not every suggestion applies to you, but many will. Just choose which is useful to you.

John Doe, one of my students, told me his story, which is quite different. "I am thankful," he said, "that my parents' divorce came when I was very young. I grew up in two homes, two Christmases, two birthday parties, two Thanksgivings. ... I had it very good. My parents lived their entire divorced lives within 10 miles of each other. I would spend four days a week with Mom and three days a week with Dad. All things considered, it worked out pretty well for me. I believe I had some advantages as a child of divorce, but I always have felt that I would trade any opportunity for the advantages of growing up watching my parents love one another." His was one of the brighter stories I have heard from children of divorce.

Kateland, age 15, reveals in the following poem some of the tug of war that children of divorce often experience.

> I am the product of Two Nations.
> They have blended easily in the past.
> But now, as I come of age,
>> when I begin to live for myself,
>> Two Nations want me,
>> fight for me. Why?
> Two Nations use me for revenge,
>> each giving a pull for a pull,
>> a push for a push.

Two Nations treat me as a pawn,
 a mere toy to entertain.
Both want something, but what?
Two Nations promise they care and
 swear they are the best for me.
How can this possibly be true?
Two Nations, both bombarding me,
 are breaking my defenses.
My walls are crumbling.
Two Nations once joined to make me.
 Now, I will stand alone,
 an island, strong with its own power.

You can see from all of this how important it is to proceed cautiously when you are picking a mate. Consider personality, mental and emotional health, values, families of origin, religion, attraction, friendship and other factors you have in common. Then, do not just try your best to pick a good mate; be a good mate. Practice the principles I have mentioned to improve your marriage. If you divorce, work hard to process the loss and the pain, learn from your mistakes and go on with your life. If you have children, please consider their needs. And remember that God still loves you and will help you overcome your divorce and live a productive and happy life.

Reflections

1. What does the Bible say about divorce?

2. Discuss how fast the divorce rate has risen since 1940 in America?

3. What effect does divorce have on the divorcing couple and their extended families?

4. What effect does it have on the children?

5. Why do some couples adjust well to divorce while others do not?

6. What helps some children adjust well to a divorce by their parents?

7. How can the church help both parents and children?

8. How can divorced parents learn not to dump their emotional baggage on their children?

9. Which suggestions for adjusting to divorce mean the most to you?

10. What do discipline, persistence and faith have to do with overcoming divorce?

CHAPTER THIRTEEN

"The Lord Is My Shepherd"

Psalm 23 is my favorite scripture. I have heard it, known it and loved it for most of my life. I say it often as I am going to sleep at night. It also meant a lot to my mom, Cleo Ann Way Flatt. In a coma the night before she died, she said a line of this Psalm. My brother Don was trying to calm her down by quoting the 23rd Psalm to her. He said, "The Lord is my Shepherd." She said, "I shall not want." When he said, "He makes me to lie down in green pastures," she added these words, "He makes me to lie down peacefully." She then settled down again and died the next day.

The writer of Psalm 23 expresses complete confidence in God's care. God is his shepherd, his host, his guide. He trusts God to take care of him in every situation. God provides green pastures, untroubled waters and rest. He is renewed, his vitality restored. He will be guided into right paths, a healthy course in life. Even in the face of death, he fears no evil, for God is with him. This means continuous blessings, security and joy because he will dwell in the house of the Lord forever.

The psalmist's trusting faith reminds me of my dad as well as my mom. As I mentioned previously, Dad's last words were, "Don't worry. Everything is all right." Perhaps some of this faith came from his mother who, the night before she died, said to Pa Flatt, "I'm going home. Tell the children to follow me." Likewise, Pa Way was extremely confident of his journey to a better world and of God's continuing presence and care beyond the grave.

Louise and I were in a car accident that broke her kneecap in three pieces and did some cartilage damage and injured my back and hip. The wreck was very disorienting. My mind raced. I could feel the sinkhole in Louise's knee. I forgot things for several days that I normally would remember. I made progress emotionally by saying to myself,

"Focus on discipline, persistence and faith." It helped.
I'm optimistic as I look toward the future. My life is meaningful. I
know what abundant life in Jesus is all about. I have gone to sleep several nights while Louise was in the hospital thinking, "God is my refuge
and strength, a very present help in times of trouble." I have visualized
him as my rock, my shepherd, my fortress and my salvation. Somehow,
he gets us through. "The Lord is my shepherd. I shall not want."

Key Shepherd Scriptures

Some key scriptures on the word "shepherd" will help you see how
biblical writers use this metaphor to reveal to us a great deal about God
and His care for us. He is worthy of our trust, which helps us to be persistent and to hold on to our faith. Most often the word "shepherd" is
used in one of three ways.

• Shepherd refers to a person who cares for wandering herds.
Shepherds were expected to show caution, find new pasture and water
and balance all of the flock's activities including rest and travel. They
were to care tirelessly for the helpless sheep and sometimes goats,
including nightly protection of the flock from animals and thieves.

Shepherds were both respected and disrespected. Some were faithful; some were not. They were suspected of dishonesty, despised, avoided and mistreated in other ways as well.

• Shepherd was used to refer to God as the only shepherd of His people, Israel (Genesis 48:15; 49:24; Psalms 23; 28:9; 68:8; 74:1; 77:20;
78:52; 79:13; 80:1; 95:7; 110:3; 121:4; Isaiah 40; 49:9; Jeremiah 23:2;
31:10; 50:19; Ezekiel 34; Micah 4; 7:14). Israel came to know that they
were safe in the care of God their shepherd. Although He maintained
unlimited sovereignty over His flock, He also loved them. They were
His chosen people (Psalms 79:13; 95:7; 100:3; Isaiah 40:11; Jeremiah
13:17; Ezekiel 34:31; Micah 7:14; Zechariah 10:3).

• Shepherd was also used to refer to Jesus, the Messiah, sent from
God as prophesied in the Old Testament (Jeremiah 3:15; 23:4; Ezekiel
34:23; 37:22-24; 12:10). He would gather the lost sheep of the house
of Israel (Matthew 9:36; 10:6; 15:24). He would become the ruler of
Israel and gather His shepherdless flock (Matthew 2:6; 9:36; Mark 6:34).
He would first die for this flock and rise again (Matthew 26:31f; Mark
14:27f – see Zechariah 13:7; Isaiah 53). As the Good Shepherd, He
stands for His people (John 10:1-16). He helps us to be spiritually resilient. As the Chief Shepherd in His church, elders, also called pastors
and bishops, serve under Him to shepherd His flock (Acts 20:17-28;

1 Peter 5:1-5; Ephesians 4:11). Today He seeks to save the lost (Luke 15). After our resurrection, He will gather His flock around His glorious throne and separate the sheep from the goats (Matthew 25:32).

Illustrations of Spiritual Resilience

Thus far I have shared my spiritual journey with you, giving numerous personal testimonies of how discipline, persistence and faith have helped me to survive and at times to thrive. I have also shared many family stories of spiritual resilience. I have also told you the stories of some of my clients whom I admire for their victorious struggles and shared some of my research with you. In all of this, I have applied spiritual resilience to common problems such as guilt, worry and anxiety, fears, depression, sexual temptations, divorce, grief, suicidal thought, and other problems as well. I have not claimed that spiritual resilience is the total answer, but it is an essential ingredient of the answer.

The greatest influences of spiritual resilience on me were my parents, grandparents and brothers and sisters. I was reminded of these spiritual roots in a letter I received from my oldest sister Rose:

> I think our parents were great examples of Christianity. By their lives they showed us how to put first things first (Matthew 6:33). I think of Daddy and his honesty in business dealings, Moma in studying her Bible. At the end of her life, she wanted to be sure everything was all right with everybody. She kept saying "preach it from the mountain tops." Daddy always believed that, whatever the situation, to do whatever you can about it and then leave it to the Lord and not worry about it. Near the end, he realized there was nothing else that could be done to heal him, he was ready to go on to his reward which he had been preparing for all of his life, which he did in a couple of days. I believe that many Christian virtues in my children and grandchildren are there because of the lives our parents lived.

I'd like to share some illustrations of such trusting faith from several special friends who mean much to me (see also Appendix D).

A Statement by Miguel Aguilar

My wife, Michelle Hernandez, and I worked together almost every day as instructors at Baxter Institute School of Preaching in Tegucigalpa, Honduras. We also worked in the administration of the school and were involved in different activities with churches of Christ in Central America, South America, the Caribbean and Mexico. Michelle worked during the 17 years of our marriage, and I have been working there for 20 years.

After being so busy with so many activities, we decided with the help of our sponsors to take a sabbatical to study the Bible at Harding Graduate School of Religion in Memphis, Tenn. We came to Memphis in order to strengthen certain areas such as the Old Testament, its theology and the Hebrew language, where we were weak at Baxter. However, 18 days after we arrived, darkness came into our lives.

On September 13, 1997, at 5 p.m., my wife was declared brain dead. Michelle died tragically without any warning. Her untimely death was a shock to me, and I confess that I was at a loss at first. She was my guiding star and my inspiration. Most importantly, she was my dear wife and my best friend. I really miss her terribly. I am happy to know that she spent her life serving others by giving generously and by teaching Christ to the people by her words, thoughts and deeds. My life has been a drama when we got married, a comedy when we laughed and were happy, and a tragedy when she departed. I was left alone in the mercy of God.

During this period of mourning, terrible things began to happen. In the beginning, I felt like a zombie or a robot because I was out of reality. This time was like a dream or another dimension such as the twilight zone. I had all kinds of pains, aches, diseases and problems that are hard to explain. I felt like Egypt under the 10 terrible plagues. Moreover, I felt as if God had forsaken me, punishing me for my behavior.

More than one year after these happenings, I fell from a chair in my apartment. My left arm and wrist were smashed and crushed. The pain was unbelievable. Up to this day, I still feel the pain although I had surgery. As a result of this accident, I was unable to finish my course work for one class because of the terrible pain and the side effects of the medication. For almost four months, I was unable to care for myself or my daughter. At this time, my younger brother came to help me.

Three months after the accident I got progressively worse because I was extremely sad. I did not want to see the people who supported me – my friends, my family or my fellow Christians. I just wanted to stare at the apartment wall for hours and be left alone. My will power became quite weak at this time. I thought I was going to die because I felt hopeless and worthless. In addition to this, I could not handle my life as before. My thoughts were very negative; I just wanted to disappear and die. At night I could not sleep; I would wake up every night by midnight and be awake all night long. I was very tired all the time. I lost my concentration, and I could not do or remember anything. Sometimes I was very hungry; at other times I lost my appetite. I lost interest in life, and I blamed myself for this misfortune. I had severe headaches, pains and stomach problems. I became anxious and fearful. I did not want to answer the phone or open the door of my apartment. I felt miserable.

One of the things that is helping me to overcome this crisis and misfortune has been my 6-year-old daughter, Anita Michelle, who gave meaning and hope to my life. She reminds me that I need to survive to care for her. Anita suffered a lot because of my illness. However, she was strong and helpful by understanding my weird behavior. I talked to Dr. Allen Black, my New Testament professor at HUGSR, and he counseled me. He suggested things I needed to do to overcome my illness. Now I am starting to do what he told me. Also, Dr. Evertt Huffard and Dr. Bill Flatt encouraged me all the time to think positively, to finish my studies and "hang in there." The rest of the professors, students, staff and Christians prayed for my recovery.

I never was left alone. I was the one who wanted to be alone. A Christian woman who is a registered nurse helped me a lot with Anita and made sure that I took my medicine. She also encouraged me to run and remain active. She helped me greatly with talk therapy. So far, I feel much better because of the medicine, running and the talk therapy with my friend. However, the side effects of the medicine make my mouth dry, my skin has developed a rash, I feel sleepy, sometimes I feel like fainting when I stand up, and my vision is blurred.

In my grief I still talk to Michelle and sometimes I cry. However, I can not hear her answers aloud. I am sure that love never dies, and Anita and I will always remember and love her.

I know that I am not alone. God cares. Others care. I'll keep trying – one step at a time. I'm beginning to feel better, to go to the library, and to look forward to my return to my mission in Honduras. That's what Michelle wanted me to do. My God is helping me to overcome grief, hardship and depression. He takes care of me.

• *My Observations:* I was there when Michelle died. What a beautiful lady she was in every way. What a great faith she had! She told Miguel before she went on to be with the Lord that this was happening to make his faith stronger. I won't argue with her. I just don't always know why terrible things happen. I'll never forget Anita's voice that night as she continually cried, "I want my Mommy." I do know that God cares for all of them and that He is showing it through people, through churches and in other ways as well. As Miguel persists through faith, God will do great things through him.

A Statement from My Brother, Dr. Don Flatt

Carolyn says my greatest book is inside me and dying to come out. It would relate to depression. Here are some thoughts which occurred to me as I meditated on this excellent book.

I have lived with a three-headed monster. I call it my Unholy Trinity, consisting of perfectionism, obsessive-compulsive behavior, and depression. Interestingly enough, the Holy Trinity has often provided me with the strength necessary for winning over this monster. While God represents everything that is good, I have experienced difficulty at times in identifying with the Supreme Being. But I know Him through the indwelling Jesus, who lives inside my heart, and the Holy Spirit constantly supplies that which is lacking in my life.

Throughout my career, I've been faced with a tremendous paradox. I had to have my doctorate, but every time I left my teaching position to return for additional graduate work, I ran into the brick wall of perfectionism ,which demanded I get straight "A's" in every course. This "need" drove me to attempt such unrealistic things as getting up repeatedly at 4 a.m. to produce superior papers or prepare well enough to attract the attention of my professors with the quality of my answers. As I kept pushing without any certainty of making "A's," my obsessive-compulsive nature would rear its ugly head to ensure a proper outcome. The situation usually helped to bring on depression.

Mornings were by far the most impossible time of day. Yet I was trying to answer the alarm clock at an unreasonable hour. Even when I secured "A's" (which was usually the case), reaching this goal never rewarded me with any feeling of security. Instead of feeling great about excelling, I immediately focused on "I wonder if I can get an A the next time." While perfectionism made me miserable, it also drove me to succeed in getting my doctorate at the age of 37.

In fact, perfectionism has been a great motivator toward other accomplishments throughout my career. Immediately after receiving my doctorate, I served eight years as chairman of the history department at our university. Leaving that position to return to full-time teaching, I was driven to spend seven years in researching and writing a 400-page definitive history of the university where I taught for 39 years. My perfectionism drove me to such lengths despite the fact that I had signed all profits over to the university. Perfectionism and having another career drove me for years to get up at 5 o'clock on Sunday mornings to finish preparation of my sermons although usually I received no remuneration. In 1997, I retired from college teaching at the age of 60. I have enjoyed the thrill of being named "Distinguished Professor" both by my students and the university. Talk about perseverance! Both honors came during my final year at the university. I told colleagues and students, "I knew I would learn how to teach if I stayed around long enough."

Here are some things which helped me to succeed:

• *Following recommended therapy.* Although unwilling to cooperate with my therapists at first and playing games with them in efforts to impress them with my progress, I eventually decided they knew best. After selecting dependable therapists, I kept detailed notes on points they made and then made frequent use of them. Upon completing my book, I proudly presented autographed copies to the two therapists who meant the most to me.

• *My "Manna for the Day" each morning.* I made great use of a 30-minute session of meditation and prayer. Later a one-minute "Good News" ministry grew out of this practice. During the 1980s and 1990s, I developed this radio program and used it in eight states and placed it on the World Radio networks.

• *Making personal application of Scripture.* For example, 2 Timothy 1:7 really spoke to me – "For God did not give us a spirit of timidity [fear], but a spirit of power, of love and of self-discipline." I also became convinced that Jesus Christ had already won for me all the perfection I would ever realize on this earth; I had to accept this through faith. Finally, I saw that God could transform my weaknesses into strength (2 Corinthians 12:1-10).

• *Having a dedicated, committed wife.* Carolyn once convinced me of how bad things were when she said in exasperation, "Don, I'd rather you have a mistress than to be controlled by your present condition." On another occasion, I told her that the analyst had said, "If there were an emergency like a plane crash behind the office right now, you'd forget everything else and rush out there to help those people." She replied, "Don, consider me as your emergency." During a third desperate situation, she got my attention when she said, "Don, there's nothing left to do but just leave you for a while." Until that time, she had been my "helpee" instead of my "helper." I now saw that she meant business. It is easy to understand why I dedicated *A Light to the Mountains* to Carolyn, who had been "a light to my life for more than 40 years."

• *Claiming the grace of God.* Claiming the grace of God in my life produced a virtual transformation of my early concepts of religion. For example, I quit dwelling on such passages as "For whoever keeps the whole law and yet stumbles at just one point is guilty of breaking all of it" (James 2:10).

• *Using great literature.* I accumulated a collection of works on religion, psychology and motivation and read from them daily.

• *Making use of music.* I became convinced of what was later called the "Mozart effect" and began listening to music constantly, especially classical music, while writing.

• *Losing myself in others' problems.* I served as a volunteer member of the pastoral care team at our local hospital, which serves a 20-county region in northeastern Kentucky. By the time I finished rounds on some days or nights, I had forgotten my own problems.

• *Throwing off my black robes of judging people.* I resigned as judge and boss of the universe after deciding that God reserved these roles for Himself. After all, He had done well in each position for centuries without any help from me.

• *Discovering that God lives inside the temple of my heart.* Someone gave me a coffee mug with an inscription of Albert Camus' statement, "In the depth of winter, I finally learned that within me there lay an invincible summer." Without sharing Camus' existentialism, I was amazed at what God was accomplishing inside my heart which became His temple the day I was baptized into Christ.

• *Being inspired by examples in history.* For instance, sidelined by depression for three years after his wife's death, Robert Browning penned those immortal words, "Grow old along with me! The best is yet to be." Also, if I had to be stranded on an island with two books, I would select the Bible and Victor Frankl's *Man's Search for Meaning.* How often this book lifted me through my darkest days, primarily because Frankl's words were not "pie in the sky" declarations but had been etched into his very soul through experiences in concentration camps! I greatly benefited from spending seven valuable hours in the Holocaust Museum across from the Washington Monument.

• *Assuming that God is author of all truth*, regardless of where it is found. Things are in the Bible because they are true.

• *Becoming convinced of the power of the human mind.* I had to use this mind at all times in such a manner as to prevent my playing the role of victim. I learned that it is not what happens to us but how we react to what happens that is most important.

• *Learning the value of exercise*, which promotes the movement of endorfins throughout the system. Having jogged for years, I once ran six miles. Later, I began making daily use of the university's Wellness Center, including lifting weights, running on an inside track and making extensive use of the treadmill.

• *Following the principles of Alcoholics Anonymous*, especially EA (Emotions Anonymous) which grew out of AA. Admitting to myself that I would always have certain tendencies. Although I've experienced no difficulty for years with either member of the Unholy Trinity, I realize I'll always be on Nardil to help prevent any reoccurrence of depression.

• *Using hymns and hymnology.* Nothing seems to move me more than the words and music of classical hymns and stories about how they came to be written.

God has indeed worked what seemed impossible in my life. "To God be the glory!"

Inspirational Stories

Since I began this project, I have become aware of other inspirational stories of spiritual resilience, some of which I will share with you as I close out this book. In all of this, I want to get you used to looking for success rather than failure, to God as well as to yourself. The key to success in life is grace plus responsibility. Neither will suffice alone.

• *Jim Bill McInteer* is an outstanding preacher and a successful businessman associated with *21st Century Christian* in Nashville and a long-time board member of Harding University. I always enjoyed hearing him preach, but my admiration has grown even more since his beloved wife, Betty, became afflicted with Alzheimer's disease 13 years ago. You see, Jim Bill has cared for her in a tender, loving and beautiful way. He dresses her, puts on her makeup, and takes her with him almost everywhere he goes.

How has he been able to do this? He mentioned Ephesians 5 and what it means to love your wife. He mentioned encouragement from family and "a world of people who pray for me."

He said that Psalm 23 reminds him of "the magnificence of God's love and the fullness of His grace toward me. God knows us individually and gives us strength." He also mentioned that God was charitable to us in our weaknesses and makes us strong. "We have our tough times, but I know that God loves me and that He is always there."

When I watch how Jim Bill cares for Betty, I say that's what love and being a real man is all about. I see in all of this discipline, persistence and faith.

• *Fred Montgomery*, an African-American, age 82, grew up in Henning, Tenn. The grandchildren of residents who once called him names using racial epithets now call him "mayor." As a child, he spent hours sharecropping with his 11 brothers and sisters. They were poor. They had little time for school due to the work their landowners required of them. When they did attend school, they applied themselves and learned all they could. They had dreams of success. At night, they prayed for their parents and their teachers. Fred did odd jobs to make ends meet. He started his own plumbing business and expanded it beyond Henning. After retirement age, he became curator of the Alex Haley Museum (Haley had been one of his classmates as a boy).

His family had several sad experiences. Two sons drowned in 1962 and in 1978. He was so devastated that he drove his car onto a bridge and tried to drive off the edge, but he just couldn't do it.

"Grown white men," he said, came up and hugged him with tears running down their faces. He learned that white people "cared as well."

When he ran for mayor a few years ago, many thought he was too old, but his experiences had just made him wiser. Respected by all ages, blacks and whites alike, he won, with more votes than his two white opponents combined.

As I heard this story, I looked for some key to his success. I found a strong clue in these lines from him: "I always felt like I would be somebody one day," he said. "No matter how tough things got, I believed I could overcome."

• *Jerri Neilsen*, a medical doctor stationed in Antarctica, discovered a lump in her breast in June but could not leave Antarctica until October because the weather was 58 degrees below zero. Her rescue was dramatic and emotional.

Dr. Neilsen was said to be calm and resolute during these months before her rescue. She treated herself with medical supplies dropped to her in July, performed her own biopsy and began chemotherapy. She also continued to treat other patients, maintaining a sense of normalcy and energy.

How did she do this? One statement from her that caught my attention was: "My spirit is strong."

• *A former client* of mine came by our house for a visit recently. When I first met him he was in a hospital being treated for major depressive disorder and obsessive-compulsive tendencies. He continually felt guilty and second-guessed himself about everything. He was hospitalized three times, went for outpatient counseling for several years and took a great deal of medication, some of which he still takes. He came by to tell me that he had grown as a result of his struggles and that he was a better man because of what he has gone through. He said he always knew that God was there to help him and that he never gave up. His visit made my day.

• *Missy Jenkins*, a beautiful Christian girl, was gunned down at Paducah Heath High School after a prayer meeting. Paralyzed from her chest down, her doctors told her that she would never walk again. Missy chose to look at her paralysis as temporary. She and her twin sister, Mandy, "knew" she would walk again some day. In November 1999, with the help of her newly fitted brace and a walker, she took her first step since December 1, 1997.

What was the key to her progress? She tried and tried and tried. Each week she tries to overcome something. She works out. She goes to the rehab clinic. She withstands pain. She prays. She forgave the boy who shot her. She said she knew that all of her anger would not solve what had happened to her. It would not make anybody better or bring anybody back. The key to her success thus far seems to be her discipline, persistence and faith.

Although Missy can't walk without assistance yet, she believes she will. She is excited about the progress being made to help people like her with spinal cord injuries. She and Mandy graduated from high school in May 2000 and are attending Murray State University in Kentucky. She wants to become a counselor for disabled children. She is thankful for the support she has received through all of this. She lives every day as though it might be her last.

I am uplifted by stories like these. They are a tribute to faith and the human spirit. Some turn against God during times of misfortune; others turn toward Him and rely on Him more. Fanny Crosby, for example, though blind wrote many songs of faith including "Praise Him, Praise Him." Surviving and thriving are a matter of discipline, persistence and faith – grace plus responsibility. "He restores my soul." He cares for you as well.

Reflections

1. What does the shepherd psalm mean to you?

2. What about Psalm 46?

3. Psalm 121?

4. Romans 8?

5. What other scriptures help you in times of need?

6. How does God use doctors, counselors and medicine in his healing process?

7. Think of some struggle you are having and focus on what you can do, what others can do and then ask God to help you grow through your difficulty.

8. What does spiritual growth mean to you?

9. Where are you in your spiritual journey?

10. What do discipline, persistence and faith mean to you?

Growing Through Grief
10 Suggestions That Often Help

1. Talk about it.

2. Cry if you feel like it.

3. Challenge your negative, irrational thinking.

4. Read good books including the Bible, especially the Psalms.

5. Force yourself to get back into circulation. Work.

6. Allow others to help you.

7. Do something constructive in memory of your loved one (scholarship, library books, city park).

8. Be of service to others.

9. Keep a journal. Process your thoughts and feelings.

10. Deepen your relationship with God – church, prayer, Bible readings, relationships.

The Suicidal Call

Persons who call represent a high suicide risk:

• *Establish a relationship.* Talk. Be honest. Empathize, communicate acceptance of the individual, listen carefully; get name, address and phone number.

• *Clarify the problem.* Ask specific questions. Offer tentative hypotheses, check accuracy of your statements, inquire about "obscure" suicidal comments or actions such as giving away possessions or buying a gun.

• *Evaluate suicidal potential.*

1. Demographic data: Age and sex; Lifestyle: job performance, interpersonal relationships, coping strategies.
2. Medical data: insomnia, anorexia, chronic illness, visits to doctors during last six months.
3. Psychiatric data: majority of those who commit suicide have past psychiatric treatment.
4. Situational factors: loss of loved one, anniversary dates, aging, divorce, unemployment.
5. Suicidal plan: Lethality and specificity of the method, details of method, availability of the means.

• *Discuss alternatives and resources.* Individual competencies; other people, places or things that can help; support group, how caller usually handles problems.

• *Make a referral.* Maintain contact, give hope concerning what can be done to help, elicit promises, arrange for transportation to the hospital.

• *Support the decision made.* Reassure caller that he or she is doing the right thing after adequate helping plan has been made.

Stress Worksheet

1. List three of the greatest causes of stress in your everyday environment and what you can do about each.

    a.

    b.

    c.

2. What is the difference between what you say and what you do?
3. How would you rate your physical, emotional and spiritual health? What can you do about it?
4. What spiritual exercises do you observe? Are there others you wish to try?
5. Are you a loner? What can you do about it?
6. Do you take regular physical exercise? What changes, if any, will you now make?
7. Take an inventory of what you eat and drink. What changes do you need to make?
8. How much sleep do you get each night? What changes do you need to make?
9. What are your career ambitions? Are they healthy? What changes would you make?
10. How do you spend your time each week?

	Hours Now	Your Goal
a. Work		
b. Family		
c. Personal Life		
d. Rest at night		
e. Other		

11. Are you insecure? What can you do about it?
12. What do you like about your work?

Interviews

An Interview with Jack and Annie May Lewis

I want to share an interview I had with two close friends. I think their experiences and spiritual insights will be encouraging to you.

Bill: I'm writing a book on Spiritual Resilience, which I define in terms of discipline, persistence and faith. I know you're modest, but I respect you guys a lot and would like your input about hard times, normal grief, and grief following suicide of a loved one. You have been heroes to me.

Annie May: But Bill, we've been given a lot more credit for things than we've ever deserved.

Bill: Looking back at your childhood, can you think of instances in your life when discipline and faith really helped you to get through?

Annie May: Jack, tell about your father losing his farm during the depression and how he persisted.

Jack: It was during the depression. They bought land and then they lost it, but everybody else did too.

Bill: There were a lot of tough times. Annie May said something to me about how you worked so hard to get through college. What all did you do while you were at Abilene to get through college?

Jack: Well, I milked cows (laughter) and graded papers.

Annie May: And he and LeMoyne lived in a room, no stove, no bath.

Jack: We had a hotplate.

Annie May: And they took showers in the gym. I saw that place and I thought, Oh, me!

Jack: Ours had a floor in it. Some of the other kids didn't have a floor!

Bill: How were you able to persist enough to get two doctor's degrees?

Jack: Well, I'd rather study than work (laughter)!

Bill: I know I've seen you over at the office when you'd come in the morning at 8 a.m. and stay until 6, just keep on working. That takes a lot of discipline and persistence.

Annie May: He'd rather study than eat. Now Clyde (Jack's brother) said that Jack would be satisfied with anything. But, I don't know of anybody that worked as hard as Jack did to get an education both at Hebrew Union and at Harvard.

Jack: It was just a matter of studying.

Bill: You still have to make yourself just keep on doing what you've set your mind to do.

Annie May: Well, a friend of ours tells a story that when he and Jack were in Abilene together that he and the other fellows would be going out somewhere, and they'd pass Jack's room and he'd just be studying. He wasn't going out with the fellows, you know, and I would not have gone through what he did to get an education, to just persist.

Bill: He is very persistent.

Annie May: He is, but that's what he wanted to do and of course it set him in good stead, but most people don't look that far ahead.

Bill: It's a matter of a goal. He had a goal, a purpose. Then, he did it.

Annie May: Yes, he did it.

Bill: Can you think of any other stories about Jack along these lines you could tell us about?

Annie May: Well, LeMoyne was his inspiration.

Bill: My parents didn't go beyond the eighth grade. They didn't have an opportunity to do so, but they somehow instilled it in us that education was important.

Annie May: His mother told the children to get an education and nobody can take it away from them.

Bill: I heard that growing up too.

Annie May: Many other things could be taken away tomorrow, but nobody can take away an education.

Bill: One of my chapters, Jack, is going to be on suicide. As a person who has lost a wife to suicide, I thought it might help our readers to know about how it hurts people who are left behind. How did you get through that?

Jack: Work.

Annie May: Well, I've heard him tell people who had just lost a loved one that their salvation would be in work. But that's true in my case as well. I don't say that I did my best work, but I did go back to work after my mother died.

Bill: Do you have any comments you are willing to share on that, Jack?

Jack: Well, you can't change what has happened. It takes discipline.

Bill: It takes a lot of discipline. You realize there's an illness involved.

Annie May: I think the people who do that though have no idea how they hurt people.

Bill: That's what I was thinking.

Annie May: They're sick, you know; they're sick, and they don't think logically.

Bill: Sure. Sure. Their brain is not working right. I know that people who are left behind have a unique feeling – helplessness, sorrow.

Annie May: They wonder what else they could have done.

Bill: Yeah. It's complicated.

Jack: Yes.

Bill: As you think about spiritual maturity, what does that mean to you, Jack?

Jack: I think spirituality should be defined in terms of obedience to the Lord and not in terms of emotion.

Bill: Okay, being Christlike. We have this idea in Scripture that we're born as a babe, you know, there is supposed to be some growth that takes place.

Annie May: Just like Jesus. I want to die to self and become like Jesus. I want to show myself approved unto God.

Bill: That's what Paul was getting at – he died to himself.

Annie May: I wish I could be like Jesus.

Bill: Well, you really are to me.

Annie May: I care too much what people think.

Bill: (Laughs.) It's hard to get past that completely. But both of you always marched to your own drummer mostly. You have persisted and marched in a constructive direction.

Annie May: I'd like to think that we have, but I know we're far from it.

Bill: Psalm 23, the shepherd psalm, has been an encouragement to a lot of people including myself.

Annie May: Also in Ezekiel 34, you have the shepherd idea.

Bill: Shepherd – how does that encourage you as you think about that idea?

Annie May: I think you almost have to go to Israel to appreciate the work of a shepherd. A shepherd doesn't let anybody come between him and his sheep. That's the main purpose of that psalm though. I think it shows the care of God for his people.

Bill: Can you think of some other chapter in the Bible that has meant a lot to you, been a lot of encouragement to you?

Annie May: (Laughs.) The whole book of Psalms. I live for the Psalms.

Bill: He's my refuge, he's my rock, he's my shield, my fortress.

Annie May: Yeah.

Bill: He's my hope.

Annie May: I told my class for years, "No matter what you read if you don't read anything else, you've got to read the Psalms," and I think most of them have tried to do that. I remember Bobbie at church. She couldn't read anything for quite a while and she said, "The first thing I did when I could read was pick up the Psalms and read all 150 of them without stopping.

Bill: Wonderful!

Annie May: But, it's really hard for me to pick out one. It used to be 103rd, but now I think it's 119, but it is really hard for me.

Bill: What is there in that one that speaks to you?

Annie May: The word. The word. I think everything goes back to that. I really think it does and, you know, it's the word that tells us about God, Jesus, the church, everything. It tells about the never failing love of God. And Irene Gatewood said one time in a devotion in Germany how she read the whole 119th Psalm. The women got pretty tired before she finished, but I think it's a wonderful selection myself.

Bill: How about you, Jack?

Jack: Well, I'll admit that I don't read the first nine chapters of 1 Chronicles but, you know, I would have difficulty picking one part above another.

Annie May: One thing, Bill, I think is really comforting, you know, is when you read the 1st chapter of Genesis and you see God's power.

Bill: I was recently studying Philippians the fourth chapter and was uplifted by Paul's emphasis on rejoicing, praying, lack of anxiety, thinking and doing.

Annie May: Yeah, and Romans 12. It's real practical.

Bill: God's going to meet our needs.

Annie May: My Momma and I used to read the Sermon on the Mount every Sunday night and say that this is a good sermon for tonight, we'll read that (laughter), and we read it every Sunday night.

Bill: It's very challenging. Also Paul's statement in Philippians 4 that he had learned to be content in whatever circumstances.

Annie May: You learn it.

Bill: Do you have any thoughts you want to share about how people can learn that? I know you never learn it perfectly, but you get to where maybe not so many things bother you as they did before.

Annie May: Well, I wish I knew a cure for that! I pray, I pray, and I worry. I know the Lord understands.

Bill: He understands. I think people have different temperaments.

Annie May: But, you know, I think in the first place my mother and father were so good, churchgoers and Bible teachers and all this: whatever needed to be done, they were willing to do it. They had the preacher in their home: he would have lunch most of the time with us. And the preacher would stay with us when he came for a protracted meeting, and so I was exposed to all that and just reveled in it. Then when I went to Harding and saw brother Armstrong and Dean Sears, and brother Rhodes and saw the lives they lived – that was marvelous.

Bill: Weren't they a good example of what I'm talking about, spiritual resilience? They had discipline, had persistence, they were people of faith, had goals. Their goals pulled them forward.

Annie May: Absolutely! I remember when Dean Sears finished at the University of Chicago, which is, you know, an outstanding institution, with his major in English and his dissertation on the evil in Shakespeare, and they tried to persuade him to stay and teach there, which was a real honor, but he said, "There is a little college in Arkansas where I am needed, you know."

Bill: He had a purpose there.

Annie May: But I asked him one time. I said, "Dean Sears, did you have to do much correction on your dissertation?" He said, "They didn't ask me to do anything."

Annie May: Jack, do you have any suggestions you think might help explain how to be content in all circumstances?

Jack: Well, I think it just means that if a person thinks he is growing patient he hasn't had anything to bother him, but then problems come.

Bill: One thing I've seen in your life is you have learned to tough it out. Can you think of anything else that has helped you to sort of accept your circumstances?

Jack: I never used the word "content" (laughter).

Bill: That's the word Paul used though (laughs).

Jack: There is something about the word "content."

Bill: One thing I've noticed about you is that you don't keep wanting more and more.

Annie May: In fact, I'd like to get rich!

Bill: You reach a certain level of modest living, and you give the rest to the Lord.

Annie May: I don't think we deserve any credit because we really don't want it.

Bill: I read one time that one way to be content is to decrease how much you want rather than getting more.

Annie May: Right!

Bill: When you think, Jack, of spiritual resilience can you think of people that you think of as being that way?

Jack: Well, I guess we all would say that we don't know very many people that have made the sacrifices that those people Annie May mentioned did. I doubt that teachers today are motivated in the same way. Those people had an ideal.

Annie May: You know brother Armstrong would go out and hold meetings and come back and divide whatever money he got with the teachers. I'm re-reading the book of James A. Harding, and I think every student who enters Harding ought to have read *Eye of Jehovah* and *For Freedom*.

Bill: I've read them.

Annie May: Yeah, I think everybody ought to read them.

Jack: Neither Harding nor Armstrong would have written such books. They were too humble.

Bill: Anything else you would be willing to share on spiritual resilience that might be encouraging to people?

Annie May: My Momma lived with me for almost eight years. I was just so sad, when she died, and I read, "Her Tears are my Salvation." She was so good to me and I went back to work the next week; but I read that first chapter of 2 Samuel over and over. She can't come back, but I can go to her. That was so sweet.

Bill: It puts things in eternal perspective, doesn't it?

Annie May: Yeah. Yeah. But I think we just really can't.

Bill: As you look toward the future, what does faith mean to you?

Annie May: Well, I think it means doing what the Lord said. He'll be with us.

Bill: Like brother E.H. Ijams said on his 87th birthday: hold to God's unchanging hand.

Annie May: You just don't ever turn loose of that, and when I lost Momma and Marty within a year, I wondered how would people bear losses like those without faith? Many I've seen who would have been beaten down by cancer and other illnesses if they hadn't had faith.

Bill: Are there any more comments from you, Jack?

Jack: Well, you don't have sympathy for people who have problems that you don't have.

Bill: You taught 2 Corinthians 4 Sunday morning. When you see the body going down, the spirit can still grow. You become more Christlike which is what spiritual maturity is all about.

Annie May: I was at the beauty shop one time. This woman had everything done that could be done in the beauty shop, and she looked at the woman and said, "Can't you do something else?" (Much laughter.) And I said, "She has done all she can do, but now we really need to work on the inside."

Bill: That's what it's all about, who the person is – whether you're wrinkled or not.

Annie May: Well, I know I've had some good Bible teachers at church and at Harding University. They influenced me a lot. One was L.K. Harding, James Harding's son. He was a wonderful teacher and example to us.

Bill: That's spiritual influence. Both of you had Christian parents, too.

Annie May: My parents, I'm sure Jack's too, believed in Christian education, but they didn't have much education. Momma said she had Latin, and she thought that would take her through the tenth grade. But, they really believed in Christian education.

Bill: It has been a blessing to both of you.

Annie May: Yeah, and your parents did too. I went to Lipscomb the first two years, and I had some wonderful teachers there. Then, I went to Harding where I really belonged.

Bill: I learned from my parents, and it was like that Deuteronomy 6 passage. It wasn't like they sat me down one day and taught me in a class but like when we were out in the field, it was do this, and don't do that. They talked about the church and the Bible. It was a constant kind of thing and, of course, as Jack was talking about a while ago, times have changed and children aren't raised that way any more.

Jack: You were around your father all day, and children may see them 10 minutes a day now.

Bill: They don't interact.

Annie May: I think of Hebrews 11; they were still living by faith when they died.

Bill: Those were spiritually resilient people. They didn't turn back just because they had some opposition.

Annie May: I think even when they didn't understand like Job, they didn't turn loose of their faith.

Bill: He held on even when he didn't understand, and I think that's what faith is all about.

Annie May: Like Paul in Romans 5, "I can rejoice in the hope of the glory of God." I have not reached the place where I can say I am rejoicing in suffering. I can't say that. I haven't really rejoiced, but one day Jack came home from work and I was crying. And he said, "You're doing better, you are," and he's not going to come home and find me like that any other time. I started counting my blessings, and I haven't felt that way in a long time.

Bill: That's great. That's understandable. You've been through a lot. That's what spiritual resilience is all about, reaffirm your faith, confidence, think you're going to be okay.

Annie May: Never did I lose confidence in God but in myself. I thought I was more spiritually mature than that.

Bill: That's a threatening thing when your body feels weak (recovering from a broken hip).

Annie May: But I had been so anxious I think.

Bill: I'm sure Paul felt that way at times.

Annie May: We were overwhelmed with dread when there was nothing to dread. I love Psalm 27. The Lord is stronger than my life. Of whom shall I be afraid?

Bill: I mentioned Don's wife, Carolyn, who is seriously ill with cancer. She says the word that she hangs on to now more than any other is hope. It means a lot to her.

Annie May: I just don't see how people do without the church.

Bill: It gives direction and meaning to our lives. God through the Bible and through his people brings hope and strength in times of trouble – grief, tough times, in all circumstances. Thanks, for your excellent input. I look up to both of you with a great deal of admiration.

An Interview with Earl West

Bill: How has spiritual resilience helped you in your life?

Earl: It's a matter of just staying with the work that you set out to do. I can remember when I was younger that Hugo McCord had me to speak at the old

Brightwood Church in Indianapolis. I worked me up a sermon on Joseph. Practiced it and thought, "My goodness, that isn't any account, and I went out someplace and I timed myself, and I spoke 37 minutes. But when I got up to deliver it, it only went seven minutes, and I was clear out of anything to say" (laughter). So, I don't know anything else to do but to recognize that here is something that is worthwhile, and you just stay with it.

Bill: How many books have you written?

Earl: Well, I've written four on *The Search for the Ancient Order*, one on the *Trials of the Ancient Order*, one on David Lipscomb, one on Ben Franklin, and one on Hugo McCord.

Bill: How do you make yourself keep researching and writing enough to get through that many books?

Earl: Well, it doesn't seem like it's been all that difficult to do, like this one on Hugo. I felt like it needed to be done by somebody, and I usually try to set aside time at home to give to this. I don't expect to get it done in one day, and my wife has been very understanding.

Bill: When I think of spiritual resilience I think of getting through the tough times, and I know Lois, your first wife, died of cancer. Did spiritual resilience help you and Lois get through that?

Earl: Yes. Also, Lois's doctor just sat down and talked to me, but it was too late for Lois.

Bill: What helped you spiritually when you found out the medication was not going to work and there was nothing anybody could do?

Earl: Well, I don't know. Prayer, I think, helps a lot – to pray about the matter and just stick close with her as I tried to do most all the time and I don't know, from a spiritual point of view, I had reached a point ultimately when I knew that there wasn't anything I could do or the doctors could do. It was the night before she died about 2 in the morning. She had the cancer that went to her lungs and she kept looking at me saying, "I can't breathe. I can't breathe." The nurse was there, and she looked over at me with a helpless look on her face. She said, "I'm doing all I can do," and so, that morning about 5 I went home and got back about 8; and when I got back her bed was situated so that it was almost against the door that I was going in. When she heard me walk in she said, "Oh, you're back, you're back." And it's always been a nightmare to me. "Why in the world did I leave?"

Bill: You didn't know.

Earl: I didn't know that she was going to go that soon. She died about 2 in the afternoon.

Bill: It's good that you got back though.

Earl: Oh, yeah

Bill: She wanted you to be there.

Earl: Oh, I did not leave with any intention of being gone but just for a few minutes. I still think of that incident with sadness, that I wish I had stayed.

Bill: I'm just glad that you got back. Obviously she was wanting you to be there, and you were. That is when faith comes in, isn't it when nothing else …

Earl: You just have to know this is the way it's going to be, and there is not much of anything you can do about it. I do think that we did everything we knew to do.

Bill: As you look toward your future, how does spiritual resilience help you?

Earl: Well, I don't know. I have never gone through my life thinking too much about the day when I was going to die or what it would be like. I have lately, not with any remorse or anything like that, but I get to thinking about it when I realize I'm getting nearly eighty now. I know older friends of mine: Hugo McCord is 88 now, and Paul Southern died at 99. But he is not remorseful. I mean you just live and think and try to say, "Well, this is what I want to do," and just wait it out and try to stay busy doing what you think is good to do.

Bill: My last chapter is on Psalm 23 – the Shepherd Psalm – which has encouraged many people over the years. How does this Psalm encourage you?

Earl: Of course, it's a faith-producing Psalm and Brother H. Leo Boles used to study it almost every day. Brother Boles would get up in the morning, and he would read it and ponder. For me, you know, the message is just one of yielding yourself to God and letting God have his way with you in your life.

Bill: It's a matter of faith.

Earl: Yeah, it's a matter of trusting, that it's the right thing to do. Brother Boles used to say that "A lot of times when I wake up in the morning, the first thing that was on my mind was the 23rd Psalm."

Bill: Paul said once that he had learned to be content in all circumstances, and that is a real challenge to me. Do you have some suggestions on how you could learn to do that?

Earl: No, I think that is a hard question. I think that Paul's idea that I'll be content in all situations, that Paul wasn't going to say that here I'm in a situation now that I don't like, but it's okay. I just think he's going to make himself not stew and fret all the time about wishing things were a lot better than they are, and I think most of us can do that. If my financial situation isn't as good as I think it ought to be, I just have to be content with it and see if I can make it any better – adjust myself to it and not worry about it.

Bill: If you had to pick one other chapter in the Bible that means a lot to you and gives you strength and courage, which one would it be?

Earl: Well, probably the eighth chapter of Romans: "All things work together for good to those that love the Lord." I've read verse 28 a lot of times in my lifetime and found it something that helps you build up your faith in the Lord, just know that whatever is going to happen that God is still in control.

Bill: If God be for us who can be against us?

Earl: … who can be against us?

Bill: He gives us the victory through Jesus Christ. That's one of my favorites too. I use the words spiritual maturity in my book. The idea in scripture is that we start out as babes in Christ, and we are to grow to become full-grown people, spiritually mature. What does that mean to you when you think about wanting to be spiritually mature?

Earl: Spiritually mature is the opposite of being upset all the time feeling like, "Well things are not going right." And maturity just means the ability to accept things for what they are and then, as far as your ability goes, to change it and make it into something that will be helpful in your life and the lives of other people. Children get awfully upset all the time about everything that doesn't go right. When they become grown up, then I think their maturity comes out. They don't let so many things throw them but say, "Well, I'm sorry I can't do it, do this job or whatever else it is," but it is simply being able to take what comes along with always being determined what you're going to do is going to be in harmony with his will.

Bill: That makes me think of what I said about my Dad – discipline, persistence, faith, sort of like keep on keeping on – that kind of thing. Even Paul I'm sure had occasions in which it was tough for him when he wasn't real happy about it, but somehow he learned to persist and live a good life though it was tough at times.

Earl: You can turn to Acts 17 and see when Paul was in Athens and saw all these images there, idols to foreign gods. That didn't throw Paul and make him decide he didn't want to be a servant of God. It was the situation that surrounded that was bad, but there was nothing he could do for that except he could still be true to God – realize that he might be able to teach other people who would do the same thing. Now when Paul preached on Mars Hill, there was just one man and one woman who accepted the gospel, and the man, so church history tells us, went on to become a bishop of the church in Athens. I don't know if that's true, but at least that's what the church historians said.

Bill: Well, you never know what's going to happen. You have taught restoration history for years and have told a lot of inspiring stories about people who were spiritual giants, people who were spiritually resilient, had a lot of discipline, persistence, and faith. Does somebody come to your mind, somebody who really survived in tough situations, that has been encouraging to you just to think about it?

Earl: Well, I think that was maybe especially true of [the restoration preacher] Benjamin Franklin. All of his life Franklin had a lot of difficulties that he had to adjust to. On the missionary society controversy, he eventually thought that it was wrong, and he said so, wrote it up in his paper that way, and he got a lot of criticism because of that.

Bill: Yeah.

Earl: And then when the Civil War came on, he didn't believe in it, and didn't want it, of course, but by the same token he simply took criticism for that. Then as he got older, he had sickness of his own. He died in 1878 in Anderson, Ind., at his daughter's home. On the top of his stone marker there is an open Bible in concrete. It's like a pulpit. And so that's the way people thought of him! He's a man who loved to preach the gospel and who was true to it as long as he lived.

Bill: He did what he believed was right.

Earl: He did always the thing that was right and people that knew him were aware of that.

Bill: One other thought I was thinking about as we were talking is that I have read how that a lot of these old time preachers used to go off and leave their wives behind to take care of the place, even do the farm work and take care of the children and that kind of thing. They must have had a lot of spiritual resilience to survive.

Earl: I don't think there is any doubt about it. Women went through an awful lot of great difficulty. James A. Harding was one of them that did that, and I guess his faith was more recognized and remembered by them than any other one that ever was. They would be gone for three or four weeks, but they didn't go away and abandon their family too much. But James A. Harding had the utmost, the most of anybody that I've ever read after, confidence in God's oversight.

Bill: Right.

Earl: And he depended on that. I can remember the story that he told his wife one day. They just had a few dollars, and he said to his wife, "Well, honey, we don't have much money. I think we're going to have to give a little more to the Lord next Sunday." And that was just his attitude, and there were times when he would have to go into a little town and catch a train, and the people gave him maybe a pumpkin, or some corn, or some kind of food to take home with him. I remember on occasions he would be at the railroad station. Somebody would see him and say, "Brother Harding, have you got any money to get home, to buy a railroad ticket?" He'd reach into his pocket, pull out 30 cents or something like that, and he'd say, "Yeah," but they'd say, "You can't go home on that kind of money. It'll take more than that to buy your ticket," and brother Harding said, "Well now that's not my worry. That's the Lord's worry. He told me to go preach and that's what I've done. It's up to him to see that I get home."

Bill: To me, that's spiritual maturity.

Earl: I think he's the grandest person like that that I've ever read after.

Bill: It makes you think of Joseph, "They meant it for evil but God meant it for good," like God has been in this plan all the time, and I can see that in the faith of people like brother Ijams and Dr. West, as they looked toward the future. They had a lot of confidence. I think that's where faith comes in. Do you have any other comments on spiritual resilience you'd be willing to share?

Earl: Well, I don't know of anything right now that would be any different. It's just that I think all of us have to decide just to trust in God and know that he is going to see us through. Sometimes we can get discouraged, which is human, and sometimes we see people do things that offend us, that we don't think they ought to be doing, but if we can just go ahead and try our best to serve God, my feeling is in the end of it all, it works out fine.

Bill: Well, I believe so too. I've had a lot of people around me who have encouraged me along those lines. I see their faith, and it has meant a lot to me – people I've associated with at Harding Graduate School as well as my family. Somehow you can see those values that have been meaningful for years, something to live for kind of thing. I appreciate your input very much Earl. Thanks.

Earl: Thanks for the honor.

An Interview with Shirley Speed

Bill: I was very sorry to hear about your illness. I know you've been struggling with brain cancer for quite a while.

Shirley: It's been about two years.

Bill: Two years?

Shirley: Uh huh, yeah. But I'm thankful to be alive still.

Bill: I'm thankful too.

Shirley: Of course, God would have taken care of me and everything, but you know especially now that I'm going to have grandchildren it's just wonderful, but you know they have done so much these days. About a year ago, they thought about a month and that would be the end of me! But they did something wonderful and now things are going and turning around and people need this so much, not just me, but it's amazing they have been able to do things in two years that will help a lot of people. You know we have so many people that have brain tumors that have suffered since I've had it.

Bill: I'm sorry to hear that. What was your reaction when they told you that you had only two months?

Shirley: Well, that God would take care of me no matter what. In the very beginning, I really felt that way. It's amazing. When I was the very sickest and I still had the surgery to go through, I was able to believe that God was going to take care of me no matter what happened, and it wasn't hard to do. That's what is so amazing is that God gave me that to begin with; and to all my friends I said, "Listen, it's going to be okay no matter what happens, you know," and really … and I don't know how I did that except that God just did that for me. He did that for me! He took care of me just like that, and I never felt bad about if I died or did not die, or whatever. I would be sad for my children, of course, but still God was going to be so good to me.

Bill: Instead you kept saying, "It's going to be all right either way."

Shirley: That's right! And you know what, I don't understand how I did that but, of course, God just took care of me like that, but that was a blessing that he gave me at the very beginning.

Bill: Wow!

Shirley: I said I was going to be so sick and all this jazz but whatever happened God was going to take care of me. I'm telling you its been almost two years and there has not been a day that people have not come to my rescue, that he has taken care of me. For almost a whole year or more people gave; every day I got a card or something. You just can't imagine what that meant and then, like I say, I did real well at first, then the medicine; I mean I got started getting sick again and everything, but still again every day I knew that God was going to take care of me whether it was going to be bad news for me. I had already had two things, and so Charlie and I decided we've got to figure out where I was going to get buried (laughter). So one Sunday after church, we didn't tell the kids or anything that we were doing that, but we took off and went to the funeral home thing that Charlie's grandfather had way back out somewhere in Memphis. Anyway, we went to the old cemetery to see if that's where I might be buried.

Bill: You can just tell them, "It doesn't matter. I'm going to be in heaven anyway!"

Shirley: (Laughs.) That's right. Yeah, that's right. After my surgery at Duke, it took me six months to heal, and I did heal so slowly but surely and got back on pretty much track.

Bill: Right.

Shirley: And that's what's been going on this whole month, year. And we go back to Duke actually in two weeks. We go to Duke maybe for the last time.

Bill: Wow! The Bible talks a lot about spiritual maturity, like, "Let us go on to maturity and grow up and be like Jesus," and all that, and I can't keep from thinking that that's been going on in your life for a long time to help you to be where you are right now. How would you define spiritual maturity?

Shirley: Mother and Daddy were so spiritually minded, and I think that helps. I'm not very mature all the time.

Bill: Not every moment.

Shirley: Right. But, Judy, my sister, has made such a difference in my life as a leader, and Rick Haynes, her husband, but Judy and I are so close and have shared things so much that you can't not believe that God touched you and has taken care of you.

Bill: You sort of see some fruit of the Spirit in people's lives and in your own life.

Shirley: Yeah, and when you finally become a little more mature you want to work for the Lord. That came to be my whole system and focus, and Germantown Church of Christ let me work, for the Lord. And so I think that helped me so much to work in the nursery. They let me do the pre-school department.

Bill: You've done a lot of good work there.

Shirley: That was my calling, but you have to find your place.

Bill: And that brings about more spiritual maturity.

Shirley: That's right. And then when I got involved in all that and then people believed that I could do things like that, well, I got more involved. God always finds a way for you to do his bidding.

Bill: Right! I love that. He helps you to do what he wants you to do.

Shirley: That's right, if you'll just listen to him.

Bill: Right. I've often been encouraged by the 23rd Psalm, "The Lord is my Shepherd ..."

Shirley: "... I shall not want." Uh huh.

Bill: I was just wondering in your situation what that really means to you as you think about it?

Shirley: It gets harder and harder for me, especially these last six months, to uh, know ...

Bill: It's a little hard to focus sometimes.

Shirley: Right. It is. It's real hard. My brain doesn't work very well anymore.

Bill: And when you think about shepherd, he's going to take care of you.

Shirley: Right. He does, but what I'm trying to say is it's harder to know now – sometimes I forget to pray, you know because my little brain doesn't work very well, and then I don't pray the prayers that I would like to pray.

Bill: God understands.

Shirley: I think so too – but still it makes me sad. It kind of makes me sad to know that, but there is another way that God will have me do things.

Bill: Right.

Shirley: That's what's happened to my life now. I will never be the speaker or the this or that I could have been earlier or with different things, but I still think that God has a purpose in my life; in fact, it is probably a bigger purpose because I can encourage other people who are sick.

Bill: Yeah, you're dealing with the big issues.

Shirley: Right, and I do that now, and we have a support group, and so, I have something completely different than I thought I would have. You know, I would do this little pre-school department, and I would be with the children and make a difference in their lives, but God said, "No, you're not going to do this. You're going to do something else now."

Bill: Right. Well, the idea of a shepherd is that a shepherd is with his sheep all the time.

Shirley: No matter what you're doing. And it changes. That's the interesting thing, that God doesn't want us to be the same and be dull or whatever but takes whatever you have given and uses it for whatever now needs to be done.

Bill: When I think of you and Judy with your exuberance and smile and faith I think of the abundant life Jesus mentioned.

Shirley: Oh. Abundant life! Right. Right.

Bill: Spiritual.

Shirley: Uh huh. Right. Right, you know, and that's what is so interesting because it just gets better and better.

Bill: It changes everything.

Shirley: Right! It sure does. It changes everything, how you want to proceed, you know, how you want to do things now, and so, its been very interesting and I say that it is different, but it's a good difference.

Bill: Right. I was studying for a class at White Station recently on Philippians 4 about rejoicing in the Lord, always ...

Shirley: Yes.

Bill: And casting all your anxiety on him, praying that God will be with you – the peace of God, and then Paul says, "I can do all things through Christ who strengthens me." Somehow, it seems like you've been doing that.

Shirley: Yeah.

Bill: Trying to find joy in tough circumstances.

Shirley: Right. But, you know, it has not been hard. God has just opened his love for me more than I deserve.

Bill: I believe you opened up to him a long time ago.

Shirley: (Laughs.) Yeah. Well you know you try to do what you can. I'm so thankful for my family. Charlie, my husband, is so good to me, and my children are just wonderful people, you know, and I've just been blessed in so many ways. It has just been a wonderful position to be in to have this kind of people that want to help you.

Bill: It may be one way that God helps you – strengthens you through other people. ...

Shirley: Right. Right.

Bill: You pray to him, and you read the Bible. Can you think of any other ways that God give you strength? It has always been tough for me to try to figure out, but I know He does.

Shirley: Yeah. Yeah. He certainly does. He just takes care of us; it's just the way that He prepares us and keeps us keeping on.

Bill: Right.

Shirley: I don't think you help others just to help yourself, but it does.

Bill: You grow, and then others help too – your children, your husband, your family, people at church, and your mission.

Shirley: Right. And so many people have told me that just having me comment when they see me at church, you know, makes them happy – they're so glad to see me.

Bill: Maybe they can make it too if you can.

Shirley: That's right! But I'm not anything very special at all, but they seem so glad to see me when I'm there. If I'm not there, they notice that I'm not there. I'm so happy, kind of satisfied with where I am because other people need some sort of help; and if I have a way to help, I'm so glad to do that.

Bill: Your showing us how to handle these tough times is inspiring to me and others as well.

Shirley: Well, you know, it's just like I said, God has just really blessed me. When all this happened he just said, "Now Shirley, this is what you're going to do now. You're not going to do what you did before. Before I could go to people's houses and clean the house or I could do whatever. Now I can't do that. Now mostly it's praying and getting people to believe that God is going to take care of them.

Bill: God is real, and he is going to be there. This ties in with another question I was thinking about. In that same Philippians 4 chapter, Paul said that he had been abased and he had abounded and he said, "I have learned to be content in whatever situation I find myself."

Shirley: Yes. That's where I am. That's really true because for a whole two years, it has been different, and it has been a wonderful blessing that God has given me in saying, "Shirley, now you can't do this anymore. This is what I want you to do now."

Bill: Wow! You're doing beautifully. Do you have any suggestions to other people about how we can learn to be content in all circumstances?

Shirley: I think the best thing is just to read and believe the Bible. What's there is so right.

Bill: Give yourself to God, and you know that you're in his hands?

Shirley: That's right. Exactly right.

Bill: Like you're in his presence whatever the circumstance.

Shirley: Right. That's right.

Bill: And he will somehow get you through it.

Shirley: Yeah, and he has just been so good to me that it's amazing how all that has worked out.

Bill: I was thinking. ... I knew your parents, of course.

Shirley: Uh huh.

Bill: I've been in their home lots of times, and I know they went through tough times economically just like I did growing up.

Shirley: Yeah.

Bill: You grew up in tough times, so you know how spiritual resilience operates in lots of different ways. I mean when finances are not there, somehow it takes discipline.

Shirley: Right.

Bill: It takes faith, persistence to get through, right?

Shirley: Right.

Bill: Do you have any other comments, you'd like to make along the line of spiritual resilience and how that faith and discipline get you through?

Shirley: Well, I think you just keep on keeping on and know that God is going to make a difference in your life if you will just continue to be the kind of person that God and Jesus want us to be, but we don't always yield. ...

Bill: We are not perfect but. ...

Shirley: Right.

Bill: Our attitude though, makes a difference.

Shirley: Right. You know, of course, obviously I cried a bucket of tears about this situation, but it always comes back that God wants me to be at a better place wherever that may be, that I will be able to be of help to somebody else or be helpful to myself, Jesus, God, I don't know how to say this but He just – I guess it's just that He loves me.

Bill: You belong to Him. ...

Shirley: Right.

Bill: He has something in mind for you now just as He did before.

Shirley: Right, and if it works out, or if it doesn't work out for whatever reason being sick or whatever, it has been a wonderful journey, you know.

Bill: Yes.

Shirley: And He has put me through all this knowing that I might be what He wants me to be.

Bill: The spiritual life is what's most important.

Shirley: That's right, and it doesn't matter if I'm dead or alive with God because He's got it all taken care of anyway.

Bill: You're still with God.

Shirley: That's right, and that's the whole thing in the very beginning. This wasn't to make me bad or to make me sick or to make me whatever. It's just something that happens. I mean a lot of people have got it a lot worse than me. I think I have had a really easy, easy two years, but God has so blessed me that no matter what happened at the very beginning I was going to be okay. God will see you through.

Bill: What you're saying is it's a matter of surrendering your will to God's will ...

Shirley: Yes.

Bill: ... somehow of letting him come into your life more fully, and surely when that happens you'll be strengthened.

Shirley: Right. That's exactly right. Yeah, that is good.

Bill: What kind of spiritual influence did your Mom and Dad have on you?

Shirley: Well, Mother was just centered on God, church and the Bible. She was so strong and then she taught Daddy; then, of course, we grew up with the church. They were faithful to God.

Bill: They lived it at home.

Shirley: Right. Yes, and Mom always had the Bible, you know, in church and worked very hard. She was a very good, good person, and she was very good with people. She did everything for people.

Bill: She had that outgoing personality, like you and Judy have.

Shirley: She had the sweetest voice. My little grandmother was good too, but somehow Mother always pulled me back to know where I came from, and I think that is her legacy to me.

Bill: Roots. You draw strength from those roots.

Shirley: Right. And Judy and I and my other two sisters …

Bill: Bobbie and Paulette?

Shirley: Uh huh. And so that's another heritage that God gave us.

Bill: That's what I'm trying to draw from in this book in looking at my heritage …

Shirley: Uh, huh.

Bill: I had that from my parents who were very strong Christians and very disciplined and hard workers.

Shirley: Right.

Bill: Your parents were too.

Shirley: Yeah, and they loved the Lord. That always came through with us whether we were good about it or not, whether we did it right or not, but we knew who we belonged to.

Bill: We belong to God.

Shirley: Right. Yeah.

Bill: He will always be there.

Shirley: That's right.

Bill: I always grew up with the strong feeling that I was really obligated to God – didn't always act that way, but I always knew it.

Shirley: Yeah, that's right. I didn't realize that all of this was so strong in me until I got a little older and saw what a blessing and what a heritage that God has given me.

Bill: It sort of becomes a part of your heart, doesn't it?

Shirley: Right. I am so blessed because of God, you know, because we could have gone off in the wrong way – It was just a blessing I think that God gave us our family and our finding you and all this all these years. It's been just a blessing that God has continued to find us.

Bill: He just works in lots of ways doesn't he?

Shirley: Yeah. Right.

Bill: He works through people, he works through the Bible and he gives us a mission.

Shirley: That's right. Yeah, that's right.

Bill: That's one of the points I make early on in the book that in order for you to grow spiritually you have to be active in some kind of ministry.

Shirley: That's good.

Bill: Everybody has his or her own calling or place in life. When you get involved in that somehow you start growing on toward maturity.

Shirley: I think so too, and it's amazing how God will let you grow. Just keep on doing what you know is right. I really believe that, and from the whole beginning, it's been an interesting situation; but like I say, I've never felt bad about being sick. I just, whatever God has in mind is what I want to be.

Bill: That's beautiful. That's what I think of as spiritual maturity. I really liked what you said. You said things change and you learn to be happy with the change – like God has a different plan for you now.

Shirley: Right! That's exactly right! Yeah that is it.

Bill: Like you said, you've had your down days and you've cried like any-body else would. That's natural because your body is hurting.

Shirley: That's right. Yeah. It has been a lot easier than you would have ever thought it would be for me, and that's what I think is a blessing that God has given me over and over and over. It's not as hard to me as it is maybe for some other people who have a lot of problems and questions and things like that. God has always kind of, I don't know if that's dumb or what, but anyway God has always kind of kept me. I don't know how to say this, but you know, it's not been too hard.

Bill: Well, that has a lot to do with you and your faith and all that. That's why this is so inspiring to me, so uplifting, because I know that's what God has in mind for us. His intentions are not evil but good.

Shirley: That's right. And he has a perfect way for us to do things.

Bill: All right.

Shirley: Thank you so much. I love you.

Bill: I love you too.

Shirley: Isn't it interesting that you married Charlie and me – all those years now – now you're going to have us in your book?

Bill: You know, I had your sister Paulette in Bible Class.

Shirley: You did?

Bill: A Bible class with teenagers.

Shirley: Right. Fourteen or 15 or something like that.

Bill: I remember I baptized her.

Shirley: Uh huh. Well, you know, I didn't remember that either. Judy was telling me yesterday.

Bill: Thanks, Shirley. You have been very helpful.

Shirley: Thank you. I hope this helps somebody. Things change. You just have to change too, and realize that it's all right. God has something else in mind for you, and he will be right there with you to help you along. That's what I really want to say. It's hard, but he is strong and loving.

Bill: God bless.

That interview profoundly moved me more than any interview I have ever conducted. Somehow, when I left, I felt like I had been on holy ground. I don't know how I would handle Shirley's struggles, yet I do know that she has a lot of discipline, persistence and faith. I admire her very much. I admire you too for your continued efforts. God bless.

APPENDIX E

Endnotes

Chapter 1

[1] Bill Flatt, *Building a Healthy Family* (Nashville: Christian Communications, 1993) 59-70.

[2] Duane Schultz, *Theories of Personality* (Belmont, California: Brooks/Cole Publishing Company, 1990) 59-65, 285-311.

[3] P. Scott Richards and Allen E. Bergin, *A Spiritual Strategy for Counseling and Psychotherapy* (Washington, D.C.: American Psychological Association, 1997).

[4] Schultz, 48-50.

[5] Schultz, 123-145.

Chapter 2

[1] Jane Middleton-Moz, *Shame and Guilt: The Masters of Disguise* (Deerfield Beach, FL: Health Communications, Inc., 1990) 14-17.

[2] June Price Tangney, Patricia Wagner, and Richard Granzow, "Proneness to Shame, "Proneness to Guilt, and Psychopathology," *Journal of Abnormal Psychology 101*, no. 3 (1992): 469-472.

[3] Howard Clinebell, *Basic Types of Pastoral Care and Counseling: Resources for the Ministry of Healing and Growth* (Nashville: Abingdon Press, 1992) 141.

[4] Bruce Narramore, *No Condemnation* (Grand Rapids: Zondervan, 1984) 37-45.

[5] Bill Flatt, *From Worry to Happiness* (Nashville, TN: Christian Communications, 1979) 11-18.

Chapter 3

[1] *Diagnostic and Statistical Manual of Mental Disorders*, IV (Washington, DC: American Psychiatric Association, 1994) 395.

[2] Flatt, 19-27.

Chapter 4

[1] DSM-IV, 405-408.

[2] DSM-IV, 408-411.

[3]DSM-IV, 408-411.
[4]DSM-IV, 408, 409, 414.

Chapter 5

[1] DSM-IV, 317-391.
[2] DSM-IV, 349.
[3] David Burns, *Feeling Good* (New York: Penguin Books USA, Inc., 1980) 40-41.
[4] Aaron Beck, *Cognitive Therapy and the Emotional Disorders* (New York: International Universities Press, 1976) 264, 271-272.
[5] Albert Ellis, ed., *Handbook of Rational Emotive Therapy* (New York: Springer Publishing, 1977) 3-6.
[6] P. Scott Richards and Allen E. Bergin, *A Spiritual Strategy for Counseling and Psychotherapy* (Washington, DC: American Psychological Association, 1997).

Chapter 6

[1] Stanley Coopersmith, *The Antecedents of Self-Esteem* (San Francisco: W.H. Freeman and Co., 1967).
[2] Morris Rosenberg, *Society and the Adolescent Self-Image* (Princeton, New Jersey: Princeton University Press, 1965).
[3] Bill Flatt, "Building Self-Esteem in Children," *Upreach* December, 1987: 8-11,22.
[4] Eric Erikson, *Identity and the Life Cycle* (New York: W.W. Norton and Co., 1980).
[5] Robert Shakelford, "Loving Your Child Is Not Enough," *Moody Monthly* 75 November 1974: 41,107-109.
[6] David Adcock and Susan Noaker, "A Comparison of the Self-Esteem Levels in Evangelical Christian and General Population," *Journal of Psychology and Theology* 13, no. 3 (Fall 1985): 199-208.
[7]Brian Barber, "Marital Quality, Parental Behavior, and Adolescent Self-Esteem," *Family Perspective* 21, no. 4 (1987): 301-316.
[8] David Carlson, *Counseling and Self-Esteem* (Dallas: Word Publishing, 1988) 72-93.
[9] Scott Peck, *The Road Less Travelled* (New York: Simon and Schuster) 311.
[10] David Burns, *Feeling Good, The New Mood Therapy* (New York: Signet, 1989) 75-90.
[11] James Dobson, "Practical Advice for Parents of Teenagers." *Fundamentalist Journal* 6, no. 3 (March 1987): 33-36.
[12] James Dobson, *Hide or Seek* (Old Tappan, New Jersey: Fleming Company, 1974) 50-100.
[13] Albert Ellis and Michael E. Bernard (eds.), *Clinical Applications of Rational-Emotive Therapy* (New York: Plenum Press, 1985).
[14] Cecil G. Osborne, *The Art of Learning to Love Yourself* (Grand Rapids: Zondervan Publishing House, 1976) 115.

Chapter 7

[1] Gary Collins, ed., *Resources for Christian Counseling*, vol. 2, *Counseling for Anger*, by Mark P. Cosgrove (Dallas: Word Publishing, 1988) 46-47.

[2] Frederick G. Lopez and Christopher W. Thurman, "High-trait and Low-trait Angry College Students: A Comparison of Family Environments," *Journal of Counseling and Development* 71, no. 5 (1993): 526.

[3] C.L. Hogland and K.B. Nicholas, "Shame, Guilt, and Anger in College Students Exposed to Abusive Family Environments," *Journal of Family Violence* 10, no. 2 (1995): 154.

[4] H. Norman Wright, *An Answer to Anger and Frustration* (Irvine, Calif.: Harvest House, 1977) 31.

[5] Michael Bullard, "Sexual Violence and Coercion," *Church and Society* 80, no. 2 (November-December, 1989): 78.

[6] Lindon Moody, "In Search of Sacred Spaces," *American Baptist Quarterly* 8 (June 1999): 110-111.

[7] Marie Fortune, *Sexual Violence: The Unmentionable Sin* (New York: The Pilgrim Press, 1983): 7, 146-151.

[8] S.I. McMillen, *None of These Diseases* (Westwood, NJ: Spine Books, 1973) 72.

[9] Leo Meadow, *Anger* (New York: Charles Scribner's Sons, 1972), 85.

[10] H. Norman Wright, *An Answer to Anger and Frustration* (Irvine, Calif.: Harvest House, 1977) 31.

[11] William H. Cormier, and L. Sherilyn Cormier, *Interviewing Strategies for Helpers* (Pacific Cove, CA: Brooks/Cole Publishing, 1991) 422-430.

[12] William H. Cormier, and L. Sherilyn Cormier, *Interviewing Strategies for Helpers* (Pacific Cove, CA: Brooks/Cole Publishing, 1991) 422-430.

Chapter 8

[1] Neil Howe, *13th Generation* (New York: Vintage Books, 1993) 83.

[2] George Barna, *The Invisible Generation: Baby Busters* (New York: Barna Research Group, 1992) 32.

[3] CDR Charles R. Eis, "Thirteenth Generation," *The Navy Chaplain*, Vol. 8, no. 2 (February, 1994): 26.

[4] Barna, 67.

[5] Nick Stinnett and John DeFrain, *Secrets of Strong Families* (Boston: Little, Brown, and Company, 1985) 5, 8, 14, 23, 155.

[6] David H. Olsen and John DeFrain, *Marriage and the Family: Diversity and Strengths* (Mountain View, Calif.: Mayfield Publishing Company, 1994) 40-50.

[7] Herbert Otto, "The Minister and Family Strengths," *Pastoral Psychology* 17, no. 163 (April 1966): 10-23.

[8] Froma Walsh, *Strengthening Family Resilience and Challenge* (New York: Guilford Press, 1998) 5-300.

[9] Froma Walsh, *Spiritual Resources in Family Therapy* (New York: Guilford Press, 1999) 3-291.

[10] Ibid., 3.

[11] Bill Flatt, *Building a Healthy Family* (Nashville: Christian Communications, 1993) 1-319.

Chapter 9

[1] Michel L. Dandeneau and Susan M. Johnson, "Facilitating Intimacy: Interventions and Effects," *Journal of Marital and Family Therapy* 20 (1994): 17-33.

[2] H. T. Reis, "Social Interaction and Well-being," in *Personal Relationships 5: Repairing Personal Relationships*, ed. S. Duck, 21-45 (London: Academic Press, 1986): 34.

[3] L. M. Horowitz, "Cognitive Structure of Interpersonal Problems Treated in Psychotherapy," *Journal of Consulting and Clinical Psychology* 47 (1979): 5-15.

[4] Maggie Scarf, *Intimate Partners: Patterns in Love and Marriage* (New York: Random House, 1987) 59-71.

[5] Ibid, 62.

[6] Lynn A. Rankin-Esquer et al, "Autonomy and Relatedness in Marital Functioning, "*Journal of Marital and Family Therapy*, 23, no. 2 (1997): 175-90.

[7] Michael Kerr and Murray Bowen, *Family Evaluation* (New York: W. W. Norton, 1988) 1-50.

[8] Ibid, 1-50.

[9] William Masters et al, *Heterosexuality* (New York: Harper Collins, 1994) 16.

[10] Deborah Tanner, *You Just Don't Understand: Men and Women in Conversation* (New York: William Morrow, 1990) 26.

[11] Masters et al, 20-22.

[12] David Schnarch, *Constructing the Sexual Crucible* (New York: W. W. Norton, 1991) 89-119.

[13] Kerr and Bowen.

[14] W. R. Beavers, *Psychotherapy and Growth: A Family Systems Perspective* (New York: Brunner/Mazel, 1977) 52, 76.

[15] L. C. and A. R. Wynne, "The Quest for Intimacy," *Journal of Marital and Family Therapy* 12, 4 (1986): 838-94.

[16] T. P. and P. T. Malone, *The Art of Intimacy* (New York: Prentice-Hall, 1987) 16.

[17] Kerr and Bowen, 10-40.

[18] Bill Flatt, *Building a Healthy Family* (Nashville: Christian Communications, 1993) 85-102.

[19] William H. Masters and Virginia Johnson, *The Pleasure Bond* (Boston: Little, Brown, 1970) 176-92.

[20] Bill Flatt, "The Misuses of Power and Sex in Helping Relationships," *Restoration Quarterly* 36 (2d Quarter 1994): 101-

Chapter 10

[1] Elizabeth Kübler-Ross, *On Death and Dying* (New York: Macmillan Publishing Company, 1969) 38-137.

[2] Judy Tatelbaum, *The Courage to Grieve: Creative Living, Recovery, and Growth Through Grief* (New York: Harper and Row Publishers, 1980) 25-47.

[3] Harold Bauman, *Living Through Grief* (Batavia, Illinois: Lion Publishing Corporation, 1960) 12-32.

[4] Catherine M. Sanders, *Grief: The Mourning After: Dealing with Adult Bereavement*, Wiley Series on Personality Processes (New York: John Wiley and Sons, 1989) 45-108.

[5] Robert W. Bailey, *The Minister and Grief* (New York: Hawthorne Books, Inc., 1976) 77-81.

[6] Robert James St. Clair, "Don't Short-Circuit Grief," in Death: Jesus *Made it All Different*, ed. Miriam G. Moran (New Canaan, CT: Keats Publishing Company, 1977) 114-17.

[7] Granger E. Westburg, *Good Grief: A Constructive Approach to the Problem of Loss* (Philadelphia: Fortress Press, 1971) 21-64.

[8] Bill Flatt, *Growing Through Grief* (Nashville: Christian Communications, 1987) 15-54.

[9] Bill Flatt, *From Worry to Happiness* (Nashville: Christian Communications, 1979), 77-79.

[10] Bill Flatt, "Some Stages of Grief," *Journal of Religion and Health* 26 (1987): 143-148.

[11] Bill Flatt, "Factors Affecting Grief Adjustment," *Journal of Religion and Health* 27 (1988): 8-18.

[12] William Rogers, "Needs of the Bereaved," *Pastoral Psychology* 1 (June 1950): 17-21. See also Ralph L. Underwood, "Ministry in the Midst of Grief," *Insights: A Journal of the Faculty of Austin Seminary* 110 (Fall 1994): 28-34; Bill Flatt, "Grief Counseling," *Pastoral Psychology* 36 (Spring 1988): 133-145.

Chapter 11

[1] Christopher Lukas and Henry M. Seiden, *Silent Grief* (Northvale, N.J.: Jason Aronson, Inc., 1997) 5.

[2] Marjorie E. Weisharr, "Cognitive Risk Factors in Suicide." In Paul M. Salkovskis, *Frontiers of Cognitive Therapy* (New York: Guilford Press, 1996) 243.

[3] Frankl, Victor. *Man's Search for Meaning: An Introduction to Logotherapy* (New York: Simon and Schuster, 1962).

Chapter 12

[1] Jack O. Balswick and Judith K. Balswick, *The Family: A Christian Perspective on the Contemporary Home* (Grand Rapids, Mich.: Baker Book House, 1989) 55-66.

[2] *Diagnostic and Statistical Manual of Mental Disorders*, Fourth edition (Washington, D.C.: APA, 1994) 658-661.

[3] Judith S. Wallerstein and Sandra Blakeslee, *Second Chances: Men, Women, and Children a Decade After Divorce* (New York: Ticknor & Fields, 1989). See also Elizabeth P. Benedek and Catherine F. Brown, *How to Help Your*

Child Overcome Your Divorce (Washington, D.C.: American Psychiatric Press, 1995) 2-10.

[4] Ibid.

[5] Ibid., 300-301.

[6] Ibid., 301.

[7] Ibid., 297-303.

[8] Ibid., 305. See also Lawrence A. Kurdek, *"Divorce: Effects on Children,"* in Encyclopedia of Marriage and the Family 1, ed. David Levinson (New York: Simon and Schuster Macmillan, 1995) 194-196.

[9] James Dycus, "Caring for Children of Divorce," *Leadership* 10 (Fall 1989): 30-36. See also Terry Bell, and Steve Joiner, *Common Sense Recovery: Dealing With Divorce* (Abilene, Texas: Abilene Christian University Press, 1990).

[10] Duane Warden, "The Words of Jesus on Divorce," *Restoration Quarterly* 39, no. 3 (1997): 141-153.

[11] David J. Rolfe, "Preparing the Previously Married for Second Marriages," *The Journal of Pastoral Care* 39 (June 1985): 116-124.

[12] Christopher L. Hayes, Deborah Anderson, and Melinda Blan, *Our Turn: Women Who Triumph in the Face of Divorce* (New York: Pocket Books, 1993) 6, 127-128.

[13] Florence W. Kaslow, "Divorce and Divorce Therapy," in *Handbook of Family Therapy*, ed. Alan S. Gurman and David Kniskern (New York: Brunner/Mazel Publishers, 1981).

Appendix F

Bibliography

Adcock, David and Susan Noaker. "A Comparison of the Self-Esteem Levels in Evangelical Christian and General Population." *Journal of Psychology and Theology* 13, no.3 (Fall 1985): 199-208.

Bailey, Robert W. *The Minister and Grief.* New York: Hawthorne Books, Inc., 1976.

Balswick, Jack O., and Judith K. Balswick. *The Family: A Christian Perspective on the Christian Home.* Grand Rapids: Baker Book House, 1989.

Barber, Brian. "Marital Quality, Parental Behavior, and Adolescent Self-Esteem." *Family Perspective* 21, no. 4 (1987): 301-316.

Barna, George. *The Invisible Generation: Baby Busters.* New York: Barna Research Group, 1992.

Bauman, Harold. *Living Through Grief.* Batavia, Illinois: Lion Publishing Corporation, 1960.

Beavers, W. R. *Psychotherapy and Growth: A Family Systems Perspective.* New York: Brunner/Mazel, 1977.

Beck, Aaron. *Cognitive Therapy and the Emotional Disorders.* New York: International Universities Press, 1976.

Bell, Terry, and Steve Joiner. *Common Sense Recovery: Dealing With Divorce.* Abilene, Texas: Abilene Christian University Press, 1990.

Benedek, Elizabeth R., and Catherine F. Brown. *How to Help Your Child Overcome Divorce.* Washington, D.C.: American Psychiatric Press, 1995.

Bullard, Michael. "Sexual Violence and Coercion." *Church and Society* 80, no. 2 (November-December, 1989): 76-82.

Burns, David. *Feeling Good, The New Mood Therapy.* New York: Signet, 1989.

Carlson, David. *Counseling and Self-Esteem.* Dallas: Word Publishing, 1988.

Clinebell, Howard. *Basic Types of Pastoral Care and Counseling.* Nashville: Abingdon Press, 1992.

Collins, Gary, ed. *Resources for Christian Counseling.* Vol. 2, *Counseling for Anger* by Mark P. Cosgrove. Dallas: Word Publishing, 1988.

Coopersmith, Stanley. *The Antecedents of Self-Esteem.* San Francisco: W. H. Freeman and Company, 1967.

Cormier, William H., and L. Sherilyn Cormier. *Interviewing Strategies for Helpers*. Pacific Cove, California: Brooks/Cole Publishing, 1991.

Dandeneau, Michael L., and Susan M. Johnson. "Facilitating Intimacy: Interventions and Effects." *Journal of Marital and Family Therapy* 20 (1994): 17-33.

Diagnostic and Statistical Manual of Mental Disorders-IV. Washington, D.C.: American Psychiatric Association, 1994.

Dobson, James. *Hide or Seek*. Old Tappan, New Jersey: Fleming Company, 1974.

Dobson, James. "Practical Advice for Parents of Teenagers." *Fundamentalist Journal* 6, no. 3 (March 1987): 33-36.

Dycus, James. "Caring for Children of Divorce." *Leadership* 10 (Fall 1989): 30-36.

Eis, CDR Charles R. "Thirteenth Generation." *The Navy Chaplain 8*, no. 2 (February 1994): 20-27.

Ellis, Albert, ed. *Handbook of Rational Emotive Therapy*. New York: Springer Publishing, 1977.

Ellis, Albert, and Michael E. Bernard, eds. *Clinical Applications of Rational-Emotive Therapy*. New York: Plenum Press, 1985.

Erikson, Eric. *Identity and the Life Cycle*. New York: W. W. Norton and Company, 1980.

Flatt, Bill. *Building a Healthy Family*. Nashville: Christian Communications, 1993.

Flatt, Bill. "Building Self-Esteem in Children." *Upreach* (December 1987): 8-22.

Flatt, Bill. "Grief Counseling." *Pastoral Psychology* 36 (Spring 1988): 133-145.

Flatt, Bill. *Growing Through Grief*. Nashville: Christian Communications, 1987.

Flatt, Bill. "Factors Affecting Grief Adjustment." *Journal of Religion and Health* 27 (1988): 8-18.

Flatt, Bill. *From Worry to Happiness*. Nashville: Christian Communications, 1979.

Flatt, Bill. "Some Stages of Grief." *Journal of Religion and Health* 26 (1987): 143-148.

Flatt, Bill. "The Misuses of Power and Sex in Helping Relationships." *Restoration Quarterly* 36 (Second Quarter 1994): 101-110.

Fortune, Marie. *Sexual Violence: The Unmentionable Sin*. New York: The Pilgrim Press, 1983.

Frankl, Victor. *Man's Search for Meaning: An Introduction to Logotherapy*. New York: Simon and Schuster, 1962.

Hayes, Christopher L., Deborah Anderson, and Melinda Blon. *Our Turn: Women Who Triumph in the Face of Divorce*. New York: Pocket Books, 1993.

Hoglund, C. L., and K. B. Nicholas. "Shame, Guilt, and Anger in College Students Exposed to Abusive Family Environments." *Journal of Family Violence* 10, no. 2 (1995): 152-157.

Horowitz, L. M. "Cognitive Structure of Interpersonal Problems Treated in Psychotherapy." *Journal of Counseling and Consulting Psychology* 47 (1979): 5-15.

Howe, Neil. *13th Generation*. New York: Vintage Books, 1993.

Kerr, Michael, and Murray Bowen. *Family Evaluation*. New York: W. W. Norton, 1988.

Kübler-Ross, Elizabeth. *On Death and Dying*. New York: Macmillan Publishing Company, 1969.

Lopez, Frederick G., and Christopher W. Thurman. "High-trait and Low-trait Angry College Students: A Comparison of Family Environments." *Journal of Counseling and Development* 71, no. 5 (1993): 521-528.

Lukas, Christopher, and Henry M. Seiden. *Silent Grief*. Northvale, New Jersey: Jason Aronson, Inc., 1997.

Malone, T. P., and P. T. Malone. *The Art of Intimacy*. New York: Prentice-Hall, 1987.

Masters, William et al, *Heterosexuality*. New York: Harper Collins, 1994.

Masters, William H., and Virginia Johnson. *The Pleasure Bond*. Boston: Little, Brown, 1970.

McMillen, S. I. *None of These Diseases*. We twood, New Jersey: Spine Books, 1973.

Meadow, Leo. *Anger*. New York: Charles Scribner's Sons, 1972.

Middleton-Moz, Jane. *Shame and Guilt: The Masters of Disguise*. Deerfield Beach: Health Communications, Inc., 1990.

Moody, Linda. "In Search of Sacred Spaces." *American Baptist Quarterly* 8 (June 1989): 110-111.

Kurdek, Lawrence A. "Divorce Effects on Children." In *Encyclopedia of Marriage and the Family* 1, ed. David Levison. New York: Simon and Schuster Macmillan, 1995.

Narramore, Bruce. *No Condemnation*. Grand Rapids, Michigan: Zondervan Publishing House, 1984.

Olsen, David H., and John DeFrain. *Marriage and the Family: Diversity and Strengths*. Mountain View, Calif.: Mayfield Publishing Company, 1994.

Osborne, Cecil G. *The Art of Learning to Love Yourself*. Grand Rapids: Zondervan Publishing House, 1976.

Otto, Herbert. "The Minister and Family Strengths." *Pastoral Psychology* 17, no. 163 (April 1966): 10-23.

Peck, Scott. *The Road Less Travelled*. New York: Simon and Schuster, 1980.

Rankin-Esquer et al. "Autonomy and Relatedness in Marital Functioning." *Journal of Marital and Family Therapy* 23, no. 2 (1997): 175-90.

Reis, H. T. "Social Interaction and Well-being." In *Personal Relationships 5: Repairing Personal Relationships*, ed. S. Duck, 21-45. London: Academic Press, 1986.

Richards, P. Scott, and Allen E. Bergin. *A Spiritual Strategy for Counseling and Psychotherapy*. Washington, D.C.: American Psychological Association, 1997.

Rogers, William. "Needs of the Bereaved." *Pastoral Psychology* 1 (June

1950): 17-21.

Rolfe, David J. "Preparing the Previously Married for Second Marriage." *The Journal of Pastoral Care* 39 (June 1985): 116-124.

Rosenberg, Morris. *Society and the Adolescent Self-Image*. Princeton, New Jersey: Princeton University Press, 1965.

Saint Clair, Robert James. "Don't Short-Circuit Grief." In *Death: Jesus Made All the Difference*, ed. Marian G. Moran. New Canada, CT: Keats Publishing Company, 1977.

Sanders, Catherine M. *Grief: The Mourning After: Dealing with Adult Bereavement*. New York: John Wiley and Sons, 1989.

Schultz, Duane. *Theories of Personality*. Belmont, California: Brooks/Cole Publishing Company, 1990.

Schnarch, David. *Constructing the Sexual Crucible*. New York: W. W. Norton, 1991.

Scraf, Maggie. *Intimate Partners: Patterns in Love and Marriage*. New York: Random House, 1987.

Shakelford, Robert S. "Loving Your Child Is Not Enough." *Moody Monthly* 75 (November 1974): 41, 107-109.

Stinnett, Nick, and John DeFrain. *Secrets of Strong Families*. Boston: Little, Brown, and Company, 1985.

Tangney, June Price, Patricia Wagner, and Richard Gramzow. "Proneness to Shame, Proneness to Guilt, and Psychopathology." *Journal of Abnormal Psychology* 101, no. 3 (1992): 469-472.

Tanner, Deborah. *You Just Don't Understand: Men and Women in Conversation*. New York: William Morrow, 1990.

Tatelbaum, Judy. *The Courage to Grieve: Creative Living, Recovery, and Growth Through Grief*. New York: Harper and Row, 1980.

Underwood, Ralph L. "Ministry in the Midst of Grief." *Insights: A Journal of the Faculty of Austin Seminary* 110 (Fall 1994): 28-34.

Wallerstein, Judith S., and Sondra Blakeslee. *Second Chances: Men, Women, and Children a Decade After Divorce*. New York: Ticknor and Fields, 1989.

Walsh, Froma. *Spiritual Resources in Family Therapy*. New York: Guilford Press, 1999.

Walsh, Froma. *Strengthening Family Resilience and Challenge*. New York: Guilford Press, 1998.

Warden, Duane. "The Words of Jesus on Divorce." *Restoration Quarterly* 39, no. 3 (1997): 141-153.

Weisharr, Marjorie E. "Cognitive Risk Factors in Suicide." In Paul M. Salkovskis, *Frontiers of Cognitive Therapy*. New York: Guilford Press, 1996.

Westburg, Granger E. *Good Grief: A Constructive Approach to the Problem of Loss*. Philadelphia: Fortress Press, 1971.

Wright, H. Norman. *An Answer to Anger and Frustration*. Irvine, California: Harvest House, 1977.

Wynne, L. C., and A. R. "The Quest for Intimacy." *Journal of Marital and Family Therapy* 12, no. 4 (1986): 838-894.

APPENDIX G

Biographical Sketch

B ill Flatt, Ed.D. is a minister, a licensed marriage and family therapist, a licensed counseling psychologist, and professor of counseling at the Harding University Graduate School of Religion in Memphis, Tenn. He has authored five books: *From Worry to Happiness, Since You Asked, Growing Through Grief, Building a Healthy Family* and *Restoring My Soul: The Pursuit of Spiritual Resilience*. He co-authored *Counseling Homosexuals* and *Personal Counseling*, and has narrated an audio cassette album titled "Relax and Feel Better." He has also done video cassette albums on "Growing Through Grief," "Building Better Homes," and "From Worry to Happiness," produced and marketed by The Way of Life TV Studio of Jackson, Tenn.

An Approved Supervisor and Fellow of the American Association for Marriage and Family Therapy and a member of the American Psychological Association, he has published articles in many papers and in several journals. He served as president of the Tennessee Association for Marriage and Family Therapy and as a member and consultant of the state licensure board for professional counselors and marriage and family therapists.

Dr. Flatt has served as a minister in Spencer, Tenn.; Brownsville, Tenn.; and Indianapolis, Ind. Since coming to the Harding University Graduate School of Religion in 1965, he has preached for several congregations in the Mid-South. He led in the planting of the Ross Road Church of Christ in Memphis and served the church as an elder and minister for some five years. He presents special lectures at colleges and churches. He is in private practice as a counseling psychologist and marriage and family therapist. Since 1963, he has participated with his brothers Leamon, Don and Dowell in the Flatt Brothers Campaigns for Christ in various parts of the country. Dr. Flatt holds several weekend meetings each year on "Spiritual Resilience" and "Building Healthy Families." He also conducts seminars on "Growing Through Grief" and workshops on counseling for church leaders.